"In this transformative and groundbreaking book, Sameera Qureshi offers a deeply spiritual, yet practical and comprehensive guide to sexual health in the life of a Muslim. Grounded in the rich Islamic tradition, this book equips readers with valuable tools to center God while navigating their sexual well-being. A true gift to the field, and a must-read for Muslims, clinicians, and anyone seeking a spiritually rooted and holistic approach to sexual health."

Amal Killawi, LCSW, *The Family & Youth Institute, USA*

"In this innovative and important book, Sameera Qureshi dialectically unites Islamic traditions of the soul with our contemporary understanding of sexual health. This unification allows the reader to center their soul as a mandatory element for their sexual health, liberating them from the polarizations of repression and permissiveness. An extraordinary work!"

Waleed Sami, PhD, *assistant professor, Department of Psychology, City College of New York*

Soulful Sexual Health for Muslims

This transformative book offers a holistic approach to sexual health for Muslims, rooted in Islamic traditions of the soul. By addressing sexual health as an integrative journey connecting physical, emotional, and spiritual dimensions, it reframes this aspect of life as a sacred practice aligned with the soul's connection to God.

Introducing the Soulful Sexual Health Model as a framework for navigating sexual health challenges throughout the developmental journey of the soul, Sameera Qureshi integrates Islamic values of compassion, self-accountability, and spiritual alignment into holistic frameworks for sexual health education and support. Chapters explore foundational topics such as anatomy and puberty, empowered abstinence, marital intimacy, and parenting approaches to sexual health. Special sections address challenges like sexual trauma, infertility, and sexual dysfunction, offering practical and faith-centered strategies for healing and growth. This book also provides tailored guidance for professionals supporting Muslims, emphasizing the importance of integrating faith-based frameworks into their practice. Through reflective questions, personal narratives, and practical activities, readers are equipped to embrace sexual health as an essential and sacred part of their journey with God.

Intended for Muslims seeking a holistic understanding of sexual health, as well as educators, therapists, imams, and other professionals who serve Muslim communities, this book bridges the gap between contemporary sexual health needs and Islamic faith-based approaches. It is an invaluable resource for those committed to fostering healing, growth, and spiritual connection in their personal lives and professional work.

Sameera Qureshi, MS OTR, is a trauma-informed occupational therapist and founder of Sexual Health for Muslims. She centers Islamic Psychology for therapeutic, educational, and program development frameworks aimed at Muslims and professionals who serve them.

Soulful Sexual Health for Muslims

A Developmental Approach for Individuals and Clinicians

Sameera Qureshi, MS OTR

NEW YORK AND LONDON

Designed cover image: Getty Images

First published 2026
by Routledge
605 Third Avenue, New York, NY 10158

and by Routledge
4 Park Square, Milton Park, Abingdon, Oxon, OX14 4RN

Routledge is an imprint of the Taylor & Francis Group, an informa business

© 2026 Sameera Qureshi

The right of Sameera Qureshi to be identified as author of this work has been asserted in accordance with sections 77 and 78 of the Copyright, Designs and Patents Act 1988.

All rights reserved. No part of this book may be reprinted or reproduced or utilised in any form or by any electronic, mechanical, or other means, now known or hereafter invented, including photocopying and recording, or in any information storage or retrieval system, without permission in writing from the publishers.

Trademark notice: Product or corporate names may be trademarks or registered trademarks, and are used only for identification and explanation without intent to infringe.

Library of Congress Cataloging-in-Publication Data
Names: Qureshi, Sameera author.
Title: Soulful sexual health for Muslims : a developmental approach for individuals and clinicians / Sameera Qureshi.
Description: New York, NY ; Abingdon, Oxon : Routledge, 2025. | Includes bibliographical references and index.
Identifiers: LCCN 2025005188 (print) | LCCN 2025005189 (ebook) | ISBN 9781032675855 (hardback) | ISBN 9781032663470 (paperback) | ISBN 9781032675862 (ebook)
Subjects: LCSH: Sex—Religious aspects—Islam. | Sexual health. | Soul—Islam.
Classification: LCC BP190.5.S4 Q774 2025 (print) |
  LCC BP190.5.S4 (ebook) | DDC 297.5—dc23/eng/20250520
LC record available at https://lccn.loc.gov/2025005188
LC ebook record available at https://lccn.loc.gov/2025005189

ISBN: 978-1-032-67585-5 (hbk)
ISBN: 978-1-032-66347-0 (pbk)
ISBN: 978-1-032-67586-2 (ebk)

DOI: 10.4324/9781032675862

Typeset in Sabon
by Apex CoVantage, LLC

Table of Contents

Acknowledgements   ix
Glossary of Terms   xi

Introduction: My Soulful Journey   1

1 Contextualizing Islam and the Soul   11

2 A Soulful Model of Sexual Health for Muslims   30

3 Foundations of Soulful Sexual Health for Muslims   49

4 A Soulful Model of Empowered Abstinence   74

5 The Soulful Search for a Spouse   99

6 Soulful Sexual Intimacy in Marriage   123

7 Soulful Parenting Approaches for Sexual Health   155

8 Soulful Sexual Health and Spiritual Maturity   185

9 A Spiritual Legacy of Soulful Sexual Health   207

10 The Soulful Navigation of Female Sexual Health Challenges   218

11 The Soulful Navigation of Male Sexual Health Challenges   249

12	Soulfully Seeking Sexual Health Support	281
13	Soulfully Providing Sexual Health Support	303
	Conclusion: A Soulful Vision for Sexual Health	322
	Additional Readings	*325*
	Index	*328*

Acknowledgements

In the Name of Allah, the Most Gracious, the Most Merciful.

This book is the culmination of my professional and personal journey, made possible by the love, support, and prayers of those who have walked alongside me. To each of you, I owe my deepest gratitude. First and foremost, all praise is due to Allah, who has guided and sustained me through every step of this journey. This work is a trust, and I pray it benefits others and draws them closer to Him. Thank You for the strength, clarity, and inspiration to carry this work forward and for the many signs You have shown along the way.

My husband, my soulmate and anchor, has been my greatest strength. Your unwavering love and belief in me have held me steady. Thank you for providing soulful space for my journey. My parents, brothers, in-laws, and extended family—your endless prayers, sacrifices, and encouragement have laid the foundation for everything I do. I hope this book makes you proud. To my spiritual guide and all those on the spiritual path, from whom I continue to draw inspiration and support, I am grateful. My dear friends, near and far, have cheered me on, lifted me in moments of doubt, and offered heartfelt advice when I needed it most—you are my extended family. A special thanks goes to DRR, for your wonderful company over miles, hills, and coffee stops; and to my hometown Calgary crew, Virginia friends, and those living across the globe for their encouragement and support.

Val, your belief in my bold vision of an Islamic sexual health curriculum planted the seeds for this work, and my many mentors—past and present—have nurtured its growth. Natasha, your soulful presence has been a profound source of strength and healing for me. My Cambridge Muslim College classmates and teachers, especially Dr. Abdallah Rothman, continue to inspire me with our shared journey. I pray this book furthers Dr. Malik Badri's legacy in Islamic Psychology. My close colleagues (you know who you are!) have enriched this journey with their insights and support. A special and heartfelt thank you to Heather Evans, my gifted editor, for holding soulful space and offering invaluable guidance; and to the

Routledge team, particularly Julia, for believing in this book and guiding it to publication with patience and care.

Finally, to those who have engaged with my work through social media, webinars, therapy, or this book—you are at the heart of everything I do. Your willingness to reflect, heal, and grow inspires me to continue. This acknowledgement barely scratches the surface of the gratitude I carry. For the many who are unnamed, please know you hold a cherished place in my heart. May Allah reward you all abundantly, and may this work serve as a source of benefit for years to come, guided always by His Mercy and Wisdom.

Glossary of Terms

The following terms appear throughout the book and are defined below. Note that within the chapters, Arabic terms are *italicized* with the English definition appearing in parentheses.

Allah The Arabic term for God, used universally by Arabic-speaking Muslims and Christians alike to refer to the One Supreme Being, the Creator and Sustainer of the universe. Throughout this book, "Allah" and "God" are used interchangeably to respect the linguistic and cultural diversity of the audience while maintaining the essence of Islamic theology. The use of "Allah" emphasizes the personal and profound connection Muslims have with their Creator, aligning with the soulful contexts explored in this book.

akhlaq Refers to Islamic ethics or moral character, emphasizing virtues such as kindness, humility, patience, and honesty. Rooted in the Quran and Sunnah, *akhlaq* guides Muslims in cultivating noble character and relationships, which are central to the soulful approaches explored in this book.

Alhamdulillah An Arabic phrase meaning "Praise be to Allah." It is commonly used by Muslims to express gratitude, contentment, or recognition of Allah's blessings in all circumstances, whether good or challenging. The phrase reflects a deep sense of thankfulness and acknowledgement of Allah's sovereignty.

amanah A trust or responsibility entrusted by Allah to humans, emphasizing accountability in life, including in matters of health and sexuality.

'awrah The parts of the body that must be covered with clothing as per Islamic guidelines for modesty, differing by gender and context.

barakah Blessing or divine grace that brings goodness and abundance, often sought in marriage and daily life.

Bismillah "In the name of Allah." This phrase is the beginning of the full Islamic invocation *Bismillah-ir-Rahman-ir-Raheem* ("In the name of Allah, the Most Gracious, the Most Merciful"). It is a phrase of immense spiritual significance in Islam and is used by Muslims to begin almost every task, activity, or recitation, including the Quran. It serves as a reminder of Allah's presence and guidance in all actions, invoking blessings, protection, and the intention of performing an act for the sake of Allah.

bulūgh The stage of physical and spiritual maturity, marked by puberty, when a Muslim becomes accountable for their actions.

dhikr Literally meaning "remembrance," *dhikr* refers to the spiritual practice of remembering Allah through spoken or silent recitation. This can include litanies—repeated phrases such as *SubḥanAllah* (Glory be to Allah), *Alḥamdulillah* (All praise is due to Allah), and *Allahu Akbar* (Allah is the Greatest). *Dhikr* nurtures presence, calms the heart, and draws the soul closer to Divine awareness, whether done individually or in community.

dua A personal supplication or prayer made directly to Allah. It is a way of turning the heart toward the Divine—whether in times of need, gratitude, or reflection. *Dua* can be spoken in any language, at any time, and is considered a deeply intimate act of connection between a Muslim and God.

fiqh Refers to Islamic jurisprudence, the understanding and application of Islamic laws derived from the Quran and sunnah. *Fiqh* provides practical rulings for daily life, including acts of worship, transactions, and personal conduct, and is a foundational framework in discussions of sexual health and ethics throughout this book.

fitrah The natural disposition or innate purity with which every human being is created, serving as a foundation for spiritual and moral guidance.

Five Pillars of Islam The foundational acts of worship and practice in Islam, representing the core framework of a Muslim's faith and devotion. They include: 1) *Shahadah* (Testimony of Faith)—declaring belief in the oneness of Allah and the prophethood of Muhammad (Peace and Blessings be Upon Him); 2) *Salah* (Prayer)—performing five daily prayers; 3) *Zakah* (Almsgiving)—giving a portion of one's wealth to those in need; 4) *Sawm* (Fasting)—abstaining from food, drink, and other physical needs from dawn to sunset during Ramadan; and 5) *Hajj* (Pilgrimage)—performing the pilgrimage to Mecca at least once in a lifetime, if physically and financially able.

futuwwah Often translated as "spiritual chivalry," *futuwwah* refers to a code of ethics in Islamic tradition that emphasizes noble character, selflessness, and service to others. It encourages individuals to prioritize the well-being of others while cultivating inner purity and alignment with Divine values.

ghadab Translated as "anger," *ghadab* refers to the intense emotional state triggered by feelings of injustice, harm, or frustration. In Islamic teachings, *ghadab* is a natural human emotion, but it must be managed with self-control and wisdom.

ghusl The ritual full-body purification performed in specific circumstances, such as after marital intimacy or menstruation.

hadith Refers to the recorded sayings, actions, and approvals of the Prophet Muhammad (Peace and Blessings be Upon Him). Hadiths (the plural form) are a key source of Islamic knowledge, second only to the Quran, and provide practical examples of how to live according to Islamic teachings. In addition to verses from the Quran, hadiths are cited throughout the book.

hajj The major pilgrimage to the sacred city of Mecca, required once in a lifetime for all Muslims who are physically and financially able. It is performed during the Islamic month of *hajj* (*Dhul-Hijjah*) and includes a series of sacred rites that commemorate the legacy of Prophet Ibrahim (Abraham) and his family.

haya Modesty or a sense of shame rooted in faith, guiding behavior and interactions in line with Islamic values.

hayd The Arabic term for menstruation or a woman's period, referring to the natural cyclical process of uterine bleeding. In Islamic contexts, *hayd* carries both physical and spiritual significance, as it is accompanied by specific rulings related to worship, such as exemptions from prayer (*salah*) and fasting (*sawm*) during this time.

ibadah Acts of worship or devotion to Allah, which include not only formal prayers but also actions like fostering a healthy marital relationship.

ihsaan A term meaning "excellence" or "perfection." In an Islamic context, it refers to worshipping Allah as if you see Him, and knowing that even if you cannot see Him, He sees you. *Ihsaan* signifies striving for the highest level of sincerity and mindfulness in actions and worship.

ihtilam A term referring to a nocturnal emission or a wet dream. It is a natural occurrence that marks the transition into adulthood in Islamic jurisprudence, signifying the onset of puberty. Following *ihtilam*, a *ghusl* (ritual purification bath) is required to regain a state of ritual purity.

inshaAllah A phrase meaning "If Allah wills." It is used by Muslims to express hope or intention for something to happen in the future, acknowledging that all outcomes are ultimately subject to Allah's will and decree.

jalal Majesty or the divine attribute of strength, often associated with traditionally "masculine" qualities of Allah.

jamal Beauty or the divine attribute of gentleness and mercy, often linked with traditionally "feminine" qualities of Allah.

khushu' A state of humility, focus, and mindfulness in worship/prayer, reflecting deep spiritual connection.

kiraman katibin The noble recording angels who document a person's deeds, emphasizing the importance of self-accountability.

Maqasid al-Shariah Refers to the higher objectives of Islamic law, which aim to preserve and promote human dignity and well-being. These core principles include the protection of faith (*hifz al-deen*), life (*hifz al-nafs*), intellect (*hifz al-aql*), lineage (*hifz al-nasl*), and wealth (*hifz al-mal*). Together, they ensure the right to spiritual growth, safeguard human life, encourage education and critical thinking, uphold family and moral relationships, and promote justice in economic matters.

ma'roof A term meaning "that which is good, recognized, or accepted." In an Islamic context, it refers to actions, behaviors, and practices that are considered virtuous, just, and in accordance with moral and social norms as guided by the Quran and Sunnah. *Ma'roof* emphasizes the importance of fostering goodness and fairness in relationships and societal dealings.

muhasabah A term meaning "self-reckoning" or "self-accountability." In the Islamic tradition, muhāsabah refers to the practice of regularly reflecting on one's thoughts, actions, intentions, and spiritual state in relation to Allah. *Muhāsabah* invites believers to turn inward with sincerity, compassion, and truthfulness, recognizing both their shortcomings and their striving on the path toward nearness to Allah.

muwaddah A Quranic term often translated as "affection" or "loving kindness." It refers to a deep, compassionate form of love that is rooted in care, tenderness, and emotional connection. In the context of marriage, *muwaddah* is one of the key foundations of the marital bond, alongside *rahmah* (mercy). It reflects not just romantic love, but a soul-nurturing love that fosters spiritual companionship and mutual support.

nafs The self or soul, often discussed in its different states. Within the Islamic Psychology model presented, the *nafs* refers to observable behaviors.

nafs al-ammarah The commanding self, inclined toward base desires and evil, requiring discipline and refinement.

nafs al-lawwamah The reproaching self, a state of self-awareness and accountability, where the soul begins to recognize and regret its shortcomings.

nafs al-mutma'innah The tranquil self, at peace with itself and aligned with Divine will, representing the highest state of spiritual contentment.

nikah   The sacred contract of marriage in Islam, establishing rights and responsibilities between spouses. *Nikah* is often used in the context of the Islamic marriage ceremony as well, officiated by an imam.

OB/GYN   An abbreviation for Obstetrician-Gynecologist, a medical doctor specializing in women's reproductive health, pregnancy, and childbirth. OB/GYNs provide care related to menstrual health, fertility, pregnancy, childbirth, and menopause, as well as addressing gynecological conditions such as hormonal disorders, infections, and reproductive system health.

Prophet Muhammad (Peace and Blessings be Upon Him)   The final messenger of Allah in Islam, sent to guide humanity with the message of the Quran and to exemplify a life of worship, ethics, and compassion. Muslims add the phrase "Peace and Blessings be Upon Him" after mentioning the Prophet's name as an act of respect and a supplication for blessings upon him, in accordance with Quranic instruction "Indeed, Allah and His angels send blessings upon the Prophet. O you who have believed, ask [Allah to confer] blessing upon him and ask [Allah to grant him] peace" (Quran 33:56).

Quran   The holy book of Islam, believed to be the word of Allah revealed to the Prophet Muhammad (Peace and Blessings be Upon Him) through the Angel Jibreel (Gabriel). The Quran serves as the primary source of guidance for Muslims, encompassing theological, ethical, and legal teachings. Its verses are referenced throughout this book to frame discussions on sexual health within a soulful and Islamic context.

rahmah   A term meaning "mercy" or "compassion." In Islam, *rahmah* is a central attribute of Allah, often mentioned in the Quran, such as in the phrase *"Ar-Rahman Ar-Raheem"* (The Most Merciful, The Most Compassionate). It represents Allah's boundless mercy and care for all creation. Muslims are encouraged to embody *rahmah* in their actions, reflecting kindness, empathy, and compassion toward others. It is a quality deeply rooted in relationships, community, and worship, aligning with the prophetic example of mercy toward all beings.

riyadat al-nafs   Often translated as "disciplining the soul," this term refers to the effort of training and refining one's lower desires and instincts to align with higher spiritual goals. It complements *tazkiyat al-nafs* by emphasizing proactive discipline and intentionality, concepts that are woven into the discussions of self-accountability and empowerment throughout the book.

sakinah   A term meaning "tranquility," "peace," or "serenity." In an Islamic context, *sakinah* refers to a deep sense of calm and spiritual comfort that comes from a connection with Allah. It is often used to describe the tranquility found in relationships, particularly within marriage.

Salafiyya An Islamic reform movement that seeks to emulate the practices and beliefs of the *Salaf* (the first three generations of Muslims, including the Prophet Muhammad [Peace and Blessings be Upon Him], his companions, and their successors). Salafiyya emphasizes a return to what it considers the pure and unaltered teachings of Islam, rejecting later innovations (*bid'ah*) in religious practices and interpretations. It is often characterized by a focus on strict adherence to the Quran and Sunnah, literalist readings of Islamic texts, and an effort to eliminate cultural or historical influences perceived as deviations from original Islamic teachings. The movement has influenced various Islamic groups and ideologies, ranging from moderate reformists to more rigid interpretations.

shahadah The foundational declaration of Islamic belief, affirming that there is no god but Allah and that Muhammad (Peace and Blessings be Upon Him) is His Messenger. It is the first pillar of Islam and signifies entry into the faith.

shahwah Translated as "desire" or "lust," *shahwah* encompasses a range of human desires, particularly those related to physical and sexual appetite. *Shahwah* is part of the lower-soul, the *nafs al-ammarah*, which single Muslims are tasked with balancing and managing until marriage, when it is channeled into mutually pleasurable sexual intimacy.

shariah The comprehensive Islamic system of guidance encompassing law, ethics, and spirituality.

sunnah The sunnah is preserved through *ahadith*, which are documented reports of the Prophet's (Peace and Blessings be Upon Him) words, actions, and approvals transmitted by his companions. The *sunnah* complements the Quran by providing context and exemplifying how its teachings were implemented. It is integral to shaping the soulful frameworks and ethical principles explored in this book.

taharah A term meaning "purity" or "cleanliness." In Islamic practice, it refers to both physical and spiritual purification. *Taharah* is essential for acts of worship, such as prayer, and is achieved through specific rituals like *wudu* (ablution) or *ghusl* (ritual bath). It emphasizes the importance of maintaining cleanliness to uphold one's spiritual and physical well-being in accordance with Islamic teachings.

tassawuf Commonly translated as "Sufism" or "Islamic mysticism," *tassawuf* focuses on the inner, spiritual dimensions of Islam, fostering closeness to Allah through self-purification, mindfulness, and devotion. This term underscores the importance of soul-centered growth and spirituality in the context of sexual health and beyond.

tawakkul Trust in Allah while taking necessary action, a principle that applies to navigating life's challenges, including sexual health.

tazkiyat al-nafs Translates to "purification of the soul," referring to the process of cleansing one's heart, and thus soul, from spiritual diseases such as arrogance, envy, and heedlessness. It is an integral concept in Islamic spirituality, linked to personal and spiritual growth, and frequently referenced as part of the soul's journey in this book.

umrah Often called the "lesser pilgrimage," *umrah* can be performed at any time of year and involves a set of rites performed in Mecca. While not obligatory like *ḥajj*, it is a highly recommended and spiritually uplifting journey that invites closeness to Allah and a break from worldly distractions.

zina Illicit sexual activity outside the bounds of marriage, prohibited in Islam to preserve individual and societal well-being.

Introduction
My Soulful Journey

I still remember the moment I finished writing on the whiteboard, my hand trembling slightly as I turned to face the class. 12 curious fifth-grade Muslim girls sat before me, some fidgeting with their pencils, others swinging their legs under their desks. I was their Muslim sexual health teacher—the familiar face they saw in the hallways—and today, I was about to teach them.

On the board were the words "Gender Education," and as I smiled nervously at their expectant faces, I had no idea that this moment would shape the trajectory of my career.

This memory from 2011 marked the start of my journey at the intersections of Islam and sexual health with Muslims. By then, I had already completed my Master's in Occupational Therapy in 2007 and transitioned into a school-based role. In 2008, I joined a mental health promotion and prevention team serving Islamic schools and Muslim-populated charter schools in Calgary, Canada. For the first time, my personal faith and professional work collided in a way that challenged and inspired me.

As project coordinator for the mental health initiative, I worked alongside social workers, supporting schools that were grappling with the complexities of Islamic perspectives on sensitive topics like sexual and mental health. Many schools avoided these discussions altogether or postponed them until the last week of school, hoping the topic would quietly fade into the summer holidays. But I saw this as an opportunity—a door waiting to be opened.

I pushed it wide open—and I haven't looked back since.

Over the years, my work has evolved. I've taken on roles as a school therapist, community educator, and nonprofit leader, focusing on sexual violence prevention and addressing the gaps Muslims face in sexual health education. I've trained on college campuses, in mosques, and with community organizations across North America and internationally. Each experience has deepened my understanding of how to integrate Islamic perspectives with sexual health education, highlighting the importance of addressing this vital topic in a way that honors both faith and well-being.

A Soulful Turn

In December 2019, I walked out of the Reviving the Islamic Spirit (RIS) Conference in Toronto feeling like my professional world had been turned upside down. At the time, I was working with a Muslim-led nonprofit in the United States, focusing on sexual health education and violence prevention. With over ten years of experience in this field, my work felt fulfilling—yet, after one transformative three-hour lecture, I realized a vital piece of the puzzle had been missing.

That missing piece was the soul.

Up until that point, my work relied on two primary approaches: "top-down" and "equivalency." The top-down approach involved integrating Islamic perspectives into existing secular sexual health concepts, like teaching Islamic guidelines about menstruation to fifth-grade girls, adapted from mainstream curricula. The equivalency approach sought to draw parallels between secular and Islamic frameworks, such as stating, "Islam also centers sexual pleasure, for example, within marriage." While functional and effective in some ways, these approaches lacked the essence of Islam—the soul.

This realization marked a turning point. I recognized the need for a bottom-up approach to sexual health for Muslims—one that *begins* with the soul as its foundation. For Muslims, the soul is the lens through which we view the world and the essence of our purpose in this life. Sexual health, I realized, cannot be meaningfully framed, addressed, or discussed without anchoring it in this soulful foundation.

For the next six months after the conference, I immersed myself in works by classical and contemporary Islamic scholars—Imam al-Ghazali, Malik Badri, Laleh Bakhtiar (may Allah elevate their souls)—alongside present-day scholars and teachers. Their insights reshaped my understanding of the soul as the center of all health: sexual, emotional, physical, and spiritual. Inspired and invigorated, I resigned from my nonprofit role and launched my own initiative in September 2020 and called it *Sexual Health for Muslims*. Through social media and a dedicated website, I began sharing soul-centered Islamic sexual health content. What started as a modest experiment quickly gained traction, with my audience growing rapidly and increased demand for educational content, trainings, and therapy services.

Around this time, I discovered Islamic Psychology through a serendipitous series of events (i.e. signs from God) that led me to Cambridge Muslim

College. In 2021, I joined the inaugural cohort of their Postgraduate Diploma in Islamic Psychology. This program deepened my understanding of the interconnectedness of the soul and all aspects of our health while transforming my approach as a therapist and educator. It reinforced the importance of centering the soul—not just in my work, but in every aspect of life.

This book is the culmination of that journey. It represents my commitment to rediscovering sexual health as a sacred, soulful responsibility rooted in the timeless traditions of Islam.

A New Mission

The soul-centered framework has reshaped not only my professional practice but also my own journey. I've learned that as a soulful professional, I can only guide others as far as I've gone myself. This realization led me to prioritize my own healing, heart purification, and inner connection to Allah. Gone are the days of believing that my worth as a Muslim was tied to how much I could support and empower others. Now, the soul is at the center—not just of my work, but of my existence.

Through this soulful lens, I've seen how Islamic Psychology transforms clients' relationships with their inner wounds. I've seen parents step out from behind shame to hold developmentally appropriate conversations about sexual health with their children. I've held space for Muslim men and women who, through tears, realize that childhood wounds underlie their sexual health struggles—and who feel hopeful that healing is possible, because Allah is with them. Because sexual health issues are ultimately caused by wounds on the heart that require healing. And for Muslims, healing requires an inward journey within the soul, with the main purpose being to actualize the spiritual potential contained within us.

What This Book Offers: A Cumulative Journey of Soulful Sexual Health

This book is a comprehensive, soulful exploration of sexual health across the lifespan of a Muslim, contextualizing it not only for this world but also for the Hereafter. At its core, it bridges theory with practice, encouraging both individuals and professionals to approach sexual health through the lens of compassionate self-accountability. Rooted in Islamic teachings, this book serves as an invitation to embark on a soulful journey—one that integrates sexual health into our relationship with Allah.

Drawing on over 16 years of professional, educational, and personal experience, this work synthesizes insights from my roles as an educator, therapist, and speaker, alongside my studies in Islamic Psychology and my reflective journey as a Muslim navigating these deeply personal and complex topics. It integrates classical Islamic teachings, contemporary research, and the lived realities of individuals and communities I've had the privilege of working with, offering a resource that is both spiritually resonant and practically applicable.

Readers often ask, "Where can I exactly find what you're sharing?" While references are included throughout, the frameworks and approaches presented here extend beyond any single source. They reflect the cumulative knowledge Allah has allowed me to gain through education, practice, and deep commitment to this field. This book bridges gaps that many Muslims experience, providing clarity, comfort, and courage for navigating sexual health in a soulful and holistic way.

Whether you are a parent, grandparent, or someone seeking to better understand your own sexual health, I invite you to approach this book with an open heart. Every step you take toward healing and growth is a step toward Allah, guided always by His mercy and wisdom.

The Soul Is at the Center

At its core, this book is anchored in a soulful lens that prioritizes compassion, self-accountability, and spiritual growth. Compassion is emphasized as a starting point—for oneself and for others—particularly when navigating the sensitive and often stigmatized topics related to sexual health. Self-accountability encourages readers to reflect deeply on their own actions and intentions, aligning them with their faith and values. Spiritual growth serves as the ultimate goal, reminding readers that every challenge and triumph in sexual health is part of their journey back to Allah.

The integration of physical, emotional, and spiritual dimensions is central to this book's approach. Sexual health is not treated as a standalone topic but as part of the larger tapestry of a Muslim's life. Whether addressing abstinence, marital intimacy, or sexual health challenges, the book invites readers to see their experiences through a holistic, soul-centered perspective that nurtures both their faith and well-being.

This multifaceted approach ensures that the book is not only a guide for personal growth but also a resource for building deeper connections—with oneself, with others, and ultimately, with Allah.

Approaches Used in the Book

This book is grounded in a bottom-up approach, which means the soul is the starting point and guiding framework for understanding and addressing sexual health. In every chapter, the soul is the lens through which sexual health is framed, emphasizing its connection to our ultimate purpose as Muslims: worshipping Allah and growing closer to Him. This perspective ensures that every aspect of sexual health—whether physical, emotional, or spiritual—is explored holistically, aligning with Islamic teachings and the journey of the soul.

While this book prioritizes the bottom-up approach, it also acknowledges the continued relevance of top-down and equivalency approaches. Top-down methods, such as infusing Islamic perspectives into secular sexual health concepts, provide practical entry points for educators and professionals. Similarly, the equivalency approach, which draws parallels between Islamic values and contemporary frameworks, helps bridge gaps for Muslims navigating both Islamic and secular contexts. However, these methods alone often fall short of addressing the deeper spiritual needs of Muslims. By centering the soul, this book offers a more integrated, transformative approach that goes beyond surface-level solutions.

The Soulful Structure of the Book: A Developmental Journey

This book is thoughtfully structured to guide readers through a developmental journey (i.e. from birth to death), with the soul as the foundation. Each chapter builds upon the one before, weaving together Islamic teachings, ethical principles, and spiritual practices. From foundational chapters that introduce soulful sexual health, to those addressing specific challenges like abstinence, marital intimacy, and parenting, the content reflects the interconnectedness of physical, emotional, and spiritual dimensions.

You will see a timeline image at the beginning of each chapter to show the stage of the soul's journey that the chapter pertains to. As you read through the book, you will notice that the moon symbol will follow your journey through the soul's main developmental stages: Birth, Spiritual Accountability, Spiritual Maturity, Spiritual Legacy, and the Hereafter.

The book's structure also reflects a commitment to both practicality and reflection. Each chapter includes questions, strategies, and actionable steps alongside thought-provoking questions for personal growth. For professionals, the book offers a deeper understanding of how to integrate Islamic

The Journey of the Soul

Birth | Spiritual Accountability | Spiritual Maturity | Spiritual Legacy | The Hereafter

values into their work, making it a valuable resource for therapists, educators, and community leaders.

A Soulful Integration of Islamic Traditions and Teachings

Throughout the book, Islamic theology, ethics, and spirituality are seamlessly woven into the content. Quranic verses, Prophetic traditions, and Islamic ethical principles serve as foundational elements, providing guidance and inspiration for navigating sexual health in a way that aligns with the teachings of Islam. For example, concepts like purification of the soul (*tazkiyat al-nafs*), compassion (*rahmah*), and self-accountability (*muhasabah*) are explored as essential values in developing a soulful relationship with one's sexual health. The book also addresses common misconceptions about Islam and sexual health, offering clarity on topics such as the permissibility of sexual pleasure within marriage and the spiritual significance of empowered abstinence. By grounding these discussions in Islamic teachings, the book affirms that sexual health is not separate from faith but an integral part of the Muslim's journey toward Allah.

This book ultimately bridges Islamic teachings with evidence-based practices, ensuring that its guidance is both spiritually resonant and scientifically sound. Drawing on contemporary research in sexual health, psychology, and medicine, the book provides readers with a well-rounded understanding of key topics, from sexual development to reproductive health. For example, scientific insights into sexual response are paired with Islamic perspectives on marital sexual intimacy. This integration reassures readers that Islam and science are not in conflict but can work together to promote holistic well-being. Professionals will find this approach invaluable for applying both faith-based and clinical knowledge in their work.

Soulful Elements of the Book

This book is written with a gentle, compassionate tone, with the understanding that challenges related to sexual health are natural and deeply personal. The intention is not to judge or criticize but to offer soulful tools that foster healing, growth, and connection with Allah. Rather than striving for perfection, I invite you to see this journey as one of progress and discovery. Struggles with sexual health, like all areas of life, are opportunities to realign with our Creator and cultivate self-compassion.

As you read through the chapters, you will notice that "God" and "Allah" are used interchangeably to reflect the diverse language preferences of Muslim audiences. Additionally, Arabic terms such as *qalb* (heart) are sometimes introduced in Arabic first, followed by their English translation, while in other instances, the English term appears first. This variation is intentional and aims to provide a balance between linguistic authenticity and accessibility for readers.

At the beginning of each chapter, you will find narratives that share personal and professional reflections on the chapter's topic. These narratives, presented in italics, offer a personal lens into the themes and ideas explored in the book, providing a deeper connection to the material and encouraging readers to reflect on their own experiences. Throughout a few chapters, you will also notice that case studies are presented, which have been created from a compilation of common issues arising within my therapy practice. The names used within the case studies were selected randomly.

Throughout the book, you will notice boxes that highlight several topics, including key definitions, myth busting, commonly asked questions, and nuanced considerations that are crucial for the topics being discussed. You will also notice images throughout the chapters, some of which encourage writing and reflecting to integrate the content. Tables are provided for key concepts, some of which have spaces for your own reflections. To deepen your connection with the material, I encourage you to actively engage with the reflections, prompts, and insights provided in each chapter. Consider journaling your thoughts, jotting down key takeaways, or discussing what resonates with a trusted friend, spouse, or family member. This reflective practice can help you uncover new insights and apply what you've learned to your own journey.

Wherever possible, take moments to pause and reflect. These pauses are not interruptions but opportunities for your heart and mind to process and grow.

To support readers in fully engaging with the content of this book, a Glossary of Terms and Additional Readings have been included. The glossary provides definitions of commonly used Arabic terms that appear throughout the book, ensuring that readers of all backgrounds can connect with and understand the concepts discussed. These terms reflect key Islamic teachings, rituals, and principles that are integral to the soulful sexual health framework presented here. The additional readings list offers a curated selection of books and online resources for those who wish to deepen their knowledge or explore specific topics in greater detail.

Considerations for Reading and Using the Book

As you engage with this book, it's important to approach its content with openness and reflection. This work is not merely an informational manual but an invitation to embark on a deeply personal and spiritual journey, centering your connection to Allah and your own soul's development. Sexual health is often misunderstood or compartmentalized, yet it intersects with every dimension of our well-being—emotional, physical, and spiritual.

Recognizing this interconnectedness is crucial for embracing the holistic approach presented here, including the following considerations.

Our Unique Destiny and Timeline

Allah has a unique plan and timeline for every soul, making each journey distinct and incomparable to others. This understanding invites us to embrace compassion—not only toward ourselves but also toward others—reflecting a Prophetic virtue that fosters understanding and kindness in our interactions. While the chapters in this book are presented in a soulful developmental order, it is essential to *remember that life as a Muslim is rarely linear*. Marriage, for instance, can occur at any age, if it is destined for us, including during the later stages of life during our spiritual legacy years. Divorce, too, can occur at different points along our journey. Parenthood—whether through biological means or adoption—may occur at or after spiritual maturity or before.

Not all of us are destined to marry, stay married, marry once, marry when we're young, or raise children. These realities underscore the truth that there is no single timeline for the soulful life stages explored in this book. Each of our journeys reflects a unique and Divinely guided path, unfolding according to Allah's wisdom.

Furthermore, Allah has gifted each of us with a unique spiritual, emotional, physical, and sexual capacity. For example, many Muslims navigate mental health challenges or illnesses; acute and chronic physical conditions; and a variety of learning or neurodevelopmental needs. Readers are encouraged to keep their individual capacities in mind, understanding that Allah only expects from us what aligns with our God-given abilities. This perspective fosters self-compassion and helps us approach life's challenges with patience and gratitude, knowing that our path is uniquely tailored by the wisdom and mercy of Allah. This perspective encourages us to approach both ourselves and others with patience, compassion, and gratitude for the individualized nature of our spiritual journey.

Centering the Soul: *Fitrah as Our Identity*

A key emphasis of this book is the centrality of the soul—your *fitrah*, the pure and innate nature created by Allah, which carries the capacity to turn toward Him, embody noble character, and return to a state of spiritual alignment and nearness. Regardless of individual circumstances, the soul's journey toward God in this life is a common theme uniting all Muslims. It is this shared foundation that forms the basis of this work, guiding the discussions and frameworks presented throughout.

This book is grounded in traditional Islamic texts and perspectives, and the language and examples reflect heteronormative contexts, aligning with the normative Muslim spaces where much of my professional experience has been rooted. While this focus underpins the frameworks presented, I also want to acknowledge the diversity within Muslim communities and the unique experiences of individuals that often remain unaddressed in public forums. For instance, some Muslims may experience same-sex attraction but choose not to act on or identify through these feelings, while others in same-sex relationships may seek soulful guidance to realign their lives with their religious values. Readers may find resonance with different aspects of this book depending on their personal, cultural, or spiritual contexts, as it aims to provide compassionate insights while remaining rooted in Islamic principles.

For those navigating conversations on LGBTQ+ topics, chapter 7 offers a section with soulful frameworks for parents and educators to approach these discussions compassionately and thoughtfully. Additionally, chapter 4 provides insights into empowered abstinence, framing it as an intentional, soulfully grounded practice. Together, these chapters aim to provide tools for fostering understanding within the spiritual framework of *fitrah* and the values of Islam, ensuring that the guidance shared remains rooted in compassion and relevance for all.

Navigating Sensitivities

Some topics in this book may feel challenging or uncomfortable, especially for readers who have experienced trauma or carry cultural and personal stigmas around sexual health. Rather than avoiding discomfort, I invite you to engage with it in a way that fosters self-awareness and growth. When you feel activated or unsettled, pause. Place the book down, take deep breaths, and ground yourself in the present moment using your senses. This practice can help you reconnect with your body and emotions without judgment.

There's no rush to move through these chapters. Give yourself the time and space you need to process what arises. If you find certain sections particularly overwhelming, consider seeking the support of a trusted professional or someone who can hold space for your reflections. Remember, discomfort is often a sign of growth and approaching it with compassion and intentionality can lead to meaningful transformation.

Ultimately, this book is here to support you—not only in learning but in navigating your unique journey with soulful sexual health. Read it in a way that feels meaningful to you, trusting that your path will unfold as it's meant to.

Your Journey Through the Book

This book is designed to meet you where you are and has been written for individuals (and couples!) at any stage of life who want to integrate faith, spirituality, and practical tools into their understanding of sexual health.

I encourage you to approach this book with a reflective heart and an open mind. Allow space for personal growth, connection, and, most importantly, compassion toward yourself. Sexual health is a deeply personal and often sensitive topic, but it's also an integral part of your spiritual and emotional well-being. As you read, you may find certain chapters resonate with your current stage of life or specific challenges. Some sections may feel particularly relevant now, while others might become more meaningful later.

This book is not meant to be rushed through; it's a companion for your journey. If a chapter stirs something within you, pause and take the time to reflect. Come back to it when you're ready. Revisit chapters as you move through different stages of life, as they are designed to grow with you.

While the chapters build upon one another in a developmental progression, this book is flexible enough to meet various needs. You can read it sequentially for a comprehensive understanding or dive into specific chapters based on your interests or circumstances.

- **Professionals:** Chapter 13 provides tools and insights for those supporting Muslim clients.
- **Parents:** Chapter 7 equips you with strategies for soulfully guiding your children's sexual health education.
- **Couples:** Chapters on marital intimacy (chapter 6) and the search for a spouse (chapter 5) offer practical and soulful perspectives.
- **Individuals:** Foundational chapters on sexual health (chapter 3), empowered abstinence (chapter 4), and overcoming challenges (chapters 10 and 11) provide guidance tailored to personal growth.

As you read, I encourage you to approach the book with an open heart and a willingness to explore your relationship with sexual health through the lens of Islam. Reflect on how the soulful frameworks presented here resonate with your personal journey and allow them to inspire growth in alignment with your values and connection to Allah.

Ultimately, this book is a companion for your journey—a resource to support you in understanding, reflecting on, and nurturing the sacred trust of your sexual health, inseparable from your spiritual self.

On this note, *Bismillah-ir-Rahman-ir-Raheem* (In the name of Allah, the Most Gracious, the Most Merciful). Let's begin!

1 Contextualizing Islam and the Soul

We cannot address soulful sexual health for Muslims without first starting with the foundations of the Islamic tradition. So often, I've seen religion and sexual health pulled apart and viewed as irreconcilable—or even worse, that religion has negative impacts on sexual health. While there are many reasons for this disconnect—both globally and within our families and communities—I in good faith cannot ignore Islamic contexts. Each workshop or conference presentation I've ever given—whether in Muslim or mainstream spaces—starts with a section on Islam. Whether we were born Muslim or converted to Islam later in life, we all need to unlearn and relearn about Islam to some degree. Some Muslims refer to this as "taking your shahadah" (i.e. testimony of faith) in adulthood, which is a conscious turning toward enhancing our knowledge about Islam to become closer to God. And since no aspect of life as a Muslim can be understood without a holistic framework of the soul, it is here that we start our soulful sexual health journey.

The Journey of the Soul

Birth — Spiritual Accountability — Spiritual Maturity — Spiritual Legacy — The Hereafter

Introduction

This chapter marks the official beginning of our journey into soulful sexual health for Muslims! The term "soulful" is intentional, as this chapter will explore how Islam and the frameworks of the soul are deeply intertwined. Yet, many Muslims—and non-Muslims—have varying degrees of exposure to accurate and holistic understandings of Islam. If you were to ask the average person about Islam, responses might range from mentions of rituals like fasting, prayer, or the pilgrimage to Mecca, to perceptions of Islam as a set of rules or restrictions. Discussions about Muslims often touch on God but rarely offer a comprehensive view of the spiritual depth that defines the Islamic tradition.

When it comes to the soul, many Muslims might associate it primarily with the Afterlife or link it vaguely to their spirituality and connection with God. However, these perspectives often lack the depth needed to fully integrate the soul into one's worldview—including sexual health. That's why this book exists: to bridge this gap and provide a holistic understanding of soulful sexual health considering Islamic teachings.

This chapter lays the foundation for what's to come. To explore sexual health from a soulful perspective, we must first understand the soul within the Islamic tradition. I invite you to use this chapter as an opportunity for deep self-reflection, which is something you'll be encouraged to do throughout this book. Many of us have been shaped by Islamic education framed in overly simplistic or fear-based narratives. Here, we'll begin the work of unlearning those limiting perspectives and replacing them with an integrative, soul-based understanding of Islam—especially as we address the shame and fear that often surround sexual health.

Let's start this journey by returning to the roots of Islam. Together, we'll explore a brief history of the religion, key historical developments that have shaped Muslim identity, and finally, the Islamic framework of the soul. Before we dive in, though, I invite you to pause and reflect: What do you already know about Islam, and how might this knowledge shape your journey ahead?

Reflection Questions

What do you currently know about Islam's origins and its connection to other Abrahamic religions? How might this shape your understanding of Islam's place in the broader religious context?

_____
_____
_____

When you think about the Prophet Muhammad (Peace and Blessings be Upon Him), what aspects of his life and teachings come to mind? How do these perceptions influence your view of Islam as a faith and practice?

_____
_____
_____

Have you encountered any misconceptions or myths about Islam, either in your own learning or through societal narratives? How have these shaped your understanding of the faith?

_____
_____
_____

At the Beginning: Islam's Birth in the 7th Century

Contrary to common perceptions, Islam is not an isolated or standalone religion. As the final Abrahamic tradition, it is deeply rooted in the legacy of the Prophet Abraham, following in the footsteps of Judaism and Christianity. These three faiths, collectively known as the Abrahamic religions, share far more in common than is often recognized. For the purposes of this chapter—and this book—our focus will remain on Islam.

Islam's origins trace back to the 7th century in the Arabian Peninsula, a region marked by tribal societies and polytheistic practices. The foundation of Islam was laid through the life of the Prophet Muhammad (Peace and Blessings be Upon Him), who was born in Mecca around 570 CE into the respected Quraysh tribe. Known for his integrity and wisdom, the Prophet (Peace and Blessings be Upon Him) earned the title al-Amin (The Trustworthy) among his people. At the age of 40, during one of his retreats in the Cave of Hira, he received the first revelation from the angel Gabriel. These revelations, continuing over 23 years, became the Quran, Islam's holy book. The central message was monotheism, justice, and moral uprightness, urging Meccans to abandon idolatry and embrace the worship of one God, Allah.

As the number of Muhammad's followers grew, so did resistance from Meccan leaders who viewed this new faith as a challenge to their social and economic systems, alongside their worship of idols. This opposition led to the pivotal event of the Hijra in 622 CE, when Prophet Muhammad (Peace and Blessings be Upon Him) and his followers migrated to Yathrib, later renamed Medina. This migration marked the beginning of the Islamic calendar and the establishment of the first Islamic state. In Medina, Prophet Muhammad (Peace and Blessings be Upon Him) served as both spiritual and political leader, uniting diverse tribes under the principles of Islam. It was here that key Islamic practices, including the Five Pillars of Islam, took shape to guide Muslims in their faith and daily lives.

The spread of Islam during the Prophet's (Peace and Blessings be Upon Him) lifetime involved peaceful propagation as well as defensive battles, particularly against the Quraysh of Mecca. After years of conflict and strategic alliances, Prophet Muhammad (Peace and Blessings be Upon Him) returned triumphantly to Mecca in 630 CE. The Kaaba, a cube-shaped structure in Mecca believed to have been built by the Prophet Ibrahim (Abraham) and his son Ismail as a house of monotheistic worship, was cleansed of its idols and reestablished as the central place of worship for Muslims. By the time of the Prophet's (Peace and Blessings be Upon Him) passing in 632 CE, Islam had firmly taken root in the Arabian Peninsula, paving the way for its rapid expansion beyond. His successors, the caliphs, continued spreading Islam's teachings, profoundly shaping history and the lives of millions.

With this brief history of Islam in mind, I encourage you to take a moment to reflect on any myths or misconceptions about Islam you may have internalized. Use the box below as a guide for this reflection. This process of unlearning and relearning is central to the journey of this book and is needed to understand who Muslims are in the 21st century.

Myth Busting: Islam 101

Myth: Islam oppresses women.

Fact: Islam granted women rights in the 7th century that were revolutionary for the time, including the right to own property, inherit wealth, seek education, and engage in business. The Quran emphasizes equality in spiritual and moral responsibility: "Whoever does righteous deeds, whether male or female, while being a believer—those will enter Paradise" (Quran 4:124). Cultural oppression often stems from patriarchal traditions, not Islamic teachings.

Myth: Muslims worship a different God than Christians and Jews.

Fact: Muslims worship the same monotheistic God of Abraham, referred to as Allah, meaning "God" in Arabic. Arab Christians also use the term "Allah." Islam honors previous revelations and highly respects prophets like Moses and Jesus (Peace be Upon Them).

> **Myth: Islam is a religion of rules and restrictions.**
>
> **Fact:** Islam is a balance of theology, ethics, and spirituality, a harmony explored in chapter 2. At its core, Islam encourages Muslims to trust and surrender to the Divine wisdom embedded in its rulings, transcending mere intellectual knowledge. It is not a religion of dogmatic rules and behaviors, but a way of life rooted in a journey toward God. Islam's guidelines aim to foster a deep spiritual connection, inner peace, and societal harmony. Practices like prayer, fasting, and charity nurture mindfulness, gratitude, and empathy. These guidelines are not restrictions but pathways to a balanced and soulfully purposeful life, aligning believers with the Divine will while enabling them to navigate the world with clarity and fulfillment.

Who Are Muslims in the 21st Century?

When the term "Muslim" is mentioned, the stereotype of a light-skinned Arab often comes to mind. This misconception—fueled by popular media—fails to reflect the reality of Muslims as one of the most ethnically diverse religious groups in the world.

Globally, the Muslim population is expected to grow from 1.6 billion in 2010 to 2.2 billion by 2030, representing nearly 26% of the world's population (Pew Research Center, 2011). Muslims live in every corner of the world, with 79 countries projected to have over a million Muslim inhabitants by 2030. While regions such as Europe and North America will see a growing share of this population, most Muslims remain in Asia and Africa, representing a wide array of ethnicities, cultures, and languages.

In addition to ethnic diversity, Muslims vary greatly in their practice of Islam. Popular media often categorizes Muslims into simplistic "conservative" or "progressive" monoliths, but their observance reflects a dynamic spectrum of personal and cultural interpretation. This diversity in practice mirrors the ways Islam spread globally from its birth in the 7th century. It also hints at how Muslims today engage with—or remain unaware of—holistic Islamic perspectives on the soul.

Despite these differences, a unifying thread among Muslims is their relationship with God. At its core, Islam is about striving to submit to God's will and preparing for the eternal life of the Hereafter. Submission is symbolized in the daily obligatory prayers, where Muslims bow their foreheads—home to the complex frontal lobe of the brain—to the ground in humility. This act embodies the choice that defines humanity: the free will to follow God's commandments and actively strive to refine the soul.

For Muslims, life is a Divine gift accompanied by responsibilities, including the call to actualize their spiritual potential. This requires continuous effort to work on the soul, moving beyond the "what" of faith to understanding the deeper "why" and "how." Yet, many Muslims lack awareness of Islam's deeper soul-based frameworks, a gap that is often rooted in and shaped by historical forces like colonization, which reshaped Islamic education and practice worldwide. It is to this critical topic of colonization and its impact on Muslims' understanding of Islam that we now turn.

Colonization's Impact on the Soulful Islamic Tradition

Many Muslims today have limited exposure to Islam's soul-centered traditions, a gap shaped significantly by colonization. Colonization systematically dominated Muslim societies, introducing foreign frameworks that disrupted authentic Islamic spiritual traditions. This process fostered rigid, patriarchal interpretations of Islam, often prioritizing cultural or societal/secular norms over the religion's inherently compassionate principles, especially in matters of sexual health and relationships.

Historically, Islam provided holistic guidance on sexuality, encouraging open, respectful discussions. For example, *hadiths* narrate the Prophet Muhammad's (Peace and Blessings be Upon Him) advice on intimacy, emphasizing compassion and foreplay in marital relations. For instance, he advised, "One of you should not fulfill one's [sexual] need from one's wife like an animal; rather, there should be between them foreplay of kissing and words" (Musnad al-Firdaws, 2/55). Yet, colonization shifted this openness to silence, rendering sex a taboo subject in many Muslim communities.

Medieval Christian views, contrasting with Islam's sex-positive stance, labeled Islamic teachings as "barbaric." Thinkers like St. Augustine framed sexual pleasure as sinful, shaping Western societies and influencing colonized Muslim regions. The Enlightenment further marginalized spirituality, fragmenting the integration of the mind, body, and soul—hallmarks of Islamic traditions. Colonization deepened this fragmentation, with pivotal moments such as the Napoleonic conquest of Egypt and the fall of the Ottoman Empire leading to European domination of Muslim lands.

Islamic leaders and civilizations responded in three ways:

1. **Returning to Fundamentals:** The rise of Salafiyya movements emphasized a return to the practices of the early Muslim community, advocating for strict interpretations of Islamic texts. This approach often led to the implementation of legalistic measures, including mandatory dress codes and restrictions on women's mobility (Khan, 2019).

2. **Modernizing Islam:** Islamic Modernism emerged as an effort to reconcile Islamic faith with Western ideologies, advocating for liberal interpretations and the adoption of secular perspectives. This movement sought to reform Islamic thought to align with contemporary values and challenges (Khan, 2019).
3. **Preserving Authenticity:** Islamic traditionalism emphasizes adherence to classical Sunni schools of law, integrating law, spirituality, and ethical behavior. This approach seeks to preserve Islam's holistic teachings, including its perspectives on sexuality and ethics (Khan, 2019).

This book aligns with the third approach, aiming to revive Islam's authentic and soulful perspective on sexual health. While colonization disrupted these traditions, exploring Islam's theological and spiritual framework can guide Muslims toward a holistic understanding of sexuality, nurturing both the body and soul.

Subsequent chapters will delve deeper into these topics, exploring how Islam's compassionate stance on intimacy and its practical guidance can address modern sexual health challenges while reclaiming its soul-centered legacy.

Reflection Questions

How has your understanding of Islam's traditions—especially regarding the soul—been shaped by modern influences or historical narratives?

_____
_____
_____

How does it feel to know that the Islamic tradition has never shied away from addressing sexual health topics?

_____
_____
_____

How might colonization have influenced your own or your community's views of Islam and sexual health?

_____
_____
_____

> Reflecting on this brief history of Islam, what new insights or connections stand out to you? How might this understanding influence your journey into soulful sexual health?
>
> _____
> _____
> _____

Traditional Islamic Perspectives of the Soul

With a foundational understanding of Islam and Muslims in place, we can now delve deeper into an Islamic framework of the soul. This understanding is crucial because the chapters to come will approach sexual health through the lens of the soul—an often overlooked perspective in contemporary discourse.

When sexual health neglects the soul, it tends to be reduced to something purely physical, focusing solely on the body (*jism* in Arabic)—specifically the genital structures and reproductive systems. This reductionist view falls far short of Islam's holistic model of the soul, which not only encompasses the body but also transcends it. In Islamic thought, the soul (*nafs*) contains the body, not the other way around, as is typically assumed in modern frameworks. The body is an integral aspect of the soul's journey, serving as its vessel, expression, and means of interaction with the world.

As you explore the forthcoming Islamic frameworks, you'll see that the body's connection to the soul is not merely functional but deeply spiritual, reflecting the soul's broader purpose and aspirations.

Understanding the Term "Soul"

The term "soul" (*nafs* in Arabic) appears 295 times in the Quran—more frequently than Heaven or Hell, which are often the focus of Islamic discussions! Traditional Islamic texts sometimes use *nafs* interchangeably with *ruh* (spirit). However, for clarity and to reflect nuanced understandings, this book distinguishes between *nafs* and *ruh*.

In Islamic thought, the soul (*nafs*) is the inner witness to all that a Muslim experiences in this world—a world that is only one stage in the soul's existence. According to Imam al-Haddad's (1991) *The Five Lives of Man*, the soul traverses five stages of existence:

1. **Preconception Stage (*'Alam al-Arwah*):** Souls exist in the realm of spirits before entering the physical world.

2. **Life in This World (*Dunya*)**: From birth to death, the soul experiences life through its physical body.
3. **Intermediate Realm (*Barzakh*)**: After death and before the Day of Judgment, the soul resides in a transitional state influenced by its earthly deeds.
4. **Resurrection and Judgment (*Yawm al-Qiyamah*)**: The soul is reunited with the body and held accountable for its actions.
5. **Final Abode (*Dar al-Akhirah*)**: The soul's eternal destination in Paradise or Hell, based on its judgment.

These stages, as summarized in Table 1.1, emphasize the soul's ongoing journey and evolution toward its ultimate destiny in the Hereafter. This cyclical and eternal perspective underscores the soul's centrality in Islamic thought.

The Distinction Between Nafs and Ruh

In Islamic tradition, the soul (*nafs*) is formed at 120 days of gestation with the entry of the spirit (*ruh*), signifying the union of body and Divine essence. The *ruh* embodies Allah's pure and sacred presence, while the

Table 1.1 A summary of the five stages of the human soul, as described by al-Haddad

Stage	Description	Key Features
Preconception Stage	Souls exist in the realm of spirits before entering the physical world.	Known as '*Alam al-Arwah*, this stage emphasizes the soul's origin in the Divine realm.
Life in This World	From birth to death, the soul experiences life through the physical body.	The soul interacts with the physical world, making choices and fulfilling its purpose.
Intermediate Realm (*Barzakh*)	The soul resides in a transitional state after death and before the Day of Judgment, shaped by its earthly deeds.	The soul experiences consequences of earthly actions and awaits resurrection.
Resurrection and Judgment	The soul is reunited with the body and held accountable for its actions.	The final judgment determines the soul's ultimate destiny based on its deeds.
Final Abode	The soul's eternal destination in Paradise or Hell, based on its judgment.	Represents eternal existence, either in blissful Paradise or in punishment.

nafs bridges the Divine and earthly realms, reflecting human free will and accountability. With its dual capacity to incline toward goodness (*taqwa*) or evil (*fujur*), the *nafs* represents the human struggle for spiritual refinement amid worldly desires. This dynamic highlights the soul's role in connecting this life to the Hereafter, carrying the weight of actions accountable on the Day of Judgment. It motivates Muslims toward self-purification, emphasizing the soul as a key to understanding the link between the transient and eternal.

Exploring an Islamic Model of the Soul

The study of the soul has been a central focus in Islam since the religion's inception, forming the foundation of what is now known as Islamic Psychology (IP). Traditionally referred to as *'ilm al-nafs* (the science of the soul), this field encompasses the study of the soul's constitution and journey through an Islamic lens. Interestingly, many Muslims may not realize that various models of the soul have existed throughout Islamic history, each offering unique insights into its nature and progression.

There are different models and types of Islamic Psychology in present-day discourse, and the model that will be the focus of this book is a bottom-up framework. This framework centers traditional Islamic perspectives of the soul. This is in contrast with top-down frameworks, which sprinkle Islamic perspectives and practices into a secular framework, or the equivalency approach, which attempts to reconcile secular/mainstream models by providing an "equivalent" from within Islam. Dr. Malik Badri's (2018) work *The Dilemma of Muslim Psychologists* highlights the challenges inherent in these approaches and underscores the importance of grounding Islamic Psychology in authentic Islamic traditions.

For this book, we'll draw on the scholarly work of Dr. Abdallah Rothman, a leading figure in applying traditional Islamic Psychology frameworks to contemporary Muslim contexts. His model of the soul, of which Figure 1.1 shows an adapted version, offers a comprehensive view of the soul's structure and dynamics, particularly in relation to psychotherapy (Rothman, 2022; Rothman & Coyle, 2020). Throughout this book, we'll apply Rothman's model to center traditional teachings of the soul, toward a soulful sexual health paradigm for Muslims.

Understanding the Iceberg Model of the Soul

Rothman's model (see Figure 1.1) conceptualizes the soul as an iceberg, with four distinct yet interconnected layers. Each layer provides unique insights into behaviors, emotions, and spiritual growth.

Contextualizing Islam and the Soul

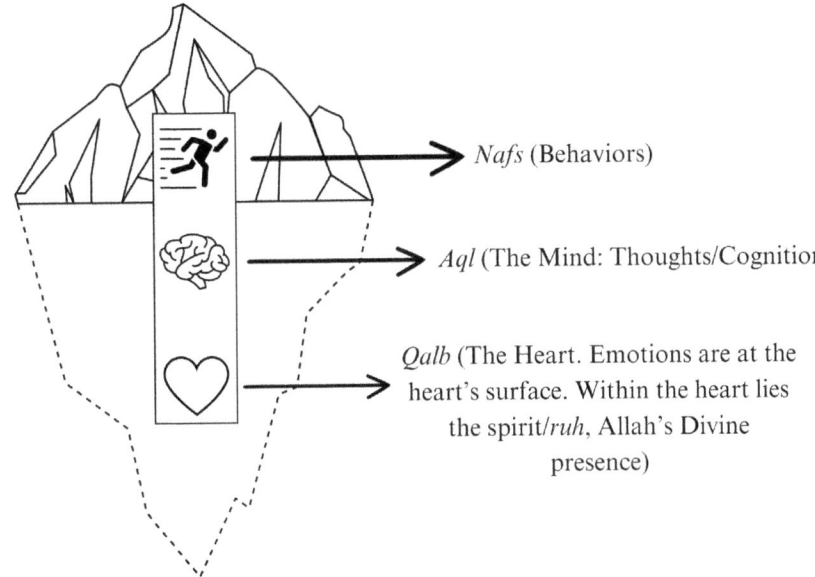

Figure 1.1 An adapted version of Rothman's model of the soul based on traditional Islamic Psychology

***Surface-Level Behaviors* (Nafs):** The visible tip of the iceberg represents the *nafs* at its most apparent level—observable behaviors. For example, in the context of sexual health, this could include engaging in premarital sexual activity (chapter 4) or displaying sexualized behaviors during the search for a spouse (chapter 5). While behaviors are the easiest to notice and often the focus of efforts to change, they are only a symptom of deeper underlying processes.

***The Mind* (Aql):** Beneath the surface lies the mind, which governs thoughts and cognition. The ʿ*aql* plays a critical role in processing experiences and making decisions, but it does not operate in isolation. Within this model, the mind works closely with the heart (*qalb*), which will be explored in detail in the following section.

***The Heart* (Qalb):** The heart is the seat of emotions, spiritual intuition, and connection with the *ruh* (spirit). It serves as the bridge between the mind and the deeper aspects of the soul, guiding a person toward alignment with their spiritual nature.

***The Spirit* (Ruh):** At the core of the iceberg lies the *ruh*, the Divine essence within every individual. The *ruh* represents the *fitrah* (natural disposition)

that Muslims strive to actualize throughout their lives. It is the purest aspect of the soul, constantly seeking closeness to Allah.

It's important to note that while these layers are presented as distinct, they are deeply interconnected and work in harmony. By exploring each layer, we can better understand which aspects of the soul are implicated in various sexual health challenges and, more importantly, how to address them holistically.

A Quranic Model: The Journey of the Soul

The Quran outlines a developmental journey of the soul through three distinct stages (Bakhtiar, 2019). While other models within the Islamic tradition offer additional complexity, this three-stage Quranic model provides an accessible framework for understanding the soul's progression through these three distinct but constantly cycling phases (see Figure 1.2).

The *Nafs al-Ammarah* (The Soul That Commands to Evil)

"Indeed, the soul is a persistent enjoiner of evil" (Quran 12:53).

Often called the "lower soul" or "animalistic soul," this stage reflects the base instincts of humanity—sexual desire (*shahwah*) and anger (*ghadab*). These instincts, while sometimes viewed as negative, serve essential purposes: sexual desire preserves the species and provides pleasure, while anger protects the individual. The challenge at this stage is to avoid being dominated by these instincts, striving instead for balance through self-accountability.

The *Nafs al-Lawwama* (The Self-Reproaching Soul)

"And I swear by the self-reproaching soul" (Quran 75:2).

At this stage, the soul begins to gain awareness and self-reflect on its behaviors, thoughts, and emotions. It seeks alignment with spiritual values but may struggle with guilt, self-criticism, or shame. While these emotions can motivate growth, they can also lead to stagnation if not channeled productively, resulting in becoming "stuck" at this stage of the soul.

The *Nafs al-Mutma'innah* (The Soul at Peace)

"O soul that is at peace, return to your Lord, well-pleased and pleasing to Him" (Quran 89:27–28).

This final stage represents a state of spiritual harmony and contentment. At this level, the soul aligns fully with Divine will, experiencing peace both inwardly and outwardly. While achieving this state can be challenging, glimpses of it can inspire further growth and dedication to the spiritual path.

It's important to remember that the soul's journey is rarely linear. Life's challenges and experiences often cause fluctuations between stages, and this dynamic process is part of the human condition. Instead of striving for perfection, use this model as a tool for reflection.

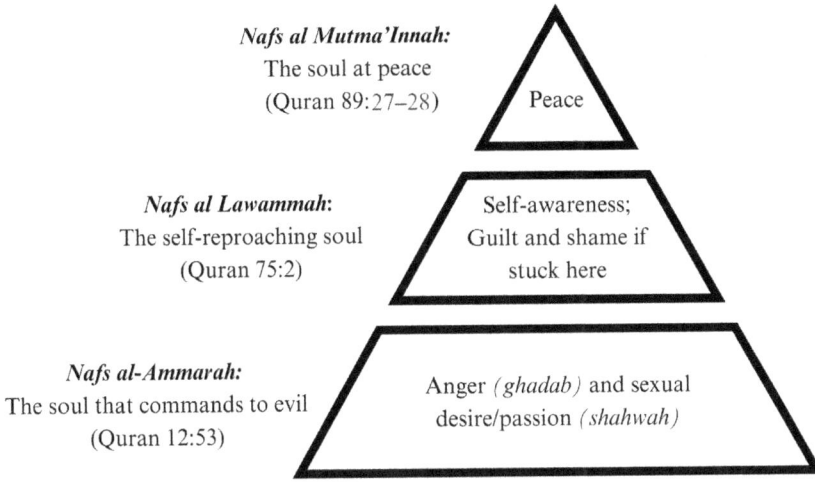

Figure 1.2 The three-stage journey of the soul, as outlined in the Quran

The stages of the soul are summarized in Table 1.2, providing key characteristics and reflective prompts to guide your understanding. This model will serve as a cornerstone for the discussions in chapter 2, where we contextualize sexual health within these soulful frameworks.

In the next section, we'll turn our focus to the heart and its role within this model of the soul, exploring what it means to "work" on the soul in the context of sexual health.

Table 1.2 An overview of the journey of the soul, as outlined in the Quran

Level of the Soul	Description and Overview
Nafs al-ammarah (The soul that commands to evil) Quran 12:53	Also known as the "animal soul," this level is where God instills two foundational drives: sexual desire (*shahwah*) and anger (*ghadab*). Sexual desire serves to preserve the species and provides the pursuit of sexual pleasure, while anger protects the individual and acts as a defensive mechanism. As Muslims, the goal is not to suppress or "conquer" these drives but to cultivate balance and moderation. This approach will be explored in greater depth in future chapters, particularly as it relates to navigating sexual health challenges.

(*Continued*)

Table 1.2 (Continued)

Level of the Soul	Description and Overview
Nafs al-lawammah (The self-reproaching soul) Quran 75:2	At this stage, the soul begins to develop greater self-awareness. We start to gain valuable insights into our thoughts and behaviors, which is an essential first step in working on the soul and aligning ourselves with the journey toward God. However, if guilt or shame becomes overwhelming and remains unresolved, we risk becoming stuck at this level of the soul, struggling to find peace with our challenges and hindering our spiritual growth.
Nafs al-mutma'innah (The soul at peace) Quran 89:27–28	This stage represents the ideal that Muslims aspire to reach and strive to maintain, though it can be challenging. At this level, the soul attains peace in and with the presence of God, free from the "inner challenges" that disrupt its spiritual journey. While most who consistently embody this state were exemplary figures such as the Prophet Muhammad (Peace and Blessings be Upon Him), his companions, and other enlightened individuals in Islamic history, we may still experience moments of this profound peace in our own lives, offering glimpses of the soul's ultimate potential.

The Heart as the Center of the Soul

In Islamic tradition, the heart plays two essential roles: it is the seat of emotions (*ihsaas*) and the container of the *ruh* (spirit). Scholar Imam al-Ghazali (2010) highlighted the heart's transformative nature, symbolized by the Arabic word *qalb* (heart), which signifies both the physical organ and the center of emotions and spirituality. This dual role underscores the heart's significance in the soul's journey.

The *ruh*, described as the Divine spark or breath of life, is breathed into the body at around 120 days of gestation, as detailed in *hadiths* from Sahih al-Bukhari and Sahih Muslim. This moment imbues the heart with *fitrah*—an incorruptible, innate inclination toward goodness, truth, and recognition of Allah. The *fitrah* represents humanity's natural state of purity, guiding individuals toward righteous behavior and God-consciousness unless impacted by external influences.

The *qalb* and *aql* (intellect) work closely together in this journey. For example, engaging in learning and seeking Divine knowledge can illuminate the heart, turning it toward Allah and strengthening its journey. The interaction between the heart and intellect is reciprocal; our thoughts significantly impact the heart's state. Positive, God-conscious thoughts can soften and purify the heart, while lower-soul, shame-based, or self-critical thoughts can cloud and harden it, creating barriers to spiritual growth.

Understanding that the heart contains the *ruh*—a Divine and incorruptible manifestation of Allah's presence—provides a profound foundation for "working" on the soul. The heart is not merely an organ or a metaphor; it is the bridge between the physical and spiritual dimensions of our existence.

To work on the soul means to actively purify the heart, clearing it of distractions, sins, and negative emotions that obscure its connection to Allah. This purification involves constant remembrance of Allah (*dhikr*), seeking forgiveness, and striving to align our thoughts, emotions, and actions with our *fitrah*. It also requires an awareness of the heart's state: Is it tranquil and reflective, or restless and clouded?

As Imam al-Ghazali beautifully articulates, the process of working on the heart is both challenging and rewarding. It is through this inner work—integrating both the heart and intellect—that the soul aligns with its higher purpose, enabling us to journey closer to Allah and actualize the peace and balance described in the Quranic model of the soul.

The Heart's Need for Purification

At birth, the heart exists in a pure state of God-consciousness, fully connected to the *ruh* and capable of actualizing the *fitrah*, the innate inclination toward goodness and truth. However, as we grow, life's nurturing and harmful experiences shape the heart. Positive interactions strengthen our connection to Allah, while negative experiences or sins create "occlusions" on the heart, described by Imam al-Ghazali as "black spots." He likened the heart to a mirror: when clean, it reflects the Divine light from our *fitrah*, but as it becomes clouded by sins, trauma, or distractions, our sense of Allah's presence diminishes. This disconnection often leads to the feeling that Allah is distant, though it is the barriers within the heart that obscure His presence (Ghazali, 2010).

Purifying the heart—removing the barriers created by unresolved pain, shame, or trauma—is essential for restoring our spiritual connection and achieving inner harmony. A weighed-down heart not only impacts our relationship with Allah but also affects how we relate to our body and others, including in matters of sexual health. The process of healing, like polishing a mirror, allows the light of the *ruh* to shine through. As Muslims, our lifelong task is to continually cleanse the heart, striving to return to

Allah in the best spiritual state. In the next section, we'll explore practices for heart-centered inner soul work, inviting reflection on what your heart might need to feel Allah's presence more fully.

> **Reflection Questions**
>
> What life experiences—both nurturing and challenging—have shaped the "mirror" of your heart? How might these experiences be influencing your connection with God today?
>
> _____
> _____
>
> Are there specific emotions that feel like "dust" on your heart, blocking you from fully accessing your *ruh* and *fitrah*? How might you begin to address them?
>
> _____
> _____
>
> Reflect on a time when you were present and felt at peace—and, therefore, were connected to Allah's presence within you. What practices or experiences helped you feel this way, and how can you bring them into your life more intentionally?
>
> _____
> _____

Compassionate Purification of the Soul

As we've discussed, maintaining a close connection with Allah through our *ruh* requires ongoing purification of the heart. This purification is essential for navigating the journey of the soul and addressing any sexual health challenges we encounter. We'll explore these connections in greater depth in the chapters to come!

The Islamic tradition offers a wealth of terms and mechanisms for this inner work, many of which were articulated by great scholars of the past. For the purposes of this book, which centers on soulful sexual health, we'll

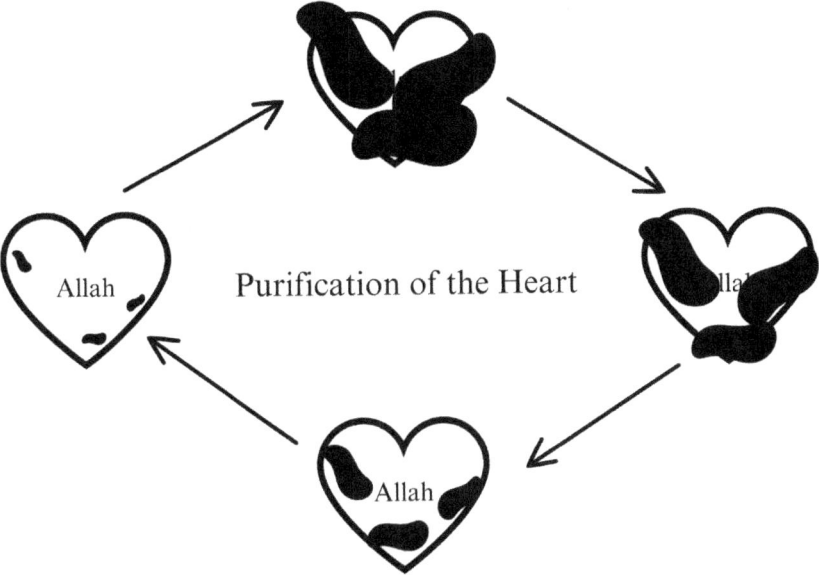

Figure 1.3 A depiction of cleaning the window of the heart and removing the dust that accumulates through life's challenges

focus on a few key concepts that illuminate the process of purifying the heart and allowing our connection with Allah to shine through. Refer to Figure 1.3, which provides a visual representation of this metaphor.

Purification of the Soul: Tazkiyat al-Nafs *and* Riyadat al-Nafs

Tazkiyat al-nafs, or purification of the soul, is the process of cleansing the heart from spiritual impurities to draw closer to Allah. It involves removing metaphorical "dust" from the heart through acts like *zakat* (mandatory charity), which purifies wealth and the soul. This practice extends to addressing traits like greed, envy, or arrogance and includes working through imbalanced sexual desires or healing from trauma. For example, sincere *tawbah* (repentance), cultivating modesty, fostering self-restraint, and reflecting on one's role in marital sexual challenges are key to this process. Integrating *dua* (supplication), Quranic reflection, and seeking therapeutic healing for past wounds aligns the heart with spiritual growth and inner peace.

Riyadat al-nafs, or disciplining the soul, complements purification by helping individuals manage impulses, cultivate virtues, and align behavior with spiritual goals. Practices like *salah* (prayer), fasting, self-reflection, and avoiding lower-self behaviors (*nafs al-ammarah*) promote compassionate self-accountability and moral development. Concepts like *dhikr* (remembrance of Allah), *muraqaba* (mindful self-awareness), and leaning into spiritually challenging actions strengthen this connection. Together, these practices allow the *ruh* (spirit) to shine, fostering alignment with Allah. Chapter 2 will expand on these frameworks, applying them to sexual health and laying the foundation for developmental topics in subsequent chapters.

Summary

Congratulations on completing the first chapter of this book! This chapter provided a holistic and nuanced introduction to Islam, starting with its origins and touching on key historical developments, such as colonization, that have shaped both Muslim and non-Muslim understandings of the religion today. We also explored the diversity of Muslims in the 21st century and how this impacts their spiritual and soulful journeys.

Building on this foundation, we delved into traditional Islamic understandings of the soul, discussing its multifaceted nature and journey as outlined in the Quran. We examined the pivotal role of the heart (*qalb*), its need for purification, and the core concepts of *tazkiyat al-nafs* and *riyadat al-nafs*, which are essential for cultivating spiritual development. These frameworks for soul purification and compassionate self-discipline will be woven into the discussions of sexual health throughout this book.

In the next chapter, we'll transition into an exploration of Islamic perspectives on sexual health and how Muslims in the 21st century navigate this deeply personal and often misunderstood topic. By connecting the soulful foundations from this chapter to the realities of sexual health, chapter 2 will set the stage for practical frameworks that integrate Islamic teachings with a holistic, soul-centered approach.

Reflections and Action Items

_____
_____
_____
_____
_____
_____
_____
_____
_____

Reference List

Badri, M. (2018). *The dilemma of Muslim psychologists*. MWH London
Bakhtiar, L. (2019). *Quranic psychology of the self*. Kazi Publications.
Haddad, A. I., al- (1991). *The lives of man: A guide to the human states before life, in the world, and after death* (M. al-Badawi, Trans.). Fons Vitae.
Ghazali, A. H., al- (2010). *Marvels of the heart: Book 21 of Ihya Ulum al-Din* (W. J. Skellie, Trans.; H. E. Nasr, Ed.). Islamic Texts Society.
Khan, M. A. M. (2019). Islam as identity: After a century of Islamic revivalism. In: *Islam and Good Governance*. Palgrave Macmillan. https://doi.org/10.1057/978-1-137-54832-0_3
Pew Research Center. (2011). *The future of the global Muslim population: Projections for 2010–2030*. https://www.pewresearch.org/religion/2011/01/27/the-future-of-the-global-muslim-population/
Rothman, A. (2022). *Developing a model of Islamic psychology and psychotherapy: Islamic theology and contemporary understandings of psychology*. Routledge.
Rothman, A., & Coyle, A. (2020). Conceptualizing an Islamic psychotherapy: A grounded theory study. *Spirituality in Clinical Practice*. Advance online publication. https://doi.org/10.1037/scp0000219
Sahih International. (1997). *The Quran: Arabic text with corresponding English meanings*. Abul-Qasim Publishing House.

2 A Soulful Model of Sexual Health for Muslims

Earlier in my career, my approach to sexual health for Muslims primarily involved incorporating Islamic content into existing sexual health frameworks. For instance, when discussing puberty or marital sexual intimacy, I would "sprinkle" Islamic perspectives into the broader sexual health content, creating a "top-down" approach. While this method felt valuable at the time, I noticed gaps—particularly in how these frameworks addressed the deeper, spiritual dimensions of our existence. They provided information but often failed to speak to the core of what it means to navigate sexual health as a Muslim whose life is inherently tied to the soul's journey toward Allah. Through my own study of the Islamic tradition, I came to realize that the missing piece was the soul. The soul is not just a theological concept; it is the foundation of our identity, influencing not only our sexual health but also how we understand ourselves as Muslims and how we live in alignment with our Creator. This realization fundamentally shifted my work, leading me to embrace a "bottom-up" approach that begins with Islamic traditions of the soul and builds outward. From this perspective, sexual health frameworks are not merely infused with Islamic content but are instead deeply rooted in the theology, ethics, and spirituality of Islam.

This chapter is therefore foundational for the entire book. It conceptualizes a soulful sexual health model for Muslims, grounded in the timeless wisdom of Islamic traditions. I encourage you to revisit it as often as needed, as it provides crucial contexts for understanding the chapters to

The Journey of the Soul

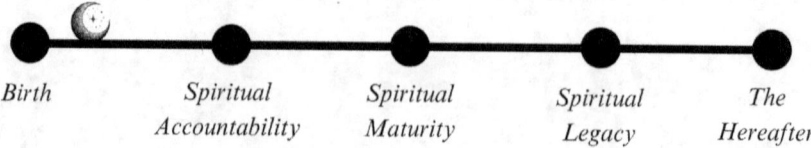

Birth — Spiritual Accountability — Spiritual Maturity — Spiritual Legacy — The Hereafter

DOI: 10.4324/9781032675862-3

come. Through centering the soul and embracing a holistic approach, this chapter lays the groundwork for navigating sexual health with purpose, compassion, and alignment with Allah's guidance.

Introduction

Sexual health is an integral part of the human experience and, for Muslims, a profound aspect of the soul's journey toward Allah. Often misunderstood as merely physical functions, sex within marriage, or a set of "do's and don'ts," it encompasses mental, physical, and spiritual dimensions. Through a soulful lens, sexual health becomes a path to self-awareness, healing, and spiritual growth, deepening our connection to Allah.

Historically, Islamic traditions embraced sexual health holistically, blending its practical and spiritual aspects. However, colonial influences introduced a narrative rooted in fear and shame. This chapter reclaims that balance, presenting a soulful framework grounded in classical Islamic teachings and adapted to modern complexities. Anchored by values of compassion, self-accountability, the soul's journey, and inseparability from Allah, this framework transforms challenges into opportunities for growth and faith-aligned relationships.

Moving forward from this chapter, the book guides readers on a developmental journey, from foundational concepts and empowered abstinence to marital intimacy, soulful parenting, and addressing sexual health challenges across life stages. Reflect on what sexual health means to you as you begin this exploration, embracing it as a Divine trust that integrates well-being with faith.

Reflection Questions

What comes to mind when you hear the term "sexual health"? How has your understanding of this term been shaped by religious teaching, cultural contexts, or society?

_____
_____
_____

How do you currently view the connection between sexual health and the soul? Are there areas where this connection feels unclear or unexplored?

_____
_____
_____

> What feelings or thoughts arise when considering sexual health as part of a holistic approach that includes mental, physical, and spiritual dimensions?
>
> _____
> _____
> _____

What Is Islam's Perspective on Sexual Health?

What exactly does "sexual health" mean, especially as it relates to Muslims? The term "sexual health" is a relatively modern construct, gaining prominence in the mid-20th century with the rise of global health initiatives. It was formalized by organizations such as the World Health Organization (WHO), which defines sexual health as "a state of physical, emotional, mental, and social well-being in relation to sexuality" (World Health Organization, n.d.). While this modern framework is valuable, it often overlooks the spiritual dimension that is foundational for Muslims. And given many Muslims' lack of understanding or misconceptions surrounding the word "sexuality," such definitions may trigger fear or shame-based reactions that prevent us from learning more about this topic.

However, it is crucial for Muslims to know that the essence of sexual health has always been integrated within the Islamic tradition. Before we dive into Islamic texts to illustrate this, let's address some myths around the Islamic faith and its approach to sexual health that I commonly see and hear as a professional.

Myth Busting: Muslims and Sexual Health

Myth: Sexual health only refers to sexual intercourse.

Fact: Sexual health encompasses physical, emotional, and spiritual well-being. For Muslims, it reflects the soul's journey toward Allah, emphasizing care of the body as an *amanah* (trust), processing emotions, and fostering compassionate relationships. It includes understanding the body, addressing challenges, and embracing intimacy as worship. A holistic view aligns sexual health with spiritual values and personal growth.

> **Myth: It is immodest for Muslims to learn or talk about sexual health.**
>
> **Fact:** Discussing sexual health aligns with Islamic principles of knowledge-seeking and intentional living. With *niyyah* (intention), these discussions become acts of worship when aimed at seeking Allah's pleasure and well-being. Historically, Muslim scholars integrated physical needs with ethical and spiritual responsibilities, showing that modesty (*haya*) means addressing essential topics with respect and soulful purpose.
>
> **Myth: Learning about sexual health may lead to sexual activity.**
>
> **Fact:** Learning about sexual health empowers value-driven, intentional choices aligned with Islamic principles. Knowledge safeguards against harm, fostering responsible navigation of desires and relationships. Islamic scholars emphasized education as integral to ethics and spirituality, with soulful understanding promoting self-awareness, growth, and alignment with Allah's guidance.

Islamic Traditions and Texts of Sexual Health

Due to the impacts of colonization, many Muslims and non-Muslims believe Islamic teachings to either condemn or shy away from sexual health topics. However, an authentic reading of the texts shows that this is far from the truth. Within Islamic teachings, while there is no direct equivalent term, aspects of sexual health are naturally embedded within discussions about life stages, such as puberty, menstruation, marital intimacy, and family planning. These discussions are not confined to legal rulings—the *halal* (permissible) and the *haraam* (impermissible)—but also encompass the soul's journey, underscoring the importance of intention, ethics, and spirituality. The ways in which Islamic tradition naturally integrates sexual health into the broader, soul-centered paradigms of life as a Muslim provide a powerful foundation to be reclaimed and applied for modern contexts. This perspective also invites Muslims to see sexual health as a holistic and dynamic process rather than a fixed state or a set of isolated behaviors.

The following section outlines crucial milestones of soulful sexual health development to exemplify its dynamic nature: puberty, premarital abstinence, marital sexual intimacy, and family planning.

Puberty: A Milestone in Spiritual Accountability

Puberty marks a crucial transition in Islamic tradition, signifying the onset of accountability (*taklif*) as individuals become *mukallaf*, responsible for their actions before Allah. This stage involves profound physical and spiritual changes, with Islamic teachings offering comprehensive guidance to navigate this transformation.

For girls, menstruation is a significant milestone explicitly mentioned in the Quran: "They ask you about menstruation. Say: It is a discomfort, so keep away from women during menstruation" (Quran 2:222). This verse emphasizes cleanliness (*taharah*) and practical considerations while acknowledging the challenges of this stage. The Prophet Muhammad (Peace and Blessings be Upon Him) and his companions modeled open, respectful conversations about menstruation. For instance, Aisha (may Allah be pleased with her) provided compassionate guidance to women seeking clarity on the end of the menstrual cycle, demonstrating the early Muslim community's supportive approach to sexual and reproductive health.

For boys, puberty is marked by signs such as seminal emission (*ihtilam*), growth of pubic hair, or reaching age 15. Wet dreams introduce the concept of ritual purity, with *ghusl* (ritual purification) required after seminal emission. Boys also learn about maintaining hygiene, fulfilling religious obligations like prayer (*salah*) and fasting (*sawm*), and fostering ethical conduct. These practices nurture discipline and align their developing sexuality with their spiritual journey.

The accountability of puberty reflects more than physical or legal changes—it signifies a profound shift in spiritual responsibility. Chapter 3 will expand on puberty's role in spiritual development, offering practical tools and soulful insights for both boys and girls navigating this pivotal stage.

Abstinence: A Soulful Practice of Self-Discipline

Abstinence, a core directive in Islam, is often framed through fear-based perspectives about the prohibition of *zina* (premarital sexual relations). While valid, these narratives can overshadow the deeper spiritual, emotional, physical, and sexual wisdom of abstinence. The Quran discourages *zina*, stating, "And do not approach unlawful sexual intercourse. Indeed, it is ever an immorality and is evil as a way" (Quran 17:32). This verse highlights abstinence as a preventive practice that safeguards the heart, body, and soul by avoiding pathways leading to sin.

At its essence, abstinence is an act of obedience to Allah that nurtures *taqwa* (God-consciousness) by cultivating self-restraint and discipline. This conscious alignment with Divine guidance strengthens the heart (*qalb*), fostering clarity, peace, and proximity to Allah. Abstinence also cultivates *sabr* (patience), an action-oriented virtue that builds resilience and spiritual growth, yielding rewards in this life and the Hereafter. Holistically, abstinence protects physical health as an *amanah* (trust), fosters emotional resilience and self-worth, and preserves the sanctity of intimacy for marriage. Far from being mere avoidance, abstinence aligns the heart, body, and soul with a higher purpose. Chapter 4 will explore empowered abstinence, offering soulful insights and practical tools to navigate this path with confidence.

Marital Sexual Intimacy and Pleasure

Islam frames marital sexual intimacy as an act of love, compassion, and mutual fulfillment, far beyond procreation. Recognized as a sacred form of worship, intimacy strengthens the emotional and spiritual bond between spouses. The Prophet Muhammad (Peace and Blessings be Upon Him) emphasized the importance of foreplay, mutual satisfaction, and care in marital relations, urging spouses to prioritize each other's desires with attentiveness and respect. The Quran highlights the intimate bond between spouses with profound tenderness, describing them as "garments for one another" (Quran 2:187), encapsulating the nurturing and protective essence of the marital relationship.

Classical scholars such as Imam al-Ghazali and Ibn Arabi explored marital intimacy as a multifaceted bond, combining physical, emotional, and spiritual dimensions. Al-Ghazali emphasized intimacy as an act of worship when approached with mindfulness and gratitude, while Ibn Arabi viewed it as a reflection of Divine unity and harmony. These teachings encourage couples to approach intimacy with mutual respect, compassion, and intentionality, aligning physical pleasure with spiritual growth. Chapter 6 delves deeper into these concepts, providing practical tools for cultivating soulful marital intimacy and fostering love, connection, and deeper spirituality.

Family Planning and Fertility

Discussions on family planning and fertility during the Prophet Muhammad's (Peace and Blessings be Upon Him) time were practical, open, and rooted in balancing human needs with spiritual and ethical principles. The permissibility of practices like *'azl* (withdrawal) was explicitly addressed, emphasizing the trust placed in couples to navigate pregnancy prevention through mutual consent and shared intention. The companions openly sought guidance, reflecting the early Muslim community's comfort in discussing sexual and reproductive health. Family planning is deeply tied to the Quran's emphasis on the sanctity of life and the responsibilities of nurturing children with spiritual, emotional, and physical care: "Do not kill your children out of poverty; We will provide for you and them" (Quran 6:151). Scholars like Imam al-Ghazali highlight parenting as a sacred trust, framing children's upbringing as an act of worship. This perspective naturally extends to preparing for soulful approaches to parenting that support children's sexual health, explored further in chapter 7.

Islamic teachings also celebrate conception and childbirth as sacred, reflecting Allah's creative power. The Quran beautifully describes human development as a sign of Divine wisdom: "We created man from an extract of clay" (Quran 23:12–14). Contemporary scholarship builds on these principles, addressing modern reproductive technologies and family planning methods within Islamic ethical boundaries. Grounded in mutual consent, collaboration, and spiritual alignment, family planning supports individual, familial, and communal well-being. To bridge the gap in holistic Islamic traditions of sexual health, the next section introduces a soulful model of sexual health, integrating Islamic teachings with modern frameworks to foster compassionate, accountable, and spiritually aligned sexual well-being.

Reflection Questions

After reading this section, how has your understanding of the relationship between Islamic tradition and sexual health evolved?

_____
_____
_____

As you reflect on Islamic traditions of sexual health, what emotions or thoughts are arising within you?

_____
_____
_____

Which topics related to your soulful sexual health journey feel most important for you to explore further?

_____
_____
_____

The Interconnectedness of Theology, Ethics, and the Spirituality: Soulful Sexual Health

Sexual health is an integral part of human life, deeply connected to the soul's journey toward Allah. For Muslims, it encompasses theology, ethics, and spirituality, offering a holistic framework that integrates physical, emotional, and spiritual dimensions. **Islamic theology** establishes sexual health as a God-given aspect of life, grounded in *taqwa* (God-consciousness) and aligned with Divine guidance. It frames sexual health challenges as opportunities for spiritual growth, fostering obedience, hope, and reverence for Allah's mercy. **Ethical** sexual health requires cultivating virtues like compassion and patience while overcoming self-gratifying behaviors stemming from the lower soul (*nafs al-ammarah*). Guided by prophetic teachings, it transforms personal desires into acts of worship and nurtures balance and harmony in relationships.

The **spiritual** dimension elevates sexual health through the heart (*qalb*), the seat of moral discernment and connection to Allah. Challenges such as shame or imbalanced desires are opportunities for inner work, cleansing the heart to reflect Divine light. Marital intimacy, when approached with *ihsaan* (spiritual excellence), becomes an act of gratitude and worship.

Together, theology, ethics, and spirituality form an interdependent framework that aligns sexual health with faith. By integrating these dimensions, Muslims can navigate challenges with compassionate self-accountability, transforming struggles into opportunities for growth and deeper connection to Allah. Table 2.1 summarizes this model, setting the stage for practical tools in the next section to realign actions with Islamic teachings.

A Soulful Model of Sexual Health for Muslims

Having explored the interconnected dimensions of theology, ethics, and spirituality, we now turn to a holistic framework for understanding and navigating sexual health as Muslims. Figure 2.1 illustrates this soulful model of sexual health, integrating three foundational aspects: spiritual, emotional, and physical health. This framework—grounded in traditional Islamic teachings and aligned with the soul's journey—provides a comprehensive approach to sexual health.

From a soulful developmental perspective, these three dimensions form the foundation of sexual health education and practice, equipping Muslims with the tools to understand their sexuality as part of their overall spiritual journey. These foundational aspects, ideally nurtured early in life, prepare individuals to navigate more complex aspects of sexual health with clarity

Table 2.1. A summary of how the key ideas of theology, ethics, and spirituality come together to inform the model of soulful sexual health for Muslims

Concept	Key Ideas	Relationship to Soulful Sexual Health
Theology	• Rooted in Divine guidance from the Quran and sunnah • Distinction between theology and *fiqh* (religious rulings) • *Taqwa* as reverential love and accountability to Allah	• Frames sexual health as a natural and sacred part of life • Encourages alignment with Allah's will through self-awareness and intentional actions • Reframes challenges as opportunities for cultivating God-consciousness and spiritual growth
Ethics	• Guided by principles of justice (*adl*) and balance (*mizan*) • Focuses on cultivating virtues (*akhlaq*) and overcoming vices • Sexual health as a moral responsibility to Allah and others	• Promotes self-discipline and purification of the heart (*riyadat al-nafs, tazkiyat al-nafs*) • Encourages ethical intimacy and abstinence as acts of worship • Integrates physical, emotional, and spiritual dimensions into ethical practices
Spirituality	• Centers the heart (*qalb*) as the seat of moral and spiritual discernment • *Ihsaan* (spiritual excellence) as a guiding principle • Struggles with sexual health viewed as spiritual challenges	• Elevates sexual health to a spiritual journey toward Allah • Highlights the role of purification and emotional healing in removing barriers to Divine connection • Encourages reliance on Allah's mercy and guidance for growth and renewal

and alignment. Let us explore each of these dimensions and how they come together to form a soulful approach to sexual health for Muslims.

Spiritual Health: The Heart of the Soulful Sexual Health Model

Spiritual health forms the core of this model, intertwining actions, intentions, and the relationship with Allah. Rooted in the alignment of theology, ethics, and spirituality, it guides the soul's journey toward Allah by

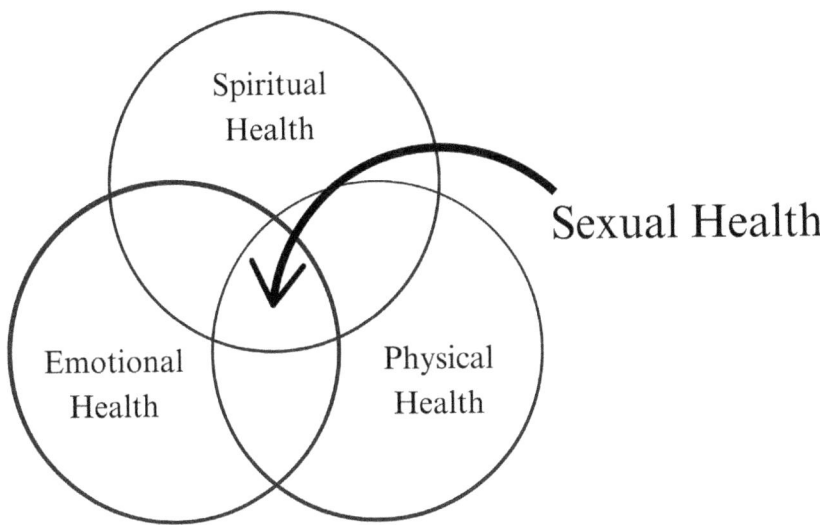

Figure 2.1 A soulful model of sexual health for Muslims

integrating belief, behavior, and moral character. Sexual health, deeply tied to the soul (*nafs*) and heart (*qalb*), directly influences the soul's development and spiritual potential. When the body and its actions are viewed as sacred trusts (*amānah*), and intimacy within marriage is understood as an act of worship (*'ibādah*), sexual health becomes deeply spiritual, fostering gratitude and mindfulness. The Prophet Muhammad (Peace and Blessings be Upon Him) emphasized this sanctity, saying, "When one of you fulfills his desire [with his spouse], it is counted as a charity (*sadaqah*)" (Sunnah.com, n.d., Muslim 1006).

Sexual health struggles, such as imbalanced sexual desire or sexual trauma, highlight the need for spiritual practices like *tazkiyat al-nafs* (purification of the soul) and *ihsaan* (mindfulness of Allah) for healing. Addressing these challenges with sincerity aligns sexual health with the soul's purpose of seeking closeness to Allah. Abstaining from prohibited behaviors serves as self-discipline, while repentance and purification realign the heart with Divine guidance. By integrating spiritual frameworks and practices, Muslims elevate their understanding of sexual health, ensuring its alignment with the primary goal of drawing closer to Allah.

Emotional Health with Soulful Sexual Health

Emotional health is integral to sexual well-being, rooted in the *qalb* (heart) as the center of emotions, self-awareness, and moral discernment.

Processing emotions such as shame, guilt, or emotional wounds (i.e. anxiety, fear, anger, etc.) on the heart is essential for nurturing healthy relationships and addressing sexual health challenges. When unresolved, these emotions can cloud the heart, disrupt its connection to Allah, and manifest as anxiety, intimacy struggles, or distorted self-perception. Practices like *dhikr* (remembrance of Allah), *tawbah* (repentance), and *muraqabah* (spiritual mindfulness) equip Muslims to address emotional wounds, fostering resilience and realigning the heart with Allah for healing and growth. Since the soul contains the body, integrating somatic practices (body-based approaches that recognize how emotions and trauma are stored in the body) can support emotional processing at a deeper level. These practices engage both the spiritual and physical dimensions, enabling a holistic approach to healing that honors the interconnectedness of the soul, mind, and body.

Emotional health also involves ethical responsibilities, such as open communication and sensitivity in addressing marital challenges. Sharing past struggles or unmet needs with honesty and compassion strengthens trust and ensures alignment between emotional and spiritual well-being. By tending to the heart and addressing emotional challenges intentionally, Muslims can align their emotional, spiritual, and physical health, transforming struggles into opportunities for growth, self-awareness, and a deeper connection with Allah.

Physical Health: Honoring the Divine Trust of the Body

Caring for the body as an *amanah* (trust) from Allah reflects its sacred role in supporting spiritual, emotional, and sexual well-being. This includes maintaining hygiene, seeking medical care for concerns like fertility challenges or sexual dysfunction, and practicing *ghusl* (ritual purification) to connect physical care with spiritual accountability. Parents can instill these values early, framing hygiene practices like brushing teeth or washing hands as acts of gratitude for the body entrusted by Allah. Such habits root practical self-care in spiritual awareness, preparing children to honor their bodies as vessels for worship and service.

Building a strong physical foundation involves balance in lifestyle choices such as healthy eating, exercise, and rest, aligning with the Prophet's guidance: "Your body has a right over you" (Sunnah.com, n.d., Bukhari 5199). For single Muslims, understanding reproductive health and bodily care fosters confidence and prepares them for marital responsibilities. Learning about the menstrual cycle, fertility, and maintaining physical wellness equips individuals to approach marriage with a holistic perspective, intertwining physical, spiritual, and emotional well-being. Caring for the body is not just personal health; it is an act of devotion to Allah, honoring responsibilities to oneself, family, and the Creator.

A Holistic Model of Soulful Sexual Health

This holistic model integrates spiritual, emotional, and physical dimensions, framing sexual health as a sacred aspect of the soul's journey toward Allah. Rooted in Islamic teachings, it aligns belief, behavior, and self-awareness with the goal of actualizing our *fitrah* (our natural, God-given disposition).

By integrating these dimensions, this model offers a balanced, intentional, and faith-centered approach, empowering Muslims to navigate sexuality as a meaningful part of their spiritual journey.

> **Reflection Questions**
>
> How do I view the connection between my physical, emotional, and spiritual health in relation to my sexual health?
>
> _____
> _____
> _____
>
> What steps can I take to ensure my sexual health practices reflect balance, intentionality, and accountability to Allah?
>
> _____
> _____
> _____
>
> How can I cultivate a deeper sense of gratitude and responsibility for my body as part of my worship of Allah?
>
> _____
> _____
> _____

How Can Muslims Practice Soulful Sexual Health in the 21st Century?

Muslims today face significant challenges in navigating sexual health due to a combination of cultural, societal, and narrow religious perspectives. The disconnect between Western ideals of sexual freedom and Islamic teachings on accountability and ethics creates confusion, especially for younger Muslims exposed to hypersexualized media during puberty (Ali Faisal, 2016; Sanjakdar, 2011). Many Muslim families avoid discussions about sexual health due to cultural taboos, leaving young people to seek guidance from secular sources, resulting in a lack of alignment with Islamic frameworks (Ali Faisal, 2014; Mirza, 2019).

Beyond puberty, many Muslims struggle with finding a spouse despite the proliferation of online matchmaking services. Unrealistic expectations, cultural barriers, and the challenges of managing sexual desires during prolonged singlehood contribute to emotional and spiritual struggles. Additionally, rising divorce rates present new challenges, including rebuilding intimacy and healing from past emotional wounds (de Rooij, 2024). Muslims also face difficulties in reconciling gender roles and societal expectations with Islamic teachings, especially within communities that practice gender segregation, which can hinder respectful and meaningful communication between genders (Sanjakdar, 2011).

Studies show a gap between Islamic values and lived realities, with on average half of young Muslims surveyed engaging in premarital sex or consuming pornography (Ahmed et al., 2014; Mirza, 2019). Current approaches focusing on external behaviors, such as abstinence or behavioral controls, fail to address the deeper emotional and spiritual struggles that lead to these actions (Schermer Sellers, 2017). There is an urgent need for a soulful sexual health model that integrates spiritual, emotional, and physical well-being, empowering Muslims to approach their sexual health through self-compassion, accountability, and alignment with Allah. The next section will introduce essential values for implementing this model, offering a comprehensive approach to sexual health that fosters spiritual growth and connection to the Creator.

Key Values of Soulful Sexual Health for Muslims

The soulful sexual health model for Muslims is rooted in four foundational values—compassion, self-accountability, the journey of the soul, and the inseparability of sexual health from Allah. These values draw upon theology, spirituality, and ethics, providing a framework that integrates the spiritual, emotional, and physical dimensions of well-being. They are designed to help Muslims navigate sexual health with purpose and alignment while fostering a deeper connection to Allah.

Compassion

Compassion is central to soulful sexual health, encompassing both self-compassion and compassion for others. It requires continuous purification of the heart to embody mercy and understanding, reflecting the mercy Allah shows as described in the Quran: "The Most Merciful, the Especially Merciful" (Quran 1:1). Self-compassion helps individuals address feelings of shame or guilt related to their sexual health without becoming stuck, allowing for growth and movement. By gently examining one's soul, Muslims can align their actions with their values and experience growth rather than stagnation in their sexual health.

Compassion for others is equally vital, as it encourages Muslims to avoid judgment and moralizing based on perceived shortcomings. This approach aligns with the Islamic principle that only Allah knows the true state of a person's heart, fostering empathy and patience in our relationships. As the Prophet Muhammad (Peace and Blessings be Upon Him) said, "The best of you are those who are best to their families" (Sunnah.com, n.d., Tirmidhi 3895).

Throughout the chapters to follow, compassion will appear as a common thread, woven into the understanding and application of soulful sexual health. By purifying the heart and practicing compassion, Muslims can build healing, understanding, and meaningful connections in their journey toward a deeper relationship with themselves, others, and Allah.

Self-Accountability

Self-accountability is a foundational concept in Islam, closely tied to *taqwa* (God-consciousness), and requires Muslims to take ownership of their actions and reflect on their intentions. The Quran advises, "And do not follow desire, for it will lead you astray from the path of Allah" (Quran 38:26), highlighting the importance of discipline. The Prophet Muhammad (Peace and Blessings be Upon Him) further emphasized self-reflection, stating, "The wise person is the one who calls their soul to account and works for what is to come after death" (Sunnah.com, n.d., Tirmidhi 2459). In the context of sexual health, this involves acknowledging the consequences of one's actions, seeking repentance when needed, and striving to align behavior with Islamic values.

Self-accountability also involves recognizing how one's actions impact others, particularly in relationships where sexual health intersects with power dynamics. Islam calls individuals to hold the impact they have on others in the highest regard, confronting trauma, owning shame, and regulating desire. The Quran warns, "Do not transgress, for Allah does not love the transgressors" (Quran 2:190), reminding believers to avoid overstepping ethical boundaries and causing harm, whether through neglect, misuse of power, or acting on unchecked desires. By practicing self-accountability, Muslims ensure spiritual growth, meaningful relationships, and alignment with Divine guidance, fostering a deep connection with Allah.

Journey of the Soul

The journey of the soul views sexual health as a dynamic, lifelong process intricately connected to spiritual development. For Muslims, navigating sexual health issues reflects the soul's alignment with Allah's guidance, transforming struggles into opportunities for self-awareness, purification (*tazkiyat al-nafs*), and spiritual growth. The Quran assures us that "Allah does not burden a soul beyond that it can bear" (Quran 2:286), emphasizing that challenges, including those related to sexual health, are meant for personal growth. As Imam al-Ghazali explains, the heart requires continual purification to reflect Divine light, and sexual health issues often reveal areas where such purification is needed.

Ultimately, soulful sexual health is about drawing closer to Allah. It transforms sexual intimacy into an act of worship when approached with mindfulness and respect for Islamic teachings. Whether managing desires during singlehood, healing from trauma, or navigating intimacy in marriage, these struggles become moments for resilience, self-reflection, and strengthening the soul's connection with Allah. Embracing the journey of the soul allows Muslims to approach sexual health with patience, resilience, and intentionality, viewing difficulties as opportunities to purify the heart and align with Divine will, all while deepening their relationship with Allah.

Compassionately Minding Your Own Soul

When Muslims face struggles—whether related to sexual health, fertility, or trauma—well-meaning family, friends, or community members often rush to offer comfort by attributing the hardship to religious or spiritual meaning. Phrases like "This is a test from Allah," "Just be patient," or "Allah gives His hardest battles to His strongest soldiers" may be intended to console, but they can unintentionally cause harm.

Such statements often fall into **spiritual bypassing**, where deep emotional pain is invalidated by overemphasizing spiritual platitudes. This can leave the person struggling feeling isolated, misunderstood, or even ashamed for experiencing difficult emotions like sadness, anger, or frustration. Religious or spiritual meaning-making is a deeply personal process, unique to each soul's journey. It cannot and should not be imposed by others.

True compassion lies in holding soulful space for those in pain, allowing them to express their emotions freely without fear of judgment

> or unsolicited advice. Instead of rushing to provide meaning or solutions, focus on listening with empathy, acknowledging their struggles, and affirming their feelings. Offer gentle support, such as: "I'm here for you, and I'll support you however you need." This approach respects their spiritual autonomy and encourages them to connect with Allah and make sense of their challenges in their own time.
>
> Remember, the most meaningful spiritual growth often arises when individuals are allowed to journey through their struggles authentically and without interference. By minding your own soul and refraining from imposing interpretations, you embody the prophetic tradition of showing mercy, compassion, and humility in the face of others' hardships.

Inseparability from Allah

Sexual health is inseparable from one's relationship with Allah, as every aspect of life is interconnected in Islam. The body is considered an *amanah* (trust) from Allah, and caring for it is an act of worship. Marital intimacy, for instance, or seeking professional support for reproductive challenges is not just a physical act but an opportunity for gratitude, compassion, and spiritual closeness. Sexual health struggles, too, are part of the spiritual journey and offer opportunities to reconnect with Allah. Challenges such as shame, guilt, or trauma can cloud the heart, but through practices like *tazkiyat al-nafs* (purification of the soul), *dhikr* (remembrance of Allah), and repentance, Muslims can cleanse their hearts and experience Allah's mercy. By aligning sexual health with Islamic principles, Muslims honor their relationship with Allah, transforming difficulties into sacred moments of growth, trust in Allah's wisdom, and spiritual closeness.

These four values—compassion, self-accountability, the journey of the soul, and inseparability from Allah—form the foundation of the soulful sexual health model for Muslims and are summarized in Figure 2.2. Together, they offer a holistic framework to navigate the intricacies of sexual health while remaining deeply anchored in Islamic theology, spirituality, and ethics. By embracing these values, Muslims can approach their sexual health with balance, intentionality, and a profound sense of sacred purpose, transforming challenges into opportunities for growth and deepening their connection to Allah.

Figure 2.2 A summary of the four soulful sexual health values

Summary

This chapter has highlighted the rich Islamic traditions that frame sexual health as a vital component of spiritual, emotional, and physical well-being. Rooted in theology, ethics, and spirituality, Islamic teachings offer profound insights into aligning desires, actions, and relationships with Allah's guidance. Far from being limited to rules, these perspectives invite Muslims to view sexual health as an integral part of the soul's journey.

Historically, Muslim societies embraced open discussions on intimacy, family planning, and relationships, balancing practical needs with spiritual responsibilities. However, colonization disrupted these traditions, replacing them with fear-based narratives that alienated many Muslims from a holistic understanding of sexual health. Revisiting these teachings through a soul-centered lens allows Muslims to reclaim this balance, fostering intentionality and confidence in addressing sexual health.

In today's complex landscape, the need for a soulful sexual health model is clear. Grounded in compassion, self-accountability, the journey of the soul, and inseparability from Allah, this framework transforms challenges into opportunities for growth. It reframes struggles as paths toward healing, aligning physical and emotional well-being with spiritual purpose.

The following chapters will explore practical tools and guidance for navigating specific aspects of sexual health, encouraging Muslims to embrace it as an act of worship and a natural, sacred part of their journey toward Allah. Through this comprehensive framework, readers are invited to transform challenges into pathways of self-awareness, healing, and closeness to the Divine.

Reflections and Action Items

_____
_____
_____
_____
_____
_____
_____
_____
_____
_____
_____

Reference List

Ahmed, S., Abu-Ras, W., & Arfken, C. (2014). Prevalence of risk behaviors among U.S. Muslim college students. *Journal of Muslim Mental Health*, 8(1).

Ali-Faisal, S. (2014). Crossing sexual barriers: The influence of background factors and personal attitudes on sexual guilt and sexual anxiety among Canadian and American Muslim Women and men (Master's thesis, University of Windsor). Electronic Theses and Dissertations. https://scholar.uwindsor.ca/etd/5051

Ali-Faisal, S. (2016). What's sex got to do with it? The role of sexual experience in the sexual attitudes, and sexual guilt and anxiety of young Muslim adults in Canada and the United States. *Journal of Muslim Mental Health*, 10(2).

Amir, H. S. (2020). The effectiveness of contemporary Islamic scholars in tackling pornography addiction: A case of Muslim students in Britain. *Asian Journal of Humanities, Art, and Literature*, 7(2). https://doi.org/10.18034/ajhal.v7i2.531

Asad, M. (2003). *The message of the Quran*. Dar al-Andalus.

de Rooij, L. (2024). Online dating for British Muslims, and the relationship with their Islamic identities. In L. de Rooij (Ed.), *British Muslims and their discourses* (pp. 221–245). Springer. https://doi.org/10.1007/978-3-031-45013-6_10

Ghazali, A. H. al- (2004a). *Ihya Ulum al-Din* (F. Karim, Trans., Vol. 2). Islamic Book Trust. (Original work published in 1096.)

Ghazali, A. H. al- (2004b). *Ihya Ulum al-Din: The book of marriage* (F. Karim, Trans.). Islamic Book Trust. (Original work published in 1096.)

Ghazali, A. H. al- (2010). *Marvels of the heart: Book 21 of Ihya Ulum al-Din* (W. J. Skellie, Trans.; H. E. Nasr, Ed.). Islamic Texts Society.

Ibn Arabi, M. A. (1989). *The Meccan revelations* (W. C. Chittick, Trans.). Pir Press.

Kawthari, M. M. I. A. al- (2008). *Islamic guide to sexual relations*. Huma Press.

Mirza, S. (2019). Behind closed doors: Porn and young Muslims. Muslim Mental Health. Retrieved November 2024, from https://muslimmentalhealth.com/behind-closed-doors-porn-and-young-muslims/

Osman, F. (2020). *How to talk to your Muslim child about sex*. Self-published.

Sahih International. (1997). *The Quran: Arabic text with corresponding English meanings*. Abul-Qasim Publishing House.

Sanjakdar, F. (2011). *Living West, Facing East*. Peter Lang Publishing.

Schermer Sellers, T. (2017). *Sex, God, and the conservative church: Erasing shame from sexual intimacy*. Routledge.

Seekers Guidance. (2014, May 26). Do the angels wait before writing down a bad deed? Retrieved November 2024, from https://seekersguidance.org/answers/islamic-belief/do-the-angels-wait-before-writing-down-a-bad-deed/

Shaker, A. F. (2001). *Al-Ghazali on poverty and abstinence: Translated from Ihya Ulum al-Din (Kitab al-Faqr wa'l-Zuhd)*. Islamic Texts Society.

Sunnah.com. (n.d.). Jami' at-Tirmidhi 2459. Retrieved January 5, 2025, from https://sunnah.com/tirmidhi:2459

Sunnah.com. (n.d.). Jami' at-Tirmidhi 3895. Retrieved January 5, 2025, from https://sunnah.com/tirmidhi:3895

Sunnah.com. (n.d.). Sahih al-Bukhari 5199. Retrieved January 5, 2025, from https://sunnah.com/bukhari:5199

Sunnah.com. (n.d.). Sahih Muslim 1006. Retrieved January 5, 2025, from https://sunnah.com/muslim:1006

World Health Organization. (n.d.). Sexual health. Retrieved December 22, 2024, from https://www.who.int/health-topics/sexual-health

3 Foundations of Soulful Sexual Health for Muslims

In 2011, I developed the first version of an Islamic sexual health curriculum for girls aged 10–12 at one of the Islamic schools where I worked. I adapted the provincial curriculum into five sessions, which included PowerPoint slides, individual and small group activities, and a question box with slips of paper. Creating and teaching the first session was a nerve-wracking experience. I felt a deep responsibility to ensure that the Islamic context was at the forefront. After all, we were Muslim, and everything we taught had to reflect our worldview and values. This chapter represents a much more refined and sophisticated version of that initial lesson plan. It builds on the foundations I introduced back then, offering a more comprehensive and holistic approach. My hope is that it provides you with the foundational knowledge you are seeking, inshaAllah *(God willing).*

Introduction

Building on from the soulful foundations of sexual health introduced in chapter 2, we now move to understand the essential knowledge required about male and female sexual health, framed within an Islamic soul-based perspective. Unfortunately, many Muslims face a lack of accurate, faith-aligned information regarding their sexual and reproductive health, often relying on incomplete or misleading sources such as peers, social

media, or generic sex education that overlooks the Islamic worldview. This gap disconnects us from the deep, soulful relationship between our bodies and our Creator.

Islam offers a profound framework for understanding the body as a sacred trust from Allah, intertwined with the five objectives of *shariah*: the protection of life, property, health, religion, and dignity. Caring for our bodies, including sexual health, is integral to fulfilling these objectives. As highlighted in the teachings of the Prophet Muhammad (Peace and Blessings be Upon Him), our bodies, including their sexual health, must be tended to with balance and moderation. This chapter will guide you through key aspects of sexual health, starting with puberty—a critical stage of spiritual accountability in Islam. By combining scientific accuracy with Islamic soul-based perspectives, this chapter empowers you to honor your body as a sacred trust from Allah.

Reflection Questions

What were you taught about the relationship between puberty, Islam, and what this means for you as a Muslim?
_____
_____
_____

Do you remember how this information made you feel?
_____
_____
_____

How has what you learned impacted your sexual health?
_____
_____
_____

Islam, Puberty, and Compassionate Spiritual Accountability

According to the *APA Dictionary of Psychology*, puberty is defined as "the stage of development when the genital organs reach maturity and secondary sex characteristics begin to appear, signaling the start of adolescence"

(American Psychological Association, n.d.). Puberty signifies a significant shift in a child's development, primarily characterized by physical and biological changes. Islam does not have a concept equivalent to "teenager" or "adolescence," as these are primarily biological and developmental terms. However, from an Islamic framework of the soul, puberty signifies a profound spiritual transformation.

Puberty in Islam marks the transition from being a child—who is not spiritually accountable—to being an adult, who becomes fully accountable to Allah for their actions. The Prophet Muhammad (Peace and Blessings be Upon Him) stated, "The pen has been raised for three persons (meaning they are not held accountable for what they do): one who is sleeping until he gets up, a child until he reaches the age of puberty, and an insane person until he becomes sane" (Sunnah.com, n.d., Tirmidhi 1423).

The term *bulūgh* is commonly understood to mean "puberty" or "maturity." It represents the stage when a Muslim boy or girl attains the capacity for spiritual accountability. The onset of puberty varies among individuals. Typically, girls begin puberty between the ages of 8 and 13, while boys start between 9 and 14 (Eunice Kennedy Shriver National Institute of Child Health and Human Development, n.d.). Islamic guidelines identify a girl's first menstrual cycle and a boy's first nocturnal emission as markers of *bulūgh*. If these milestones do not occur before age 15, this age is used to signify spiritual maturity.

Islamic texts illuminate the concept of spiritual accountability during *bulūgh*. Before puberty, children's deeds are not recorded in relation to their soul's development. However, with the onset of the first menstrual cycle, the first nocturnal emission, or reaching the age of 15—whichever comes first—a spiritual shift occurs. Two angels, known as *kiraman katibin* ("Noble Recorders"), are assigned to record an individual's deeds. One angel, on the right shoulder, records good deeds, while the other, on the left shoulder, records misdeeds. These angels remain with us from the age of spiritual accountability onward. While we often associate their role with the Afterlife, it is equally important to approach this concept with compassion. The Quran states, "But verily, over you (are appointed angels in charge of mankind) to watch you, Kiraman (honorable) Katibin — writing down your deeds, They know all that you do" (Quran 82:10–12).

Allah's compassion is particularly significant during puberty as this is a time of immense challenges and pressures, such as managing sexual desire (more on this in chapter 4). During these years, balancing compassion for oneself with self-accountability is essential for spiritual growth. How can we as Muslims nurture the journey of our soul without understanding this context? Without a compassionate framework for spiritual accountability during puberty, Muslims lack foundational, soul-based knowledge about sexual health. To bridge this gap, it is important to understand the developmental journey of our bodies, which begins at birth.

Having established a foundational understanding of puberty and its spiritual significance, we now turn our focus to the specifics of reproductive health. We will begin with an exploration of the female reproductive system, followed by the male reproductive system.

Female Sexual Health Foundations: Anatomy and Physiology

Allah has created the female and male bodies—including their intricate sexual health systems—with great intentionality and purpose. Unfortunately, many Muslim women refer to their reproductive organs with vague terms like "it," "that," "down there," or even by nicknames. It is also common for Muslim women to mistakenly refer to the vulva as the vagina and to treat the term "vagina" as if it is unspeakable. Often, this reluctance is justified under the guise of modesty, with the belief that proper anatomical terms should not be used, or that learning about one's body should wait until marriage—if it happens at all.

However, this understanding of modesty is not aligned with Islamic tradition. A well-known hadith beautifully illustrates this point. Safiyyah bint Shaybah reported: Aisha (may Allah be pleased with her) said, "How excellent are the women of the Ansar! They do not allow shyness to prevent them from understanding the religion." In another narration, The Prophet Muhammad (Peace and Blessings be Upon Him) praised the women of the Ansar, saying, "Shyness does not prevent them from seeking knowledge of the religion" (Sunnah.com, n.d., Bukhari 48).

This hadith exemplifies that true modesty, as understood in Islam, should not be a barrier to seeking knowledge, especially when that knowledge brings us closer to Allah and supports our spiritual growth. Reflecting on this *hadith*, we can imagine Aisha (may Allah be pleased with her) leading what we might now call a *halaqah*, or religious study circle, with women asking questions about their bodies. Questions such as "What color of vaginal discharge indicates the end of my menstrual cycle?" or "How do I purify myself after menstruation?" may have been asked. Perhaps they sought guidance on understanding their fertile phases or discussed the best methods of contraception available at the time, such as withdrawal (*azl*) prior to ejaculation. Such questions would reflect a dedication to aligning their lives with the worship of Allah, underscoring the importance of understanding sexual health as a dimension of spiritual development.

As you reflect on the legacy of women sitting in circles of learning with Aisha (may Allah be pleased with her), take a moment to consider your own intentions as you embark on this journey of unlearning and discovering your body. Pause and give language to your emotions, whether

Figure 3.1 A visual representation of a modern-day support group among women, facilitating a soulful connection

it's discomfort paired with trust in the process of growth or curiosity about the wisdom in Allah's creation. Visualize your modern-day support circle. Who are the women you would invite to sit with you, share in your vulnerabilities, and journey alongside you? Note their names and qualities, drawing inspiration from Figure 3.1, which illustrates a contemporary women's support circle. Let this vision remind you that you are not alone—reach out to those you trust, create spaces for meaningful conversations, and let this circle be a source of strength, growth, and joy, *inshaAllah* (God willing).

Reflection Questions

How much do you know about your reproductive system? Be honest while also showing compassion with yourself.

_____
_____
_____

> How comfortable are you with your body and how much do you know? Do you remember where you first learned about your body and how it made you feel? What is your intention to learn more about your body?
>
> _____
> _____
> _____
>
> If you were provided with a simple outlined diagram of the female and male reproductive systems, how much could you currently identify?
>
> _____
> _____
> _____

Foundations of the Female Reproductive System

Building on this historical and spiritual understanding, let us explore the foundational knowledge of the female reproductive system, an intricately designed and dynamic system created by Allah and vital throughout a woman's life. This section will provide detailed information about sexual and reproductive health relating to puberty and the reproductive years. For insights into the subsequent stages of perimenopause and menopause, please refer to chapter 8. Unfortunately, many women believe they cannot or should not learn about their reproductive system until they are married, often associating this knowledge with marital obligations. However, as discussed in the Islamic foundations earlier in this chapter, soulful learning about our bodies is an essential act of caring for the God-created body entrusted to us. By understanding and honoring our reproductive system from an early stage, we approach this knowledge with intention, modesty, and a sense of spiritual responsibility.

With this in mind, let's look at some myths before moving forward.

> **Myth Busting: Female Reproductive System**
>
> **Myth:** It is religiously impermissible to insert anything—such as menstrual products or a speculum during a pap smear or pelvic exam—into the vagina prior to being married.
>
> **Fact:** This misconception arises from the prohibition of premarital sexual intercourse, but the vagina serves multiple purposes beyond intercourse. Using menstrual products like tampons or cups is

permissible for hygiene. Similarly, pelvic exams or pap smears, recommended for menstrual or reproductive health concerns, are essential acts of self-care aligned with the Islamic principle of caring for the body Allah has entrusted to us.

Myth: If your hymen is not intact when you get married, it means you've had premarital sex and are not a virgin.

Fact: The hymen is a thin membrane that varies among individuals and can stretch or tear due to non-sexual activities like exercise, tampon use, or medical exams. Virginity in Islam is defined by abstaining from premarital sexual intercourse, not the state of the hymen.

Myth: Touching the parts of our vulva to identify and learn about our body before marriage is impermissible.

Fact: Islam encourages knowledge, including understanding one's body. Learning about the vulva's anatomy and functions is essential for health and hygiene. This differs from masturbation, which seeks sexual pleasure. Caring for and understanding the body is part of fulfilling the trust Allah has given us.

Myth: Visiting an OB/GYN prior to marriage is unnecessary since premarital sex is impermissible.

Fact: Caring for sexual health is a lifelong responsibility, distinct from the prohibition of premarital sex. The vaginal canal and reproductive organs may require medical attention for issues like pain, irregular cycles, or discharge. Consulting an OB/GYN ensures overall health and addresses concerns, regardless of marital status. Further details are in chapter 12.

Now, let's outline the female sexual developmental phases, which further emphasizes the point that as Muslims, we have sexual health responsibilities and awareness across our entire lifespan.

Female Sexual Developmental Phases

Understanding the phases of female sexual development highlights the intricacy and intentionality of Allah's creation. Each phase is marked by hormonal and physiological changes that shape a woman's reproductive and overall health.

Puberty: Puberty, typically between ages 8–16, marks the onset of reproductive maturity, signaled by menstruation, breast development, and changes in hair and body fat distribution, driven by estrogen and progesterone. Spiritually, it signifies the age of accountability (*bulūgh*), as we become directly responsible to Allah for our actions and soul's journey.

Reproductive Years: Spanning the years of fertility, this phase is characterized by the menstrual cycle, ovulation, and the potential for pregnancy, sustained by hormones like estrogen, progesterone, and hCG during pregnancy. These years reflect Allah's intricate design, allowing the body to nurture and sustain life while encompassing diverse individual experiences shaped by health and Divine destiny.

Perimenopause: The transition to menopause, often beginning in the 30s or 40s, involves irregular menstrual cycles, hormonal shifts, and symptoms like hot flashes and mood changes. This phase varies in duration and serves as a precursor to the cessation of menstruation.

Menopause: Occurring around ages 45–55, menopause signals the end of reproductive years, marked by a decline in estrogen and progesterone, cessation of menstruation, and symptoms like hot flashes and bone density changes. Islam encourages viewing this phase as a time for continued spiritual and personal growth, with self-care seen as an act of worship.

Female Genitalia: External Structures

Transitioning from developmental stages, we'll zoom in on learning the proper anatomical names and functions of the female reproductive system. Each of these structures serves specific functions related to reproduction and sexual health and works collaboratively together. We'll start with the female genitalia, which are external and visible to us, collectively referred to as the vulva. Remember that God created women with different body shapes, so Figure 3.2 is a general reference, with the location of organs slightly differing based on how we've been created.

Mons Pubis: A rounded mound of fatty tissue covering the pubic bone. It provides cushioning and protection to underlying structures and varies in size among individuals.

Labia Majora: The larger, outer folds of skin surrounding the vaginal opening and urethra. They protect internal genital structures and contribute to the vulva's overall structure.

Foundations of Soulful Sexual Health for Muslims 57

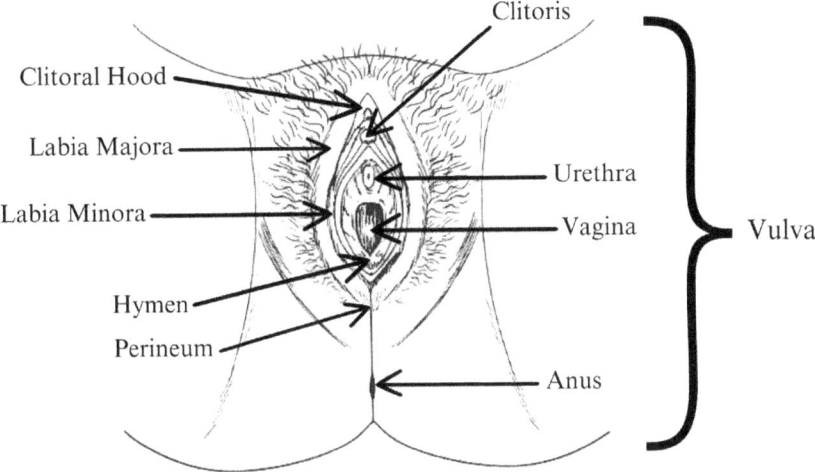

Figure 3.2 A diagram of the female genitalia, external structures, collectively known as the vulva

Labia Minora: The inner folds of skin located inside the labia majora. Functions include:

- Enclosing and protecting the openings of the urethra and vagina.
- Containing sweat and oil glands.

Clitoris: A highly sensitive organ located at the top of the vulva, where the labia minora meet. Functions and features include:

- Contains a dense network of nerve endings, with sexual pleasure as its sole purpose.
- Largely hidden from view, with nerve endings extending around the vulva and into the vaginal canal.
- Covered by the clitoral hood, a fold of skin that shields the clitoris from direct stimulation and friction while maintaining sensitivity.
- Can retract or move during sexual arousal, exposing the clitoris, which often enlarges with increased blood flow.

Urethral Opening: Located between the clitoris and the vaginal opening, it is the exit point for urine from the bladder. The urethra is a separate channel from the vagina.

Vagina (Vaginal Canal): A muscular canal around five to six inches long, consisting of intersecting pelvic floor muscles. Functions include:

- Exit point for menstrual blood from the uterus.
- Allows for sexual intercourse.
- Examined during pelvic exams and pap smears.
- Used for vaginal ultrasounds when assessing internal reproductive structures.

Hymen: A thin membrane of tissue present at birth that may partially or fully cover the vaginal canal. Features include:

- Varies widely in appearance and thickness among individuals.
- Not an indicator of "virginity" or sexual activity, as it can stretch due to non-sexual activities like physical exertion or tampon use.
- Serves no specific function but has been culturally misused, causing fear and misunderstanding about a woman's sexual status prior to marriage.

Perineum: The area of skin between the vaginal opening and the anus. It provides support to the pelvic floor muscles and may stretch during childbirth.

Anus: The point of exit for solid waste, located below the vaginal opening.

These structures collectively form the external genitalia, each playing a unique role in maintaining reproductive and sexual health. Understanding their anatomy helps to honor the God-given design and dispel harmful misconceptions.

Internal Reproductive Structures

The internal reproductive system, as depicted in Figure 3.3, is intricately linked to the external genitalia that we've just reviewed. Each structure plays a vital role in reproduction and overall reproductive health.

The **vaginal canal** extends internally from the external vaginal opening and connects to the uterus. The cervix is the point of fusion between the vagina and uterus.

The **cervix**, the lower part of the uterus that connects to the vagina, plays crucial roles in female reproductive health. It produces mucus that changes in consistency during the menstrual cycle to support fertility and protect against infections. During childbirth, the cervix dilates to allow the passage of the baby.

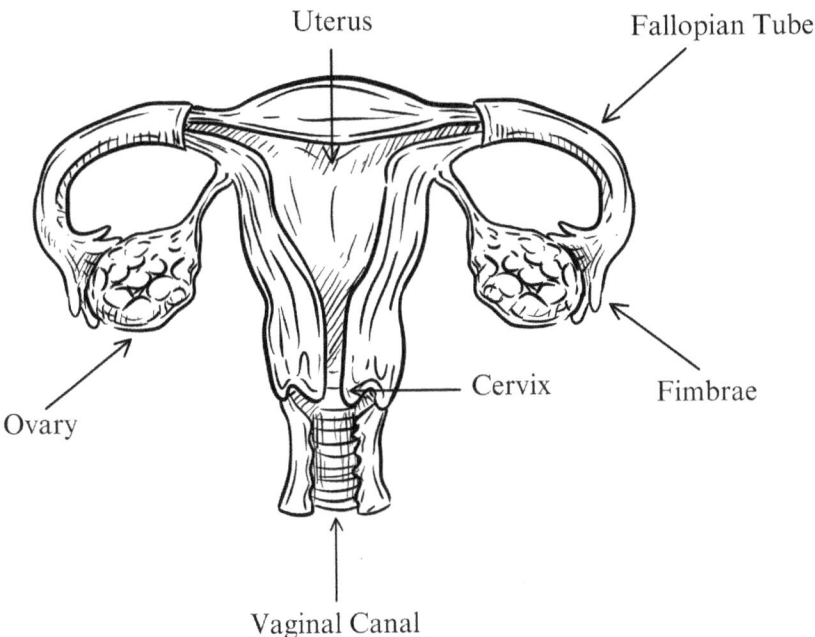

Figure 3.3 A diagram of the internal female reproductive system

The **uterus** (womb) is a muscular organ that houses and nourishes a fertilized egg during pregnancy. If fertilization does not occur, the endometrium, or inner lining, thickens during the menstrual cycle and is shed during menstruation.

The **ovaries** are a pair of organs located on either side of the uterus. They produce eggs (ova) and release them during the menstrual cycle. Additionally, the ovaries produce hormones such as estrogen and progesterone, which regulate the menstrual cycle and contribute to secondary sexual characteristics.

The **fallopian tubes** are two narrow tubes that connect the ovaries to the uterus. These tubes provide the site for fertilization of an egg by sperm and facilitate the movement of the egg to the uterus through the sweeping motion of **fimbrae**.

With this foundational understanding of the female reproductive organs, we can now explore the next phase: menstruation. This essential process reflects the intricate hormonal interactions and cyclical nature of the female reproductive system, providing further insight into how Allah has designed the female body with intentionality and purpose.

Soulful Islamic Perspectives on Menstruation

Menstruation is a remarkable process designed by Allah, reflecting Divine wisdom and serving as an important indicator of health. However, many Muslims lack the knowledge to fully appreciate this process, often influenced by cultural silence and stigma. Misconceptions, such as labeling menstruation as "dirty" or "impure," arise from colonized interpretations and cultural biases, which detract from its natural and spiritual significance.

Islamic teachings, rooted in compassion and practicality, frame menstruation as a time for rest from certain obligations like prayer and fasting. The Quran explicitly addresses menstruation in verses like, "They ask you about menstruation. Say: It is a discomfort, so keep away from women during menstruation" (Quran 2:222). This verse liberated women from pre-Islamic restrictions, emphasizing ease and understanding. *Hadiths* further affirm this perspective, offering practical guidance and highlighting the Prophet Muhammad's (Peace and Blessings be Upon Him) kindness, as seen in his interactions with Aisha (may Allah be pleased with her) during her menstruation.

By embracing menstruation with confidence and clarity, Muslim women can deepen their understanding of their bodies, nurture self-awareness, and strengthen their spiritual connection to Allah.

Soulful Foundations of Menstruation

Menstruation, which begins during puberty, marks the transition to spiritual accountability. Cycles typically range from 20 to 35 days but may vary due to hormonal imbalances or medical conditions. The menstrual cycle comprises four phases: follicular, ovulatory, luteal, and menstrual, each regulated by specific hormonal changes.

While women are often taught to call the first day of menstruation "Day 1" of their entire cycle, we'll begin with the follicular phase to reflect the underlying biological processes. Figure 3.4 provides a visual representation of the menstrual cycle, and each phase is covered in detail below.

In the **follicular phase** (Days 1–13), follicle-stimulating hormone (FSH) prompts follicle development, increasing estrogen levels and energy. One dominant follicle matures, preparing for ovulation.

The **ovulatory phase** (around Day 14) is marked by a surge in luteinizing hormone (LH), triggering the release of an egg. Ovulation can be tracked through natural methods like basal body temperature and cervical mucus changes, topics explored further in chapter 6.

During the **luteal phase** (Days 15–28), the ruptured follicle becomes the corpus luteum, producing progesterone and estrogen to prepare the uterine lining for pregnancy. If fertilization does not occur, hormone levels drop, signaling the start of menstruation.

Foundations of Soulful Sexual Health for Muslims 61

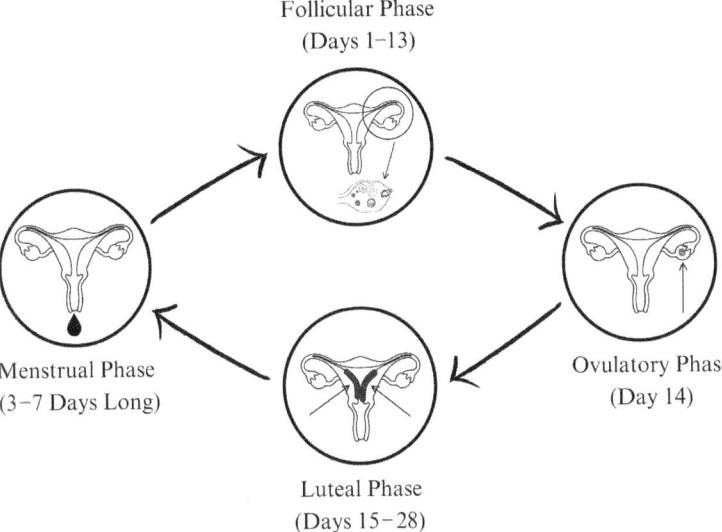

Figure 3.4 A summary of the four phases of the menstrual cycle

The **menstrual phase** (3–7 days) involves shedding the uterine lining, with typical blood loss ranging from 1 to 2.7 fluid ounces (2 to 5 tablespoons). Variations in blood color and texture depend on flow rate and duration.

By understanding these phases, women can appreciate the menstrual cycle's intricacy and its effects on health, energy, and emotions. This knowledge allows women to view their cycles as a reflection of inner harmony and a testament to Allah's perfect design.

The Menstrual Cycle: An Infradian Rhythm

The menstrual cycle is an example of the **infradian rhythm**, a biological cycle lasting longer than 24 hours, typically recurring over a month. Unlike circadian rhythms, which regulate daily cycles such as sleep and wakefulness, infradian rhythms operate over extended periods and are influenced by hormonal fluctuations. The menstrual cycle is one of the most well-known infradian rhythms, but its effects extend far beyond the reproductive system. This rhythm impacts mood, energy levels, cognitive function, metabolism, and even immune response, highlighting its influence on overall health and well-being.

> Understanding the infradian rhythm and its stages allows for greater self-awareness and the opportunity to align daily activities, nutrition, and rest with the natural ebbs and flows of the menstrual cycle. This practice, often called **cycle syncing**, can enhance physical and emotional well-being by harmonizing life with the body's biological patterns. A valuable resource to explore this concept further is *In the FLO* by Alisa Vitti, which delves into the science of cycle syncing and provides practical guidance for integrating these rhythms into daily life.
>
> To learn more while you track your cycle, consider apps, such as:
>
> **Flo:** A popular app for cycle tracking, offering insights into symptoms and health patterns.
> **Clue:** Known for its science-based approach and customizable tracking options.
> **MyFLO:** Created by Alisa Vitti, this app integrates cycle syncing with health recommendations.
> **Ovia Fertility:** Offers comprehensive tracking with a focus on fertility and reproductive health.
>
> Using these tools can help you better understand your body's rhythms, empowering you to align your lifestyle with your menstrual cycle for improved health and balance.

Menstrual Hygiene

Menstrual hygiene products are essential items designed to manage menstrual flow, providing comfort and protection during a woman's menstrual cycle. There are various types of menstrual products available, and women can choose based on personal preferences, lifestyle, and comfort. Despite what many Muslims may think, it is a myth that menstrual products worn in the vagina are impermissible (*haraam*) to use before marriage. As discussed earlier, the vagina has multiple functions, and the use of a tampon or menstrual cup/disc is for menstrual hygiene purposes.

To help clarify the different options available, Table 3.1 summarizes the most common menstrual hygiene products, their features, and factors for consideration. This overview will guide you in making an informed choice about which products may work best for your comfort and needs during menstruation.

Ultimately, the best menstrual hygiene product varies from person to person, and it may take some trial and error to find the most comfortable

Table 3.1 An overview of menstrual hygiene products related to considerations such as menstrual flow, comfort, lifestyle, and environmental impacts

Product	Description	Pros	Cons	Factors to Consider
Menstrual Pads	Absorbent pads worn externally in underwear to collect menstrual blood.	Easy to use, available in various absorbencies, suitable for different flow levels.	Can feel bulky, may cause discomfort if not changed regularly.	**Flow Level:** Wide range of absorbencies; suitable for light to heavy flows. **Comfort:** Easy to use but can feel bulky; needs regular changing. **Lifestyle:** Best for sedentary or less active routines; may shift during activity. **Environmental Impact:** Disposable; creates waste, though biodegradable options exist.
Tampons	Cylinder-shaped devices inserted into the vagina to absorb menstrual blood.	Discreet, suitable for active lifestyles, less noticeable than pads.	Requires learning how to insert, potential risk of toxic shock syndrome (TSS), should be changed every few hours.	**Flow Level:** Different absorbencies available; match to flow to avoid risks like TSS. **Comfort:** Discreet and comfortable once inserted; some may find insertion challenging. **Lifestyle:** Great for active lifestyles, including swimming and sports. **Environmental Impact:** Disposable; less waste than pads but still contributes to pollution.

(Continued)

Table 3.1 (Continued)

Product	Product	Pros	Cons	Factors to Consider
Menstrual Cups or Discs	Flexible cups or discs made of silicone or rubber inserted into the vagina to collect menstrual blood.	Environmentally friendly, can be worn for up to 12 hours, reduces waste.	Requires proper insertion and removal technique, initial learning curve.	**Flow Level:** Suitable for all flows; holds more fluid, ideal for heavy flows. **Comfort:** Requires correct insertion and removal; comfortable for extended wear once mastered. **Lifestyle:** Ideal for eco-conscious users and compatible with travel or work. **Environmental Impact:** Highly eco-friendly; reusable for years, reducing waste significantly.
Period Panties	Underwear specially designed to absorb and contain menstrual flow.	Comfortable, reusable, eliminates the need for additional products.	Limited absorbency, may not be suitable for heavy flow days.	**Flow Level:** Effective for light to moderate flows; may need extra protection for heavy flows. **Comfort:** Soft, reusable, and feels like regular underwear. **Lifestyle:** Convenient for daily routines but multiple pairs needed for busy and/or heavy flow days. **Environmental Impact:** Eco-friendly; reusable for multiple cycles, reducing waste.

and effective option for individual needs. Islam gives you permission to explore different products, recognizing that your needs and preferences may evolve during your menstrual cycle and life.

A common question many Muslims ask is how to determine when menstruation ends and what steps to take afterward. From an Islamic perspective, menstruation concludes when there is no longer any colored discharge from the vagina. At this point, *ghusl* (major ritual purification) is performed, which is the same process used after sexual intercourse. *Ghusl* is a spiritual and physical act of cleansing, symbolizing the readiness to return to acts of worship such as prayer and fasting, and to resume marital intimacy. It is important to approach this process with intention and mindfulness, as it represents a renewal of your connection to Allah.

Ghusl: Major Purification

Ghusl (a ritual bath) after menstruation, known as *"Ghusl Janabah"* or *"Ghusl Hayd,"* is a purification ritual in Islam. The following *ghusl* process is outlined from the Hanafi school of thought, adapted from Seekers Guidance (2022).

1. *Niyyah* (**Intention**): Begin by making a sincere intention in your heart to perform *ghusl* for the purpose of purification.
2. Say *Bismillah* (**In the name of Allah**): Start by saying *"Bismillah"* before beginning the *ghusl*.
3. **Remove any physical impurities from your body** and cleanse the private parts. Wash your hands thoroughly, including wrists, ensuring that no part is left dry.
4. **Perform *wudu* (ablution):** Perform a complete ablution as you would for daily prayers, washing your face, hands, arms, head, and feet.
5. **Pour water over your head three times.**
6. **Pour water over the right side of your body, starting from your right shoulder.** Repeat three times.
7. **Pour water over the left side of your body, starting from the left shoulder.** Repeat three times.

It's important to note that the specific practices may vary slightly among different Islamic schools of thought. It is therefore recommended to follow the guidance of scholars for precise details and variations in the ritual. This same process of *ghusl* will be explored in the next section on the male reproductive system, once we explore the foundations of its functions.

Before we move forward to explore the male reproductive system, diving into its unique aspects and how they are shaped by both physical development and spiritual accountability in Islam, let's take a moment to reflect on this section.

> **Reflection Questions**
>
> What insights have you gained from this section on menstrual hygiene, and how do you feel about menstruation now, both from a physical and spiritual perspective?
>
> _____
> _____
> _____
>
> How can you apply the concept of compassionate accountability in your own life or in the lives of those you support when it comes to understanding and managing menstruation?
>
> _____
> _____
> _____
>
> What actionable steps can you take to deepen your soulful care of your menstrual cycle, integrating both spiritual and physical practices for better self-awareness and health?
>
> _____
> _____
> _____

Feeling All the Feelings: Sexual Desire and Attraction

Puberty brings about not only physical changes but also intense emotional experiences, including sexual desire and attraction. In Islam, these feelings are seen as natural, created by Allah, and part of our journey toward spiritual and emotional maturity. While feelings themselves are not sinful, how we respond to them reflects our spiritual growth and self-discipline.

> To navigate these emotions, Muslims are encouraged to cultivate emotional awareness by recognizing and naming their feelings, such as "I feel curious" or "I feel attracted." It's important to normalize discussing emotions and frame them as part of the spiritual journey, remembering that they are opportunities for self-reflection, not shame. Engaging in soulful practices—such as worship, hobbies, or community service—can help channel these feelings in ways that honor one's values and deepen the connection to Allah. By grounding emotions in compassion, self-accountability, and a soulful perspective, young Muslims can navigate their desires with purpose, aligning their actions with their spiritual growth. Further insights and skills for empowered abstinence will be discussed in chapter 4.

Foundations of the Male Reproductive System

When the topic of sexual health arises, there is often a tendency to focus on the female body. However, the male system is equally important to understand, as it plays a critical role in both physical health and spiritual development. Although the male reproductive system may appear simpler than the female system, it is far from basic. Many complex processes, including hormonal fluctuations and the development of key reproductive functions, occur continuously.

From an Islamic perspective, as we explored earlier, boys reach spiritual maturity and accountability at the time of their first nocturnal emission (commonly referred to as a "wet dream"). If this emission does not occur by the age of 15, the age of *bulūgh* (maturity) is reached, marking the onset of spiritual responsibility. Before we dive into these aspects, it is important to first build a strong foundation of knowledge about the male reproductive system. You may want to revisit the reflection questions that were shared earlier in the chapter, before the female reproductive system section.

The male reproductive system consists of both internal and external structures that work together to produce and deliver sperm for fertilization. Each component plays a critical role in sexual health and reproduction. Understanding these organs and their functions is essential for both physical well-being and spiritual awareness. As we explore the male reproductive system, we also recognize the Divine wisdom behind the design of the body, which Allah has created in diverse forms, each serving its purpose. Below is an overview of the external male genitalia, their respective functions, and the hormonal regulation that governs them, with Figure 3.5 as a reference.

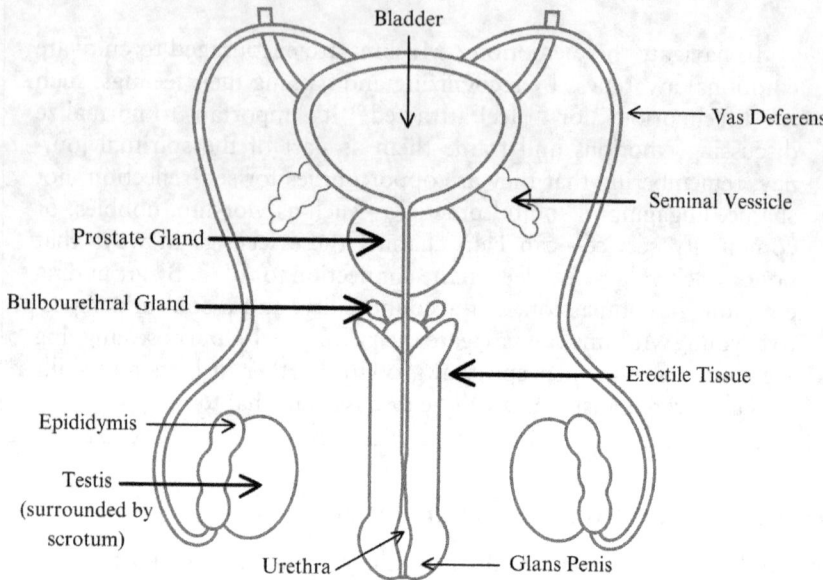

Figure 3.5 The male reproductive system, including external and internal structures

Penis: The penis serves as the external organ for sexual intercourse. It is responsible for the delivery of semen through the urethra during ejaculation and functions as the passage for urine.

Scrotum: The scrotum is a pouch of skin that houses and protects the testes. It regulates the temperature of the testes, maintaining a cooler environment necessary for sperm production.

Urethra: The urethra is a tube that runs through the penis, providing a passage for both urine and semen. It expels semen during ejaculation and urine during urination.

Testes (Testicles): The testes produce sperm through spermatogenesis and the hormone testosterone, which is vital for male sexual characteristics and sperm production.

Epididymis: The epididymis is a coiled tube that sits atop each testicle. It is responsible for storing and maturing sperm until they are ready for ejaculation.

Foundations of Soulful Sexual Health for Muslims

Vas Deferens: The vas deferens are the tubes that transport sperm from the epididymis to the urethra during ejaculation.

Seminal Vesicles: These glands produce a fluid rich in fructose and nutrients, which nourish the sperm and facilitate their motility through the reproductive system.

Prostate Gland: The prostate gland produces an alkaline fluid that mixes with sperm to form semen. This fluid helps neutralize the acidic environment of the vagina, enhancing sperm motility and protecting sperm from damage.

Male Hormone Fluctuations

The male reproductive system is intricately regulated by hormones, which fluctuate in daily and seasonal rhythms to maintain reproductive health.

Testosterone: Produced by the Leydig cells in the testes, testosterone is the primary male sex hormone. Its levels fluctuate throughout the day, typically peaking in the early morning and declining throughout the day. This daily variation is part of the natural circadian rhythm.

Luteinizing Hormone (LH): Released by the pituitary gland, LH stimulates the production of testosterone in the Leydig cells. It follows a pulsatile secretion pattern, with surges occurring every 1 to 3 hours, influencing sperm production and other reproductive functions.

Follicle-Stimulating Hormone (FSH): Also secreted by the pituitary gland, FSH plays a critical role in spermatogenesis by stimulating the Sertoli cells in the testes, supporting sperm development.

In addition to these daily fluctuations, there are seasonal variations in hormone levels. Hormonal levels are also influenced by factors such as age, stress, sleep, and overall health. Disruptions in these hormonal patterns may occur, but the natural fluctuations serve to ensure the proper functioning of the male reproductive system, aligning physical and spiritual processes within the body.

Erections and Nocturnal Emissions: A Soulful Understanding

As boys enter their preteen and teenage years, they undergo various stages of sexual development. This process, which we will explore further in chapter 7 on soulful parenting, may include experiences such as more frequent erections. It is important to approach these developments with sensitivity and compassion, understanding that these physical changes are a natural and Divinely ordained part of growing into adulthood. An erection is simply a physiological response involving the enlargement and stiffening of the penis, caused by increased blood flow to the erectile tissues. This is a process that is controlled by a delicate balance of nervous, hormonal, and vascular mechanisms, all part of the body's intricate design by Allah.

For many boys, erections may occur unexpectedly, even without sexual stimuli. These physical responses can be confusing, especially when they seem to happen at inappropriate times, such as during moments of nervousness or embarrassment. It is essential to remember that erections are a normal part of bodily functions and can occur for many reasons beyond sexual desire. For instance, boys may experience erections while bathing or dressing, or even when feeling anxious or stressed.

It is important to distinguish between an erection as a physiological response and feeling sexually aroused, which comes from the experience of sexual desire. The experience of sexual desire and premarital sexual activity will be covered in chapter 4. By understanding this distinction, we can foster a compassionate and supportive environment where boys feel comfortable as they navigate these changes.

Nocturnal Emissions: Understanding the Nighttime Release

Nocturnal emissions, or "wet dreams," are another natural phenomenon that may occur during sleep, particularly during adolescence and young adulthood. These spontaneous orgasms, often accompanied by ejaculation, are part of the body's natural rhythm and are a sign of sexual maturity. Nocturnal emissions are a manifestation of sexual arousal and the body's need to release accumulated semen.

Several factors contribute to the occurrence of nocturnal emissions:

1. **Sexual Dreams:** During REM (rapid eye movement) sleep, individuals may experience vivid dreams, some of which may be erotic. These dreams can trigger sexual arousal, leading to the physiological response of ejaculation. It is important to remember that these dreams and their resulting physical responses are part of the body's normal development.
2. **Hormonal Changes:** As young men progress through puberty, their bodies undergo significant hormonal changes, including increased testosterone levels. These hormonal fluctuations contribute to the occurrence of nocturnal emissions, particularly during sleep when the body is in a state of rest and rejuvenation.

3. **Semen Buildup:** The body naturally produces sperm, and nocturnal emissions may serve as a mechanism to release any excess semen that has built up in the reproductive system. This is part of the body's way of maintaining balance and ensuring reproductive health.
4. **Lack of Sexual Activity:** Nocturnal emissions are more common in individuals who are not sexually active or who engage in infrequent sexual activity. The body, in its wisdom, may naturally release built-up sexual tension through this process.

A Compassionate Perspective on Nocturnal Emissions

It is essential to understand that experiencing nocturnal emissions is a normal part of sexual development. These occurrences are not sinful or shameful; they are a natural and healthy response to the body's maturation. Allah has designed the body to function in this way, and it is a sign of the body's healthy reproductive system.

If a young man feels distressed by these occurrences, it is important to offer compassionate support and guidance. If these occurrences continue into adulthood or are accompanied by concerns about sexual or reproductive health, it may be beneficial to consult a healthcare professional for reassurance and support. This enables us to navigate these natural stages of life in a way that honors the body's Divine design while integrating both the physical and soulful aspects of our well-being.

Soulful Reflections on *Ghusl*

For boys, the practice of *ghusl* after nocturnal emissions or after any situation of ejaculation is a profound and soul-nurturing act. It serves as a reminder that the body is a trust from Allah, and maintaining its purity is a way to honor that trust. Just as physical cleanliness is an integral part of our faith, it is also a symbol of our commitment to living with integrity, accountability, and mindfulness. Through *ghusl*, boys are guided to transition into adulthood with a deep understanding of their spiritual responsibilities. It is a moment to connect with Allah and renew the intention to live a life that is soulfully inspired, both inside and out. This sacred act is an opportunity to reflect on the journey of the soul and the body, embracing both with humility and gratitude.

Summary

This chapter has provided foundational insights into the Islamic soulful perspectives of puberty, spiritual accountability, and the male and female reproductive systems. Puberty, marked by milestones such as menstruation and nocturnal emissions, is not just a physical transformation but a profound step into spiritual maturity, where physical changes intertwine with spiritual responsibilities. These moments remind Muslims of the Divine wisdom that governs our bodies, emphasizing accountability for actions and intentions. Practices like *ghusl* highlight the integration of physical cleanliness with spiritual purity.

Through a mindful understanding of the reproductive systems, we recognize that these bodily functions, though often private or misunderstood, are integral to Allah's design. Approaching them with respect and self-awareness connects physical knowledge with spiritual growth, reinforcing that our bodies are essential to our soul's journey. Building on this foundation, chapter 4 will delve into the concept of soulfully empowered abstinence, offering practical and spiritual tools to navigate desires with intention and alignment with one's faith, further enhancing the connection between physical, emotional, and spiritual well-being.

Reflections and Action Items

_____
_____
_____
_____
_____
_____
_____
_____
_____
_____
_____
_____

Reference List

American Psychological Association. (n.d.). Puberty. In *APA Dictionary of Psychology*. Retrieved from https://dictionary.apa.org/puberty

Eunice Kennedy Shriver National Institute of Child Health and Human Development. (n.d.). *Puberty and precocious puberty*. Retrieved from https://www.nichd.nih.gov/health/topics/factsheets/puberty

Sahih International. (1997). *The Quran: Arabic text with corresponding English meanings*. Abul-Qasim Publishing House.
Seekers Guidance. (2022, July 18). *What is the proper method of performing the ritual bath (ghusl)?* Retrieved from https://seekersguidance.org/answers/hanafi-fiqh/what-is-the-proper-method-of-performing-the-ritual-bath-ghusl/
Sunnah.com. (n.d.). Sahih al-Bukhari 48. Retrieved January 5, 2025, from https://sunnah.com/bukhari:48
Sunnah.com. (n.d.). Jami' at-Tirmidhi 1423. Retrieved April 3, 2025, from https://sunnah.com/tirmidhi:1423
Vitti, A. (2020). *In the FLO: Unlock your hormonal advantage and revolutionize your life*. HarperOne.

4 A Soulful Model of Empowered Abstinence

This chapter has been the most challenging for me to write, and it may be the most challenging for you to read. The topic of sex—especially premarital sex—tends to stir strong emotions and reactions among Muslims. When asked what they know about sex, many Muslims commonly respond that premarital sex is haraam (religiously impermissible) and that sex is reserved for marriage. However, when I've asked why premarital sex is forbidden, the explanations often focus on physical consequences, such as unwanted pregnancy or sexually transmitted infections, or religious consequences. While these reasons hold truth, the way they are typically presented—often through fear-based narratives—can create a sense of constriction in the heart. This fear can close us off from compassionately reflecting on and working toward the growth of our soul. My hope is that this chapter will help you approach this topic with openness and compassion, allowing you to engage deeply with the emotions and complexities surrounding abstinence, sexual desire, and the soul. Let's journey through this together with courage and care.

The Journey of the Soul

| Birth | Spiritual Accountability | Spiritual Maturity | Spiritual Legacy | The Hereafter |

Introduction

As Muslims, we are traditionally taught to abstain from sex before marriage, but many of us struggle to understand the deeper "why" or practical "how" in our modern context. Abstinence is often viewed as a binary behavior: either adhered to or abandoned, with labels of "good Muslim" or "bad Muslim" based on compliance. This simplistic view is compounded by challenges such as pornography and masturbation, alongside disproportionate scrutiny faced by Muslim women, despite Islamic teachings emphasizing equal standards for both genders.

When viewed through an Islamic soul-based lens, abstinence is far more nuanced than fear-based messaging suggests. Many of us were taught abstinence through warnings of dire consequences, reputational risks, or graphic cautionary tales, particularly for women. Such rigid approaches often cause emotional harm, reducing abstinence to a single decision rather than an ongoing, dynamic journey of spiritual growth and self-awareness.

This chapter reframes abstinence as a soulful endeavor, emphasizing its spiritual dimensions and offering insights and strategies to embody it as an act of self-compassion and devotion to Allah. As we explore these perspectives, take a moment to reflect on your beliefs, emotions, and experiences. This self-awareness will enrich your understanding as we embark on this journey together.

Reflection Questions

What does "premarital sex" mean to you? What thoughts and feelings come up as you hear the term "premarital sex"?

_____
_____
_____

Why do you think the religious ruling of abstinence exists?

_____
_____
_____

As you reflect, where did you learn about abstinence? How was this concept explained to you? Do you remember how it made you feel in the moment?

_____
_____
_____

> What do you hope to learn from this chapter?
> _____
> _____
> _____

Soulful Islamic Perspectives on Abstinence

Islamic tradition emphasizes the sacredness of sexual intimacy within marriage, defining abstinence as refraining from all sexual contact, intimacy, and behavior outside of this union. The Quran warns against unlawful sexual activity (*zina*), stating, "And do not approach unlawful sexual intercourse. Indeed, it is ever an immorality and is evil as a way" (Quran 17:32). This prohibition extends to avoiding behaviors or situations that might lead to unlawful sexual activity (*zina*) such as emotionally intimate conversations or exposure to sexualized content, underscoring the importance of vigilance in safeguarding spiritual goals.

Recognizing sexual desire (*shahwah*) as a natural, God-given aspect of human existence is crucial to understanding abstinence. As discussed in chapter 1, the soul encompasses the *nafs* (behaviors), *aql* (thoughts), *qalb* (emotions), and *ruh* (spirit), all of which shape how desires are managed. The soul also contains the body (*jism*). *Shahwah* serves Divine purposes, such as bringing pleasure and enabling reproduction within marriage, and its presence at any stage of life is not sinful. Abstinence, therefore, becomes a soulful practice of self-restraint, channeling desires in alignment with Islamic values. By embracing abstinence as a means of spiritual growth, Muslims can cultivate discipline and accountability, transforming their approach to sexuality into a reflection of faith and a deeper connection with Allah.

Sexual Desire and the *Nafs al-Ammarah*

The *nafs al-ammarah*—the lower soul that inclines toward harm—is central to understanding the challenges of managing *shahwah* (sexual desire). While desire itself is a God-given aspect of human nature, the *nafs al-ammarah* often distorts its balance, influenced by internal vulnerabilities and external pressures, as depicted in Figure 4.1. Cultivating self-awareness and compassion in addressing these influences is key to navigating abstinence as a path of spiritual growth. Let's take a look at these now.

Key Influences on the Nafs al-Ammarah

Whispers of Shaytaan (Waswaas – *whispers*): *shaytaan* (the devil) vigilantly seeks opportunities to exploit human vulnerabilities, whispering suggestions that frame imbalanced sexual behaviors—such as pornography or masturbation—as escapes from discomfort. The Quran reminds us, "Indeed, *shaytaan* is an enemy to you; so take him as an enemy" (Quran 35:6), urging vigilance against these whispers and the lower soul's tendencies to act on them.

External Worldly Influences: Media and societal norms glorify unrestrained sexual exploration, challenging Muslims to critically filter these messages. The Prophet Muhammad (Peace and Blessings be Upon Him) advised, "A person is upon the religion of their close companion, so let one of you look at whom you befriend" (Sunnah.com, n.d., Tirmidhi 2378), emphasizing mindful consumption of relationships, media, and influences to align external environments with spiritual values.

Wounds on the Heart (Qalb)*:* Unhealed trauma or emotional pain can disrupt the heart's connection to Allah, leading individuals to seek temporary relief through lower-soul behaviors like overindulgence in sexual desires. These actions, though momentarily soothing, deepen disconnection from Allah

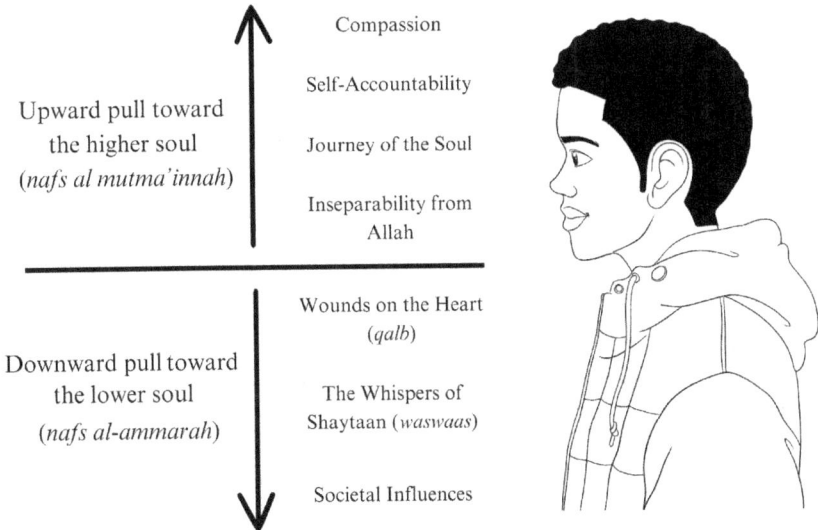

Figure 4.1 A depiction of the forces pulling Muslims down toward the lower soul, and soulful values which support the soul's journey toward Allah

and the self. Healing the heart's wounds is essential to realigning desires with spiritual growth, a theme further explored in chapters 1 and 2.

By addressing these influences, Muslims can cultivate resilience against the inclinations of the *nafs al-ammarah* and reframe their sexual desires as opportunities for spiritual discipline and connection with Allah.

Abstinence, therefore, is more than a surface-level behavior; it is a sacred journey of the soul, deeply rooted in the healing and purification of the heart (*tazkiyah al-qalb*). The *qalb*, as the center of emotions (*ihsaas*) and the seat of Divine presence (*ruh*), holds a profound role in shaping our actions and intentions. As we explored in chapter 2, the heart is both tender and transformative, capable of growth and renewal when nurtured with care. Struggling with abstinence is a reality for many Muslims—know that you are not alone in this journey. These challenges often reflect deeper wounds or imbalances within the heart, which can be addressed with compassion and sincerity.

While the journey may feel overwhelming at times, it may help to draw compassionate attention to our choices, efforts, and intentions to realign with Allah's guidance. It is equally essential to remember that the outcomes are ultimately in Allah's hands. This balance of effort and reliance mirrors the Prophetic teaching to "tie your camel and trust in Allah." Through this, abstinence becomes not just an act of willpower but an act of faith and surrender, a way to align ourselves with the Divine while trusting Him to guide and support us on this path.

A Note for Muslims Who Have Engaged or Are Engaging in Premarital Sexual Activity

A common question I hear from clients is, *"I've engaged in premarital sex—does this mean I'm going to Hell?"* This fear reflects a deeply felt spiritual and emotional struggle, and it's important to approach yourself with compassion. Remember, you are not alone, and these feelings are a natural response to reconciling your actions with your values. Let's explore this topic through the lens of *tawbah* (repentance), self-accountability, and the journey of the soul, centering the heart (*qalb*) as the root of our thoughts and actions.

The Infinite Mercy of Allah

Begin with the reminder of Allah's mercy, which encompasses all things (Quran 7:156). No matter your past, the door to repentance is always open. *Tawbah* is not just seeking forgiveness; it's a soulful commitment to renewal, transformation, and realigning your actions with Divine guidance. Compassionately exploring the root causes of your behavior—often tied to deeper emotional wounds or unmet needs—can open pathways to healing and growth. Reflect on what your heart (*qalb*) might be communicating and use this as an opportunity to deepen your connection to Allah.

Renewing Intentions and Embracing the Journey

Abstinence in Islam is a dynamic process of striving (*mujahadah*) to align your actions with your values, embracing compassion, self-accountability, and persistence. This chapter presents soulful approaches to learn more about your soul as it pertains to empowered abstinence, offering tools to deepen your understanding of the relationship between your actions, emotions, and spiritual growth. Approach this journey with compassionate self-accountability, knowing that struggling does not make you a "bad Muslim" but someone who is actively engaging in the journey of the soul. Trust in Allah's infinite mercy and in your heart's capacity to heal, grow, and realign with your soul's purpose.

Muslims and Abstinence: 21st-Century Challenges

Most Muslims are aware of abstinence as an Islamic value, often reinforced through family, community, or religious settings. While premarital sex is widely understood to be impermissible, interpretations of abstinence vary—some permit non-intercourse intimacy, while others justify sexual activity within committed relationships. Despite this awareness, premarital sexual activity, including pornography consumption, is increasingly common among Muslims globally, revealing a disconnect between Islamic teachings and lived experiences (Hald et al., 2021). A few key challenges to abstinence in the 21st century are:

A Hypersexualized World: The normalization of sexual freedom in media, technology, and online spaces exposes Muslims to sexualized content and ethical dilemmas. While much focus is placed on men's struggles with pornography, women often turn to romance media for emotional fulfillment, reinforcing unrealistic expectations. Navigating these influences requires tools that build internal resilience and reframe abstinence as a soulful commitment to spiritual growth.

Challenges with Islamic Guidance: Delayed marriages due to societal pressures or cultural practices intensify struggles with abstinence. While Islamic teachings provide practices like fasting and lowering the gaze, these are often presented as rigid rules without integrating their ethical and spiritual dimensions. Divorced Muslims face unique challenges in readjusting to abstinence, highlighting the need for compassionate support to align actions with values while navigating emotional and spiritual complexities.

Lack of Holistic Sexual Health Education: Many Muslims lack comprehensive sexual health education that integrates Islamic values, leaving them ill-equipped to navigate sexual desire and abstinence. Fear-based approaches perpetuate shame and reduce abstinence to reputation preservation rather than presenting it as a path to spiritual growth and closeness to Allah.

Oversimplification of Abstinence: Abstinence is often seen as a surface-level behavior, creating a binary view of "good" and "bad" Muslims. However, abstinence in Islamic tradition involves the purification of the soul (*tazkiyat al-nafs*) and aligning actions with Divine guidance. Addressing struggles like pornography or compulsive behaviors requires exploring their emotional and spiritual roots, fostering a deeper connection with Allah through soulful abstinence.

These challenges underscore the need for holistic approaches to abstinence that integrate theology, ethics, and spirituality.

Soulfully Bridging the Gap Between Knowing and Doing

For many Muslims, practical strategies and spiritual frameworks to uphold abstinence as a soulful practice are limited. Abstinence is not merely avoiding behaviors but an ongoing journey of intention, self-compassion, and spiritual growth. It requires external support and internal resilience, making it a continuous commitment rather than a one-time decision. To navigate modern challenges, Muslims must cultivate critical media literacy to filter pervasive messages through Islamic values, empowering them to resist harmful influences with clarity and confidence.

Reframing abstinence as a dynamic, spiritually enriching practice transforms it from a restrictive obligation into an act of self-love, self-accountability, and alignment with Allah. By understanding its spiritual, emotional, and practical dimensions, Muslims can embrace abstinence as a profound expression of devotion and soul-centered growth.

With this holistic foundation to understand the "why" behind sexual desire and abstinence, let's incorporate this to understand the "how" of empowered abstinence.

Understanding Shame and Guilt in the Context of Abstinence

For many Muslims, guilt and shame are closely linked to abstinence and sexual activity, but it's important to distinguish between the two for spiritual growth. **Guilt** arises when actions conflict with values, serving as a constructive reminder for reflection and repentance, and guiding individuals to realign with their beliefs. It motivates growth, affirming one's worth as a creation of Allah. In contrast, **shame** internalizes actions as a reflection of self-worth, leading to self-condemnation and feelings of unworthiness. Unlike guilt, which fosters growth, shame often creates cycles of avoidance and despair, hindering self-awareness and spiritual connection with Allah.

Islamic teachings emphasize the soul's capacity for purification (*tazkiyah*), but shame impedes this dynamic process. It is linked to anxiety, depression, and unhealthy coping mechanisms such as pornography or self-gratification (Grubbs et al., 2019; Hall et al., 2020). Fear-based teachings often reduce abstinence to a "good–bad" dynamic, neglecting the soul's complexity. The Prophet Muhammad (Peace and Blessings be Upon Him) modeled compassion, reminding us that no mistake is beyond Allah's mercy. To move from shame to self-compassion, Muslims should recognize Allah's infinite mercy, separate actions from identity, and replace fear with soulful accountability, using struggles as opportunities for growth. Through practices like *salah* (prayer), *dhikr* (invocation), and *tawbah* (repentence), Muslims can reconnect with Allah, fostering healing and self-compassion.

Defining Empowered Abstinence: A Soulful Perspective

Empowered abstinence is a dynamic, spiritually rooted approach that reframes abstinence not as a rigid restriction or fear-based obligation, but as a soulful journey of aligning with Allah's wisdom. This framework draws from the theology, ethics, and spirituality model introduced in chapter 2, offering a holistic way to conceptualize and practice abstinence in the modern world.

Theology, Ethics, and Spirituality: Foundations of Empowered Abstinence

Empowered abstinence begins with a comprehensive understanding of the Islamic rulings on premarital sexual activity, grounded in trust in Allah's infinite wisdom. **Islamic theology** teaches that these guidelines are not arbitrary but part of Allah's Divine design for human well-being. Abstinence protects the sanctity of the body and soul, ensuring sexual intimacy is reserved for marriage. Trusting in Allah's wisdom means acknowledging our human limits and embracing His knowledge, even when societal pressures or personal desires challenge us. By choosing abstinence, we express our faith in Allah's wisdom and submit to His Divine plan.

Empowered abstinence is also an **ethical** pursuit, fostering virtues such as patience, self-control, and gratitude. Recognizing our bodies as sacred gifts from Allah, abstinence becomes a way of honoring this trust. The struggle to maintain abstinence is not easy, but its beauty lies in the perseverance it requires. The Quran affirms, "And those who strive for Us – We will surely guide them to Our ways" (Quran 29:69). Abstinence, therefore, is about intentionality, striving to align our actions with spiritual values, and cultivating a deeper connection with Allah that benefits us in all aspects of life.

At its core, empowered abstinence is a **spiritual** journey, prioritizing long-term growth over immediate gratification. It requires a deep sense of *ihsaan* (God-consciousness), living with the awareness that Allah is always present. Abstinence is not about denying desires but channeling them to contribute to spiritual growth. The struggle against the lower soul (*nafs al-ammarah*) elevates our intentions, guiding us toward the tranquil soul (*nafs al-mutma'innah*). Each step of empowered abstinence is a step in the purification of the soul (*tazkiyah*), bringing us closer to tranquility in this life and the next.

Empowered Abstinence: A Framework for Soulful Development and Growth

Empowered abstinence is ultimately about aligning sexual decision-making with a holistic vision of Islamic theology, ethics, and spirituality. It is:

- Trusting in Allah's wisdom while accepting our human limits.
- Cultivating virtues through struggle, honoring the sacred trust of the body.
- Centering the development of the soul and prioritizing long-term spiritual fulfillment over short-term pleasure.

As we move into the practical steps for practicing empowered abstinence, let this framework guide your reflections and actions. Empowered abstinence is not about being perfect; it is about striving sincerely, trusting that

Allah sees every effort you make on this soulful journey. Table 4.1 summarizes key differences between fear-based and empowered abstinence. After reviewing this content, take a few moments to note down thoughts and feelings in the space provided.

Reflections

_____
_____
_____
_____

Practical Steps Toward Empowered Abstinence: Compassionate Self-Accountability

Empowered abstinence is a crucial part of our spiritual journey as Muslims, reflecting our ongoing development toward becoming the best spiritual versions of ourselves before returning to Allah. Struggles with abstinence and sexual desire are natural and integral to our growth.

Table 4.1 A summary of the key differences between fear-based and empowered abstinence approaches

Aspect	Fear-Based Abstinence	Soulful Empowered Abstinence
Definition	Behavior-focused.	Soul-focused.
	"Just don't have sex before marriage, it's haraam."	"Empowered abstinence is a spiritual struggle."
Strategies	Centers the anger and punishment of God.	Centers an Islamic model of the soul.
	"Sex before marriage is impermissible to avoid Hellfire in the Afterlife, and consequences in this life."	"Avoiding premarital sexual activity before marriage is an ongoing struggle, to focus on our spiritual development."
Possible Impacts	May lead to shame being projected into marital intimacy.	Helps Muslims hold themselves compassionately accountable.
	"I've been told my whole life to not have sex before marriage because it's wrong and bad. I feel like my body is wrong and bad for what it could lead me to do. The thought of sex within marriage is confusing. I don't feel comfortable in my body."	"I have learned nuanced and spiritual approaches to manage my sexual desire before marriage. As I think about marriage, I feel more confident approaching communication about and sexual intimacy with my spouse."

84 Soulful Sexual Health for Muslims

Feeling sexual desire or struggling with abstinence does not make you a weak or bad Muslim, nor are you punished by Allah for facing these challenges. Instead, these struggles are opportunities for spiritual development and self-reflection.

Empowered abstinence is rooted in compassion and self-accountability, key themes throughout this book. It encourages us to make intentional, empowered choices about sexual activity before marriage, reflecting trust in Allah and a commitment to spiritual growth. The Quran outlines three levels of the soul—*Nafs al-Ammarah*, *Nafs al-Lawwamah*, and *Nafs al-Mutma'innah*—which provide a framework for understanding how to approach sexual desire and maintain abstinence. Table 4.2 summarizes how each level influences these practices.

Table 4.2 An overview of the three levels of the soul outlined in the Quran, and roles related to empowered abstinence

Level of the Soul	*Role in Sexual Desire and Empowered Abstinence*
Nafs al-ammarah (the soul that commands to act upon increased levels of sexual desire)	The level of the soul that commands to act upon increased levels of sexual desire/*shahwah*.
	We are increasingly influenced by the world around us, and what's pulling us toward sexual gratification. There are often emotional wounds and unmet needs that may draw us toward premarital sexual activity for the purpose of feeling soothed, distracted, and some form of pleasure. Whispers and distractions from *shaytaan* are amplified—*shaytaan* (the devil) knows that we are struggling, and these inclinations will arise within us as thoughts/ideas that then snowball into emotions that result in sexual choices and behaviors.
Nafs al-lawwammah (the discerning soul that is starting to have compassionate self-accountability)	This level of the soul starts to gain awareness over the factors that are leading us to be pulled into the direction of sexual behaviors.
	We separate our behaviors from who we are as a God-created person, and compassionately start to ask ourselves questions to gain greater self-awareness about our sexual decisions:
	What thoughts and emotions are influencing this behavior? How do I feel now, and how might I feel in the future? Which part of my soul feels most active—higher spiritual self or lower self-gratification? Does this decision align with my spiritual journey or hinder it?

(Continued)

Table 4.2 (Continued)

Level of the Soul	Role in Sexual Desire and Empowered Abstinence
Nafs al-mutma'innah (the soul at peace that is at balance and equilibrium with sexual desire)	The soul is at peace. We have achieved equilibrium of sexual desire within our soul and are balancing this presence with our spiritual journey.

Empowered Abstinence Requires Soulful Sexual Decision-Making

Now that we've explored premarital sex through the lens of the soul's journey, let's shift our focus to the role of the discerning soul in sexual decision-making. For some Muslims, the phrase "sexual decision-making" may feel unfamiliar or even uncomfortable. However, rather than merely following the directive of "don't have sex before marriage," empowered sexual decision-making integrates theology, ethics, and spirituality. This holistic approach acknowledges the complexity of sexual desire, seeing abstinence not as a restriction but as a soulful practice that strengthens our connection to Allah and honors the dynamic nature of the soul.

This section offers a roadmap to guide you through empowered abstinence. First, we explore **Self-Awareness**, reflecting on your current relationship with sexual desire. Next, we address **Balancing Daily Life**, providing practical strategies for maintaining a balanced lifestyle that supports healthy sexual decision-making. The third step, **Mindful Presence**, enhances mindfulness and emotional processing to address imbalances in sexual desire. Finally, we introduce a **Self-Accountability Framework**, adapted from Imam al-Ghazali's teachings, to guide your decisions with intention and spiritual alignment. Each step builds upon the previous one, supporting your journey toward empowered sexual decision-making. As you engage in this process, remember that every effort you make is seen and valued by Allah.

Step 1: Gain Awareness About Your Struggle with Empowered Abstinence

The first step toward empowered abstinence is cultivating self-awareness about your struggle with sexual desire. This process requires compassion and self-accountability. Instead of judging yourself, approach this step with curiosity and kindness, like a detective examining your sexual desire from all angles to understand it better. Awareness is the foundation for meaningful change and a pathway to healing any shame you may hold.

Below are reflective questions to guide you in this process. Answer them with honesty and compassion, remembering that acknowledging your struggles is an act of courage and self-accountability.

Reflection Questions

What premarital sexual activity or activities am I struggling with right now? As I reflect, when did I start to struggle with this? What else was happening in and around my life at the time? (Consider family, school, community, friends, etc.)

_____
_____
_____

Reflecting on when you were younger, do you have any memories or thoughts from how you learned (indirectly or directly) about sex or sexual health? Are there any difficult or traumatic experiences that may have led you to seek sexual activity as self-soothing or numbing outlets?

_____
_____
_____

How often do I slip into this behavior? Where and when does it usually happen? What or who else is involved in this behavior?

_____
_____
_____

Think back to the most recent time this sexual decision/activity occurred:

- How were you feeling earlier in the day or right before the behavior? Were you stressed, frustrated, angry, upset, lonely, triggered, etc.?
- What types of thoughts were you having?
- What were you telling yourself about this sexual decision?
- Were there any memories of past situations that came up?
- Were you consuming any pornography or other content online that may have triggered the behavior?
- Note down anything else that may have played a role in this moment.

A Soulful Model of Empowered Abstinence   87

_____
_____
_____

How did you feel after the sexual decision was made? What do you tell yourself about the spiritual impacts of this decision?

_____
_____
_____

What do you do if you're feeling guilty or ashamed about your decision?

_____
_____
_____

What have you previously tried to address this imbalance with sexual desire?

_____
_____
_____

Table 4.3 A self-reflection activity to explore insights about sexual desire and abstinence using an Islamic model of the soul

Part of the Soul	My Compassionate Reflections	Questions or Areas of Exploration
Nafs (behaviors)		
Aql (thoughts/cognition)		
Qalb (emotions)		
Qalb (*ruh*/spirit)		

Using your responses to the questions, complete Table 4.3 to map your compassionate insights to the Islamic model of the soul covered in chapter 1. This will help you go beyond behaviors and thoughts, to the heart (*qalb*), which contains our emotions and connection to the Divine *(ruh)*.

A Compassionate Reminder: As you reflect on your responses to these questions and how they map to your soul, remember to approach yourself with gentleness. The goal of this exercise is not to dwell on mistakes but to understand the patterns and emotions that influence your sexual decisions. Self-awareness is a form of self-accountability—it allows you to reflect without judgment, learn without shame, and begin aligning your choices with your values.

Step 2: Perform an Honest Assessment of How You're Spending Your Time

With a deeper awareness of how your sexual desire is showing up, the next step is to examine lifestyle factors that may be influencing it. Imam al-Ghazali's works remind us that our senses—what we see, hear, and taste—play a significant role in shaping the balance of our sexual desire. Balancing your daily routines and activities is essential for creating the energy and focus needed to address imbalances in your sexual desire. By honestly evaluating how you spend your time, you can identify areas that may require adjustment and take proactive steps to realign your lifestyle with your spiritual goals.

Table 4.4 A self-reflection activity to assess daily activities and areas of improvement

Category	Helpful Information to Keep in Mind	Areas of Improvement
Sleep	For adults, we ideally need 6–9 hours of sleep. Sleep hygiene refers to what we do for the 1–2 hours before bedtime, such as dimming the lights or reading instead of scrolling on our phones.	
Nutrition	Ideally, we eat three meals a day and reflect on the following *hadith*: ⅓ of your stomach for food, ⅓ for water, and ⅓ with air/empty. Meals and snacks are ideally eaten at regular times each day, to ensure that we are well nourished.	

(Continued)

Table 4.4 (Continued)

Category	Helpful Information to Keep in Mind	Areas of Improvement
Exercise and Outdoor Time	Evidence suggests 150 minutes of exercise per week (moderate heart rate), and daily exposure to the sun, to help with our circadian rhythm. Exercise is also an excellent outlet for emotions which may be contributing to sexual desire imbalances: cardiovascular, strength training, or mindful movement such as yoga and tai chi.	
Religious and Spiritual/ Soulful Practices	This refers to completing the five daily prayers; making *dua* (personal supplication); spiritual practices; listening to or reciting the Quran; taking classes on religious topics; etc.	
Technology Use	Consider your daily tech habits. How often do you scroll aimlessly? Do you set boundaries, like avoiding devices an hour before bed or after waking? Reflect on patterns and adjust for balance.	
Family, Friends, Partner/ Spouse, etc.	Reflect on time spent with your spouse, family, friends, community, etc. Who is your circle or friends and support? Are you surrounding yourself with soulful companions?	
Work, Productivity, and Learning	What activities do you engage in related to work, school, learning, productivity, etc.? Do you find meaning and enjoyment in what you do or study? What are you passionate about and how you spend your time?	
Hobbies	What non-work activities—especially creative ones—do you do? What would you be interested in exploring? Particularly think about hobbies that use your hands, such as arts, crafts, woodworking, and other creative pursuits.	

Use Table 4.4 to reflect on how your time is spent and how it may be impacting your sexual desire. Approach this exercise with the same compassion and self-accountability you applied in Step 1.

As you glance over your daily activities reflections, compassionately ask yourself the following questions:

How is my status in each of these categories impacting me? Do any of these play a role in impacting my sexual desire?

_____
_____
_____

Which two to three areas are in the greatest need of improvement?

_____
_____
_____

What are two simple steps I can take to improve in each of these areas?

_____
_____
_____

How will I hold myself accountable to make these changes for at least three weeks, to build healthier routines?

_____
_____
_____

Now, let's move on to Step 3, where we'll focus on enhancing mindful presence and processing emotions that may be contributing to the imbalance in your sexual desire. Mindfulness is a powerful tool to help you deepen your connection with your emotions and bring greater awareness to your actions. Let's begin.

Step 3: Enhancing Mindful Presence and Processing Emotions

Steps 1 and 2 laid the foundation for this critical part of your journey. Now, in Step 3, we delve into enhancing mindful presence and processing emotions—key steps in understanding the deeper roots of your challenges and fostering empowered abstinence.

Through my professional experiences, I've seen that challenges with sexual desire often stem from unresolved emotional wounds or traumas.

A Soulful Model of Empowered Abstinence 91

These wounds are often connected to difficult emotions such as anxiety, guilt, shame, anger, loneliness, or sadness. If you haven't yet, I encourage you to revisit Step 2 and map your reflections to the model of the soul discussed earlier in this chapter. This will provide greater clarity about how your emotional landscape influences your sexual desires.

Recognizing Emotional Avoidance and Spiritual Bypassing

Building on the foundations laid in Steps 1 and 2, Step 3 focuses on enhancing mindful presence and processing emotions—essential practices for addressing the deeper roots of challenges with sexual desire and fostering empowered abstinence. Unresolved emotional wounds, often tied to anxiety, guilt, shame, or sadness, can amplify desires or lead to avoidance behaviors.

Many Muslims unknowingly engage in spiritual bypassing—using religious practices or beliefs to repress, ignore, or *"Alhamdulillah"* (All Praises be to Allah) our way out of feeling certain emotions. Gratitude can exist simultaneously with compassionate acknowledgement of challenging feelings. Recognizing emotional avoidance—including spiritual bypassing—is essential; relying on religious narratives to suppress emotions, rather than process them, can create a sense of disconnection from Allah and hinder spiritual growth. Compassionate acknowledgement of these emotions aligns with the understanding that they are part of Allah's creation and known to Him.

The steps outlined in the following section suggest a guided method to mindfully approach your emotions.

Practical Steps for Mindful Emotional Presence

1. **Ground Yourself in the Present Moment:** Breathe as you look around and name three things you can see. Then, listen and name two things you can hear. Finally, pick up one item nearby and hold it in your hand, noticing its weight, texture, and size.
2. **Go Inward:** Ask yourself, *what am I feeling?* Name your emotions or note bodily sensations if words don't arise.
3. **Stay with the Feeling:** Avoid analyzing or judging emotions. Acknowledge and sit with the feeling, offering compassion.
4. **Respond to the Emotion:** Allow natural releases, like tears or movement based on what your body needs. Act on insights, such as journaling or tensing and relaxing muscles to release anger, without overanalyzing.
5. **Make It a Habit:** Practice emotional check-ins during overwhelming moments or as a daily routine, fostering balance and self-awareness.

Mindfully processing emotions prevents them from compounding and unconsciously influencing decisions. This practice supports spiritual growth, deepens your connection with Allah, and nurtures inner peace. If emotions tied to past trauma feel overwhelming, consider seeking support from a trusted therapist or counselor. Reflect on this step's insights before transitioning to the final approach, centered on al-Ghazali's scholarly framework.

Reflections

_____
_____
_____
_____
_____

Step 4: Implement al-Ghazali's *Tazkiyat al-Nafs* (Purification of the Soul) Framework

In this step, we build on al-Ghazali's teachings on the interconnectedness of the heart (*qalb*), soul, and actions. Al-Ghazali explains that the heart shapes both the soul and body, and vice versa, emphasizing the need to purify the heart from elements that disturb the balance of sexual desires. He likens this purification to cleansing the "black spots" on the heart, which may arise from past trauma, early exposure to sexual content, or emotional wounds like loneliness. To illuminate the heart with Allah's presence, it's essential to engage in spiritual practices and inner struggle, committing to a gradual and consistent journey of self-reflection and self-discipline (Bakhtiar, 2019; Ghazali, 1995).

The 6M framework for purification of the soul is an adaptation of al-Ghazali's principles, tailored to address modern struggles, including challenges with sexual desire. Rooted in Islamic teachings, it integrates the purification of the heart with practical steps for self-reflection and inner work. As al-Ghazali teaches, the heart's state influences the soul and body, and it is through consistent effort to purify the heart that we can transcend traits of the lower self (*nafs al-ammarah*) and reconnect with our sacred essence (*fitrah*). This framework is inspired by the principles outlined in the book *Applying Islamic Principles to Clinical Mental Health Care: Introducing Traditional Islamically Integrated Psychotherapy (TIIP)* (Keshavarzi et al., 2021) and was further developed during my studies at the Cambridge Muslim College's Postgraduate Diploma in Islamic Psychology.

This framework offers a compassionate yet disciplined process to purify the heart and align our actions with spiritual aspirations. Through this structured approach, you engage in a transformative journey, gradually removing the impurities that hinder spiritual growth and reconnecting with Allah's guidance. This step is an essential continuation of the journey of self-awareness, balance, and mindfulness, enabling Muslims to make empowered decisions regarding sexual health and their relationship with Allah.

Let's explore each step in detail.

1. *Musharatah* (Setting Goals): The first step involves making a contract with oneself and Allah. This requires an honest and compassionate acknowledgement of what needs to change in relation to sexual desire and its consequential behaviors. Setting clear, actionable goals helps align your intentions with your spiritual journey.

Example: *"I am setting a heart-centered contract with Allah that I will work to gain insights and self-accountability over what is leading me to consume pornography and masturbate."*

2. *Muraqabah* (Self-Monitoring): In this step, you develop awareness of the thoughts, emotions, and triggers that lead to specific sexual behaviors. This process is akin to scanning the mind and heart to identify patterns and vulnerabilities. *Muraqabah* is most effective when practiced twice daily—once in the morning and once in the evening.

Example: *"What thoughts, feelings, or situations led me closer to or further away from my goals today?"*

3. *Muhasabah* (Self-Examination): Self-examination involves reflecting on your actions and thoughts to evaluate whether they align with the goals you set. Gratitude toward Allah can be expressed for progress, while forgiveness is sought for moments when actions diverged from the intended path.

Example: *"Today, I avoided a trigger that usually leads to slipping up—Alhamdulillah. I seek forgiveness for indulging in a thought that pulled me toward imbalance."*

4. *Mu'aqabah* (Spiritual Consequence): This step introduces a spiritual consequence when the contract you've set with yourself is broken. Rather than punishment, this consequence is a reminder to reconnect with Allah and turn toward Him during moments of struggle.

Example: *"If I engage in a behavior I've committed to avoid, I will perform two extra units of prayer (nafl) to seek closeness to Allah."*

5. *Mujahadah* (**Self-Struggle**): Al-Ghazali refers to self-struggle as *jihad al-akhbar*—the greatest struggle. This step emphasizes the lifelong nature of struggling with the soul. Some days will feel easier than others, and the state of the soul will fluctuate daily. *Mujahadah* requires patience, perseverance, and reliance on Allah to navigate this non-linear journey.

Example: *"I struggled today, but I will continue to strive tomorrow, knowing that each effort brings me closer to Allah."*

6. *Mu'atabah* (**Self-Admonition**): The final step is self-admonition—catching yourself in the act and course-correcting in the moment. Over time, implementing this framework enhances awareness, enabling you to recognize and address slipping behaviors earlier in the process.

Example: *"I noticed myself engaging in my anxious thought pattern that leads to imbalance. I paused and redirected my focus to name my emotions, shook out the restlessness in my arms and legs, and performed dhikr (remembrance of Allah)."*

Table 4.5 A summary of the six aspects of al-Ghazali's purification of the soul framework

6M Step	Definition	Notes
Musharatah	Setting goals to create a contract with oneself and Allah.	
Muraqabah	Bringing self-watchfulness into daily life, to notice what is going on while it is happening.	
Muhasabah	Self-examination of one's actions and associated thoughts retrospectively, to explore whether they are in line with the goals that have been set.	

(Continued)

Table 4.5 (Continued)

6M Step	Definition	Notes
Mu'aqabah	Consists of implementing an appropriate spiritual consequence toward oneself—that would have an impact—when the initial self-contract is broken. Examples include: fasting; waking up for *tahajjud* or night prayer; donating more to charity; reading a certain number of pages of the Quran.	
Mujahadah	Self-struggle and working diligently; the emphasis here is on adopting spiritual disciplines that help fortify the will.	
Mu'atabah	Self-censure: it's the ability to catch oneself in the act and course-correct in the moment.	

Applying the 6M Framework

Now that you've reviewed these six steps, complete Table 4.5 to personalize the framework to your needs. Use it as a tool to guide your journey toward a purified soul, one step at a time. Guidance is provided on how to implement your customized framework.

Practical Guidance for the 6M Framework

Integrate your personalized 6M framework into daily life by deciding on which day to start implementing it (*Bismillah*! [In the Name of God]), and by also setting a consistent time to revisit your framework each day. Focus on the process of daily effort and renewal, not perfection. Some days may feel easier than others, as Allah reminds us in Surah Inshirah: "Verily, with hardship comes ease" (Quran 94:6). Show up with intention and trust in Allah's mercy. If persistent struggles arise, revisit the previous steps, which are foundational to the 6M framework, and/or seek support from a professional for guidance.

Reflection Question

What insights have you gained about yourself while reviewing and personalizing the 6M framework? How do you feel about incorporating these steps into your daily life? Write down your thoughts and observations, allowing yourself to process them with compassion and self-awareness.

_____
_____
_____

Summary

This chapter has redefined abstinence as a dynamic, spiritually rooted practice, far beyond the simplistic directive of "don't have sex before marriage." By integrating theology, ethics, and spirituality, abstinence emerges as a journey of compassionate self-accountability, aligned with the soul's development. Empowered abstinence reframes this practice as a spiritual struggle and an opportunity for growth, addressing emotional wounds, societal influences, and the need to balance compassion with accountability. Practical tools such as self-awareness, mindful presence, and the 6M *tazkiyat al-nafs* framework rooted in al-Ghazali's teachings provide a comprehensive path to managing sexual desire in alignment with Islamic values.

This journey is not linear but a process of persistence over perfection, as there will be moments of both struggle and ease, constriction and expansion. The key is to show up sincerely, trusting Allah's mercy, and seeking support when needed. Each effort—whether through processing emotions, pausing to reflect, or reaching out for professional guidance—brings you closer to aligning your actions with your values, purifying your soul, and deepening your connection with Allah. Remember, every step of this path is seen and valued by the One who created you. With compassion and trust in Allah, you move closer to fulfilling your spiritual purpose and becoming the best version of yourself.

Reflections and Action Items

_____
_____
_____

Reference List

Ahmed, S., Abu-Ras, W., & Arfken, C. (2014). Prevalence of risk behaviors among U.S. Muslim college students. *Journal of Muslim Mental Health, 8*(1).

Ali-Faisal, S. (2016). What's sex got to do with it? The role of sexual experience in the sexual attitudes, and sexual guilt and anxiety of young Muslim adults in Canada and the United States. *Journal of Muslim Mental Health, 10*(2).

Bakhtiar, L. (2019). *Quranic psychology of the self*. Kazi Publications.

Bleakley, A., Hennessy, M., & Fishbein, M. (2017). Examining the relationship between adolescent exposure to sexual content in media and adolescent sexual behavior. *Journal of Health Communication, 16*(8), 831–852.

Bőthe, B., Tóth-Király, I., Potenza, M. N., Orosz, G., & Demetrovics, Z. (2019). Revisiting the role of impulsivity and compulsivity in problematic sexual behaviors. *Journal of Sex Research, 56*(2), 166–179. https://doi.org/10.1080/00224499.2018.1480744

Ghazali, A. al- (1995). *Al-Ghazali on disciplining the soul and on breaking the two desires: Books XXII and XXIII of the Revival of the Religious Sciences* (T. J. Winter, Trans.). Islamic Texts Society.

Grubbs, J. B., Wright, P. J., Braden, A. L., Wilt, J. A., & Kraus, S. W. (2019). Internet pornography use and sexual motivation: A systematic review and integration. *Annals of the International Communication Association, 43*(2), 117–155. https://doi.org/10.1080/23808985.2019.1584045

Hald, G. M., Mulya, T. W., & Coleman, E. (2021). Pornography consumption in Arab countries: An overview and preliminary findings. *The Journal of Sexual Medicine, 18*(3), 539–547. https://doi.org/10.1016/j.jsxm.2020.12.012

Hall, P. A., Pfaus, J. G., & Campbell, S. M. (2020). Adverse childhood experiences and problematic sexual behaviors in adulthood: A meta-analytic review. *Psychology of Addictive Behaviors, 34*(4), 398–410. https://doi.org/10.1037/adb0000516

Keshavarzi, H., Khan, F., Ali, B., & Awaad, R. (Eds.). (2021). *Applying Islamic principles to clinical mental health care: Introducing Traditional Islamically Integrated Psychotherapy*. Routledge/Taylor & Francis Group.

Mirza, S. (2019). Behind closed doors: Porn and young Muslims. *Muslim Mental Health*. Retrieved November 2024, from https://muslimmentalhealth.com/behind-closed-doors-porn-and-young-muslims/

Rothman, E. F., Kaczmarsky, C., Burke, N., Jansen, E., & Baughman, A. (2020). The prevalence of exposure to sexually explicit media among adolescents:

A systematic review. *Journal of Adolescent Health*, *56*(2), 14–21. https://doi.org/10.1016/j.jadohealth.2020.02.002

Sahih International. (1997). *The Quran: Arabic text with corresponding English meanings*. Abul-Qasim Publishing House.

Sunnah.com. (n.d.). Jami' at-Tirmidhi 2378. Retrieved January 5, 2025, from https://sunnah.com/tirmidhi:2378

Ward, L. M. (2016). Media and sexualization: State of empirical research, 1995–2015. *Journal of Sex Research*, *53*(4–5), 560–577. https://doi.org/10.1080/00224499.2016.1142496

5 The Soulful Search for a Spouse

Marriage is often the most emphasized phase in a Muslim's life. Across cultures, it is celebrated, cherished, and blessed within the Islamic tradition—not only for its religious significance, as this chapter will explore, but also because it fulfills a deep human longing. To have a life partner who shares your joys and sorrows, who helps you grow closer to Allah, and with whom you may build a family, is a profound blessing. Yet, the journey to marriage is rarely straightforward. It can be filled with challenges and frustrations, especially when so many of us grow up hearing, "Don't date!" only to be later asked, "Why aren't you married yet?!" That question often feels neither fair nor compassionate. Instead of placing blame or pressure, let's reframe it with sincerity and care: How can Muslims center their soul in the search for a spouse? This chapter will guide you through exploring that question, offering insights into the spiritual and emotional dimensions of this phase of life and equipping you with the tools to approach it with intention, alignment, and compassion. Let's begin this journey with a renewed perspective, rooted in the heart and aligned with the soul.

The Journey of the Soul

| Birth | Spiritual Accountability | Spiritual Maturity | Spiritual Legacy | The Hereafter |

Introduction

"So, when are you getting married?"

It's a question nearly every Muslim encounters, often more frequently than they'd like. While marriage is celebrated as "half of our religion,"

DOI: 10.4324/9781032675862-6

the journey to find a spouse is often clouded by rigid timelines, societal expectations, and personal insecurities. Despite Islamic reminders that Allah has a unique plan for each of us, these external pressures can overshadow the deeply personal and spiritual essence of marriage. With the rise of Muslim marriage apps and matchmaking services, the process might seem more accessible, yet it often brings new layers of confusion and frustration.

This chapter offers a soul-based perspective on marriage, focusing on spiritual and sexual health aspects that are often overlooked. By moving beyond superficial checklists, it reframes the journey to find a spouse as one of spiritual growth and soulful alignment. Modern challenges in spouse-seeking—whether navigating online platforms, addressing sexualized behaviors, or maintaining empowered abstinence—are explored with practical tools for setting boundaries, cultivating self-accountability, and fostering meaningful premarital conversations about sexual health and emotional readiness.

Through clarity, compassion, and spiritual grounding, this chapter provides a framework to approach the premarital phase with sincerity and confidence. It invites you to reflect on external influences and internal emotions that may have shaped your understanding of marriage, encouraging a perspective aligned with Allah's guidance. Together, we'll explore how to honor the sacredness of marriage while empowering your journey toward a union rooted in spiritual growth and practical readiness. Let's begin!

Reflection Questions

How do I feel about the process of searching for a spouse, and what have my experiences been like so far?

_____
_____
_____

When I hear the term "soulful marriage," what words or images come to mind, and how do they shape my perspective?

_____
_____
_____

What preparation have I done, including understanding sexual health, to align my search for a spouse with my spiritual and personal values?

_____
_____

What Is a Soulful Marriage? Centering Islamic Perspectives

For Muslims to holistically center their soul in the search for a spouse, it's essential to understand marriage from nuanced Islamic perspectives. Marriage is a significant stage of life, holding immense spiritual value—not just for this world but for the Hereafter. Islamic scriptures provide a rich and beautiful vision of marriage as a deep, soulful union:

> O mankind, fear your Lord, who created you from one soul and created from it its mate and dispersed from both of them many men and women . . .
> (Quran 4:1)

> It is He who created you from one soul and created from it its mate that he might dwell in security with her . . .
> (Quran 7:189)

> They are garments for you, and you are garments for them . . .
> (Quran 2:187)

> And of His signs is that He created for you from yourselves mates that you may find tranquility in them; and He placed between you affection and mercy. Indeed, in this are signs for those who reflect.
> (Quran 30:21)

These verses underscore that marriage, from a soul-based perspective, is far more than a legal or religious contract—it is a sacred bond between two souls. As explored in chapter 1, our existence is not limited to this life; our souls were once in the presence of Allah, connected to others in profound ways. This pre-worldly connection can manifest in our earthly lives, such as the feeling of immediate familiarity with a friend or the deep sense of knowing with a spouse. These experiences reflect the soulful bond that marriage embodies—one rooted in the heart, the center of the soul, and a reflection of Divine love.

Yet, many Muslims approach marriage as if it were a transactional arrangement, focusing solely on rights and needs. This often reduces the search for a spouse to a checklist of superficial qualities, akin to a job interview. In therapy sessions, I frequently hear statements like, "I want a good Muslim spouse," with little clarity about what "good" means, or "I want someone who is practicing," focused solely on external acts of worship without considering the quality of the person's heart. These oversimplified criteria fail to reflect the soul-based framework that Islam prioritizes for marriage—a framework that centers on spiritual growth, mutual compassion, and Divine connection.

Cultural double standards further distort Islamic perspectives on marriage. Women, for instance, often face greater scrutiny, being told to be "good Muslims" and bear the responsibility for a marriage's success. Meanwhile, men are frequently reminded only of their financial obligations, with little emphasis on emotional or spiritual preparation. These cultural narratives contradict the equitable, soul-based responsibilities Islam assigns to both spouses. A marriage rooted in the soul requires mutual accountability, where both partners engage in personal inner work to nurture their connection with Allah and each other.

A truly soulful marriage transitions from "me" to "we," centering the collective spiritual journey of both spouses. This journey involves working on the heart—polishing away emotional wounds and distractions that obstruct the soul's potential. Marriage is not merely about fulfilling a religious obligation or securing personal happiness; it is about striving toward Allah together. Loving your spouse becomes an act of worship, where you see and treat them as a Divine creation, carrying Allah's presence within their heart. From waking together each morning to falling asleep each night, every moment in a soul-centered marriage is intertwined with the remembrance of Allah.

With this perspective, let's pause to reflect on your understanding of marriage and the soul. Use these reflections as a foundation for the next section, where we will explore centering heart-based intentions for marriage.

Reflection Questions

Compared to how you answered this question earlier in the chapter, how has your understanding of a soulful marriage changed?

_____
_____

What words and images now come to mind when you think about a soulful marriage?

_____
_____
_____

What does "working on your soul within marriage" mean to you?

_____
_____
_____

Islamic Perspectives: Qualities to Look for in a Spouse

Islamic teachings emphasize that marriage is a sacred bond founded on mutual love, mercy, and spiritual growth. The Prophet Muhammad (Peace and Blessings be Upon Him) identified four qualities to seek in a spouse—wealth, lineage, beauty, and religiosity—but stressed that religiosity should be prioritized, saying, "Choose the one who is religious, so that you may prosper." (Sunnah.com, n.d., Bukhari 5090). This underscores the importance of shared spiritual values and character over material or superficial attributes.

The Quran highlights the foundation of love (*muwaddah*) and mercy (*rahmah*) in marriage, describing it as a Divine sign of Allah's blessings: "And among His signs is that He created for you from yourselves mates that you may find tranquility in them; and He placed between you affection and mercy" (Surah Ar-Rum 30:21). Emotional and spiritual compatibility is key to fostering a peaceful, nurturing relationship. Additionally, qualities such as honesty, good character, and the ability to uphold Islamic ethics are essential for a soulful partnership, as the Prophet (Peace and Blessings be Upon Him) said, "If a man comes to you whose religion and character please you, then marry him" (Sunnah.com, n.d., Tirmidhi 1084).

Ultimately, the Islamic tradition encourages Muslims to approach the search for a spouse with intentionality, focusing on qualities that support a relationship built on mutual respect, shared faith, and spiritual alignment.

Centering Heart-Based Intentions for Marriage

Marriage in Islam is not just a checklist or a legal arrangement, but a deeply spiritual journey centered on intentions, which shape both actions and rewards. The Prophet Muhammad (Peace and Blessings be Upon Him) taught that "The deeds are considered by the intentions, and a person will get the reward according to his intention" (Sunnah.com, n.d., Bukhari 1). To approach marriage from a soulful perspective, we must reflect on the spiritual and emotional dimensions of our hearts, moving beyond surface-level desires and examining the deeper purpose behind our search for a spouse.

Emotional wounds or external pressures can often cloud our intentions, making us focus on superficial traits or idealized checklists. While checklists can provide clarity and comfort, they should not define our approach to marriage. Instead, they should be viewed as tools to guide us toward a heart-centered intention, aligning with Allah's presence. By reflecting on the qualities we seek in a spouse—religion, character, emotional capacity, and values—we can identify how these preferences may be influenced by societal norms or personal expectations. Compassionately acknowledging these emotions helps refine our intentions and reconnect them to the spiritual purpose of marriage.

Ultimately, a soul-centered marriage involves two people supporting each other in their spiritual journeys, loving each other for the sake of Allah. By reframing a checklist through this lens, as Table 5.1 demonstrates, we focus on qualities that foster mutual growth and Divine love. For instance, instead of "I want someone who is financially stable," consider "I seek a partner who values financial responsibility and trusts Allah's provision." This approach deepens our understanding of our desires, ensuring that our intentions align with the spiritual, emotional, and Divine aspirations we seek in a partner.

After completing the table on a separate piece of paper, compassionately check in with how you're feeling. Acknowledge and accept these feelings and remember that you can revisit these intentions as often as you like during your spouse-seeking journey. Moving forward with these current intentions, we'll next explore the question that Muslims love to ask.

So . . . Can Muslims "Date"?

The short answer is yes—but, as you've explored, it must come from heart-based intentions centered on marriage and finding a spouse. These intentions reflect sincerity and alignment with Islamic values, emphasizing the sacredness of relationships as part of the soul's journey toward Allah. If the reasons behind dating do not align with the intention of marriage, it warrants compassionate and self-accountable exploration to ensure soulful alignment. Approaching this process with honesty and care allows us to uncover motivations and realign them with our faith and personal growth.

The topic of "dating" often provokes strong reactions among Muslims, shaped by cultural influences and varying levels of understanding from family, peers, and religious teachings. For many, dating carries connotations of physical intimacy and casual relationships, which conflict with Islamic values. This makes the concept uncomfortable or unacceptable for some Muslims.

In the 21st century, social media and digital platforms significantly shape perspectives on relationships—often without spiritual grounding. While many Muslims learn about relationships through their parents or Islamic education, these lessons are often incomplete or overly rigid. Well-meaning parents might assert that "Muslims don't date," creating a false dichotomy: either you engage in casual dating or avoid it entirely. This rigidity can suppress curiosity, leave important questions unanswered, and make open discussions about relationships challenging.

This lack of nuanced conversations often leads to confusion and frustration, with many Muslims asking, "If I can't date, how do I find a spouse?" Without holistic, soul-centered discussions and sufficient sexual health education, oversimplified narratives need to be unlearned, paving the way for healthier approaches to finding a spouse. These approaches should reflect both modern realities and Islamic teachings, ensuring they are rooted in sincerity and alignment with one's spiritual values.

In Islam, intention is key. Whether exploring relationships influenced by peers or actively seeking a spouse, a God-centered intention transforms

Table 5.1 A self-reflection activity to transform checklist qualities into heart-centered intentions for the soulful search for a spouse

Checklist Quality (the "What")	Heart-Centered Intention (the "How" and "Why")
Example: *I want a spouse who is tall with an athletic build.*	Example: *I seek someone who sees their body as a responsibility from God, and actively works to take care of their body through daily choices.*
Example: *I want my spouse to pray five times a day.*	Example: *I seek a spouse who is conscious of God both on and off their prayer mat. They align their behaviors with God-consciousness.*

dating from a superficial activity into a meaningful journey towards marriage. The real question isn't whether Muslims can date, but rather, "What is my heart-centered intention for dating?"

Reflecting on and redefining "dating" for yourself allows you to reclaim it in a way that aligns with your spiritual and emotional values. It's essential to examine your unique understanding and preferences about dating, approaching it with clarity and free from comparison to others. Whether you call it "dating," "getting to know someone," or "courtship," what matters most is that your approach honors your heart and soul.

So, let's reframe the question to "What does dating as a Muslim look like when we center heart-based intentions?"

This shift in framing opens new possibilities. Let's start by reflecting on our understanding of the term "dating." Take a moment to complete these prompts with honesty and compassion for whatever arises:

I define dating as:
_____
_____
_____

I learned about dating from:
_____
_____
_____

When I hear about Muslims who date, the following comes to mind:
_____
_____
_____

If "dating" isn't the right term for me, this is how I would describe the "getting to know someone for marriage" stage:
_____
_____
_____

As the way Muslims find spouses evolves, particularly with the rise of marriage apps and online platforms, it's important to maintain heart-based intentions in every step of the process. Whether through traditional or modern methods, let your approach reflect sincerity, spiritual alignment, and a commitment to finding a spouse whose soul complements your own, guiding you both on the path toward Allah.

The Spark/Fireworks Feeling: Does It Need to Be There?

We've all seen the movies where two people meet, lock eyes, and sparks fly, suggesting instant chemistry is a sign of a lasting marriage. However, this view overlooks the importance of a deeper connection that involves all aspects of the soul—behaviors, thoughts, emotions, and spiritual alignment with Allah. True, lasting relationships should be built on a foundation beyond physical attraction or intense emotions, avoiding the fleeting impulses of the lower soul (*nafs al-ammarah*).

While Islam encourages seeking physical attraction, it's important to remember that its presence—or absence—at the beginning isn't a reliable indicator of the relationship's future. Early stages of attraction often involve intense emotions driven by neurotransmitters like dopamine, but these feelings alone do not guarantee long-term success. A relationship grounded in heart-centered intentions and spiritual alignment is key for lasting connection.

If you don't feel an immediate spark, that's perfectly okay. As emotional and spiritual bonds deepen, physical attraction often follows naturally. Trust that a healthy relationship, built on shared values and spiritual alignment, will foster true attraction in its own time.

The Soulful Search for a Spouse: Online and IRL (In Real Life)

In the interconnected world of the 21st century—where online interactions are woven into the fabric of daily life—the ways in which Muslims search for a spouse have dramatically evolved. With Muslim communities spread across the globe, technology has become a central tool for bridging these physical distances. However, the freedom and anonymity that online platforms provide can be a double-edged sword. On one hand, these tools offer access to a broader network of potential matches and allow Muslims to connect in ways that were previously unimaginable. On the other, the same sense of freedom and privacy can give rise to concerns around sincerity, intentions, and even challenges related to sexual health and emotional boundaries. Navigating these spaces requires a thoughtful approach rooted in heart-based intentions and soulful accountability.

Before we delve into the unique sexual health challenges that arise in both in-person and online contexts of searching for a spouse, let's take a moment to reflect.

> **Reflection Questions**
>
> Which of these two methods—online or in-person—do you prefer or are actively using to find a spouse?
> _____
> _____
> _____
>
> What challenges have you encountered with these options?
> _____
> _____
> _____
>
> Do any of these challenges relate to sexual health? Are there potential sexual health concerns you foresee in the future?
> _____
> _____
> _____

Feel free to revisit these questions as you move through this section. We'll explore not only the challenges that arise in these two realms but also spiritual and soul-based approaches to address these concerns, ensuring that your journey toward finding a spouse remains aligned with your values and faith.

> **"My Therapist Is Encouraging Me to Get Out There and Date . . ."**
>
> In my work with Muslim clients searching for a spouse, it's not uncommon to hear narratives reflecting past experiences with non-Muslim therapists. Many Muslims seek therapy to address issues

within existing relationships or to process past experiences and traumas that could impact their current or future journey towards marriage. A recurring pattern in these accounts is the encouragement by therapists to adopt societal norms, such as dating to "discover what you're looking for" or to "gain relationship experience."

While these suggestions may come from a place of good intention, they often fail to consider the holistic, soul-based perspectives that are central to a Muslim's understanding of sexual health and relationships. For Muslim clients, such advice can create inner turmoil, leading to confusion, misalignment with their values, and a sense of disconnection from their spiritual framework. As explored in chapter 13, professionals working with Muslim clients must be cautious not to project their own values onto their clients. Misattribution bias—assuming that Islam itself is the source of a client's challenges—can lead to well-meaning but misguided recommendations that aim to "liberate" the client through approaches like casual dating, without considering their spiritual and cultural context.

Therapists must instead approach Muslim clients with cultural humility and an openness to understanding the soul-based perspectives that guide their lives. Compassionate care involves respecting the client's framework, helping them align with their values, and supporting their journey toward holistic growth without imposing external paradigms.

Sexual Health Challenges: Sexualized Behaviors and Empowered Abstinence

As we've explored, the two most common methods for seeking a spouse—online and in-person—often overlap, with online interactions leading to in-person meetings and vice versa. While both methods have their own dynamics, the focus of this chapter is on the sexual health challenges that arise during the spouse-seeking phase. These challenges are not limited to first-time seekers but also affect those reentering the process after divorce, those who have lost their loved one, or those who have been searching for an extended period.

In my therapy practice with Muslims, I've observed that sexual health challenges during this phase are common, yet they are often accompanied by feelings of shame or self-blame. Let's explore two key categories of challenges: 1) dealing with unwanted sexualized behaviors and 2) maintaining empowered abstinence.

Sexualized Behaviors: A Soul-Based Perspective

Sexualized behaviors, especially on marriage apps and social media, are a common challenge, particularly for Muslim women, who often receive inappropriate messages. These behaviors stem from unbalanced sexual desire (*shahwah*) and the *nafs al-ammarah*, the lower-self driven by self-gratification. When dominated by this aspect of the soul, actions prioritize immediate pleasure over mutual respect and spiritual alignment, distancing individuals from heart-centered intentions for marriage.

External factors, such as societal norms equating masculinity with sexual assertiveness and misinterpretations of Islamic teachings, further complicate these behaviors. Men may justify inappropriate actions or dismiss boundaries, while women often face pressure to comply with sexualized dynamics out of fear of rejection or emotional need for validation. These pressures can lead to behaviors that conflict with personal values, particularly when emotional wounds from past experiences are involved.

Understanding these behaviors through a soul-based lens is crucial for aligning actions with spiritual goals. Whether we've engaged in or been affected by such behaviors, the key is to approach them with compassion, identify underlying wounds, and commit to aligning our actions with our heart-centered intentions for marriage. Let's reflect on these challenges as we explore strategies for maintaining empowered abstinence and managing unwanted behaviors.

Reflection Questions

Have I engaged in sexualized behaviors toward another person? If so, what do I remember about why and what was going on at the time? What did I tell myself to justify these actions?

_____
_____
_____

Have I been on the receiving end of sexualized behaviors? How did it make me feel and what steps—if any—did I take? Use this space to write out and process any emotions that are still there.

_____
_____

If I have engaged in sexualized behaviors in the past, what signs can lead me to become more aware of my soul before I engage in these behaviors again?

___

Dealing with Sexualized Behaviors

Addressing sexualized behaviors in the spouse-seeking process requires a soul-based approach of compassionate self-accountability and realignment with heart-centered intentions. For those on the receiving end, it is crucial to set and communicate boundaries that preserve dignity and spiritual alignment. Boundaries are sacred tools that protect emotional, spiritual, and physical well-being, ensuring that behaviors outside of your values are not tolerated. This may involve expressing how behavior has affected you, blocking someone, or reporting misconduct.

To navigate unwanted behaviors, reflect on your relationship with boundaries. Consider where you stand and what steps you need to take to strengthen them. This reflection helps you honor your values while maintaining spiritual alignment. Setting clear boundaries protects your well-being and fosters respect and sincerity in your search for a spouse.

By establishing and maintaining boundaries, you cultivate an environment of respect and trust, which is foundational for a soul-centered marriage rooted in mutual respect, God-consciousness, and spiritual growth.

Complete the following as you reflect on your experiences with boundaries:

My understanding of boundaries is . . .

___

A recent example of when I set a boundary (does not need to be related to seeking a spouse) is . . .

___

After I set the boundary, I felt . . .

_____

_____

_____

When I think about setting boundaries for sexualized behaviors, I feel and think . . .

_____

_____

_____

> **It's OK to Take a Break from Marriage Apps**
>
> Setting boundaries for sexual behaviors is no easy task, and navigating marriage apps can add another layer of emotional and mental strain. The energy and time it takes to sort through profiles, initiate and maintain conversations, and balance your own needs in the process can feel overwhelming. It's completely normal to experience exhaustion, frustration, or even resentment during this journey. These feelings are important signals from your heart and soul, calling for care and rest. Taking a step back from marriage apps and the process of searching for a spouse is not only acceptable—it's an act of compassion toward yourself.
>
> Remember, taking a break does not mean you're delaying your path to engagement or marriage. Allah is in control, and your journey unfolds according to His wisdom and timing. As the Quran reminds us, "And they plan, but Allah plans. And Allah is the best of planners" (Quran 8:30).
>
> When you feel the need to pause, see it as an opportunity to reconnect with yourself, renew your intentions, and realign your heart and soul with your spiritual journey. Trust that Allah's plan is unfolding in the best possible way, even in the pauses.

Setting Soulful Boundaries

Using your responses to the reflection questions, let's delve into a simple yet powerful two-step process to set and communicate boundaries when faced with sexualized behaviors.

Setting boundaries is not just about creating rules—it's an act of **compassionate self-accountability**. By setting boundaries, you are not trying to control the other person's behavior; instead, you are honoring your values and ensuring your emotional and spiritual well-being. Boundaries are for you, and they empower you to respond thoughtfully and purposefully to how others react. By establishing and communicating them, you are actively protecting your emotional and spiritual integrity while creating space for meaningful, heart-centered connections.

STEP 1: WRITE A CLEAR DECLARATION OF YOUR BOUNDARIES

The first step is to clarify what behaviors cross your line and how you will respond. Boundaries should be specific, actionable, and reflective of your values. How others respond to your boundaries is their responsibility, but you get to decide what steps to take based on their response. Take a moment to read the example below and create your own boundary declaration.

Example: *"I am not comfortable with any suggestive or explicit sexual references during communication. This includes comments about my physical appearance or questions about it. If this happens, I will communicate my boundary. If this boundary is not respected, I will end the communication and the getting-to-know process with this person."*

My boundary declaration is:

_____

_____

_____

STEP 2: PREPARE AND PRACTICE ASSERTIVE COMMUNICATION

Having a clear boundary is the foundation, but communicating it is equally important. Assertive communication is a compassionate yet firm way to express your needs and expectations. Preparing your response in advance will help you feel confident and grounded if a situation arises. After reading the example below, create your own assertive communication statements.

Example: *"I don't appreciate being treated like a sexual object, and I'm not OK with this type of communication. Please don't send me anything like this again."*

My assertive statements are:

_____

_____

_____

If you assert your boundary and it isn't respected, take a moment to brainstorm potential next steps. These steps might include ending communication, blocking the individual, or reporting the behavior to the relevant platform. By doing so, you reinforce that you are in control of how you respond, even when you cannot control the actions of others.

If my boundary isn't respected, my next steps are:
_____
_____
_____

By creating clear and compassionate boundaries, you are affirming your worth as a soul-centered individual and aligning your actions with your heart-centered intentions for marriage. When you communicate these boundaries assertively, you protect your sacred space and model respect and sincerity in your interactions.

A Note to Those Who Receive Assertive Communication

When someone shares a boundary with you, pause and approach the situation with compassion and self-accountability. Your actions have impacted them, and responding thoughtfully fosters growth for both parties.

Begin by acknowledging their message and reflecting on its significance. If needed, ask for time to process your response. Apologize sincerely if you recognize your behavior's impact and hold yourself accountable by examining the emotions and intentions behind your actions. Were they aligned with your spiritual values and higher self?

Circle back with honesty and vulnerability, sharing your reflections and intentions. If continuing the relationship is not appropriate, communicate this respectfully. For example: *"I want to be honest—I felt guilty about those messages. My feelings toward you grew, and I got caught up in them. I'm sorry, and I'm working to manage my feelings better. I think it's best if we end our communication so I can focus on myself."*

This response reflects integrity, compassion, and alignment with your spiritual journey.

Empowered Abstinence: Values and Boundaries

As we move from discussing online sexualized behaviors to navigating in-person interactions, maintaining empowered abstinence in real-life settings presents unique challenges, especially when attraction arises. While physical chemistry and sexual desire are natural and not sinful in Islam, the focus is on how we respond to these feelings. Feelings of attraction are part of God's creation, and the emphasis is on managing these feelings in a way that aligns with our spiritual journey.

Empowered abstinence involves intentionality and clear boundaries, especially when the lower soul (*nafs al-ammarah*) pulls us away from our values. These boundaries are not merely about controlling external factors but reflect self-accountability and compassion. Setting boundaries protects your heart and soul, helping you remain aligned with your spiritual development. While how others respond is outside your control, you have the power to uphold your boundaries with respect for your own spiritual growth.

To navigate this stage successfully, let's explore a practical, soul-centered framework for setting and maintaining boundaries in person, ensuring that your actions reflect your commitment to empowered abstinence and spiritual alignment.

1. Write a Clear Declaration for Your Value of Empowered Abstinence

Clarity is essential when it comes to upholding your values. By clearly defining your boundaries for empowered abstinence, you create a point of reference to guide your actions and decisions. Reflect on your intentions and craft a declaration that aligns with your spiritual goals.

Example Declaration:

"To focus on my spiritual development and get to know someone emotionally and spiritually, I choose not to engage in any physical or sexual intimacy before marriage. I acknowledge that I may experience feelings of attraction and sexual desire, and I will use strategies to manage these feelings when they arise. It's important to me that my future spouse respects this value. If they try to challenge or undermine this boundary, I will remain firm. If I slip up, I will compassionately check in with myself and take steps to realign with my values."

My declaration for empowered abstinence:

_____
_____
_____

2. Communicate Openly with the Person You're Getting to Know

Open communication is key to fostering mutual respect and understanding. Share your values and boundaries with the person you're getting to know early in the process. This ensures clarity and allows both of you to make informed decisions about continuing the relationship.

Example Statement:

"Since we're moving forward with getting to know each other, I'd like to share some of my values. For me, it's important to not engage in physical or sexual intimacy before marriage. This helps me focus on my spiritual development and build a connection that's emotional and spiritual. I'd like to know how you feel about this and what values you hold regarding intimacy before marriage."

My communication approach:
_____
_____
_____

3. Be Assertive and Enforce Boundaries

Setting boundaries is only the first step—you also need to enforce them when necessary. Assertive communication is a compassionate yet firm way to address crossed boundaries. If you slip up, use self-accountability to reflect, revisit your values, and communicate honestly with your partner.

Example Responses:

If your partner pushes your boundaries: *"I know our feelings and attraction for each other are growing, but I shared that I don't want to engage in sexual behaviors. This value is important to me, and I would ask that you respect it moving forward."*

If you cross your own boundaries: *"I want to be honest—I feel guilty about some of the messages I sent. I felt this strong sexual pull and, in the moment, I got caught up in them. I'm working on managing my feelings better and staying true to my values."*

My assertive statements and reflections:
_____
_____
_____

4. Reevaluate Your Values and the Relationship

Relationships evolve, and so should your understanding of your boundaries and values. Periodically reflect on how the relationship is aligning with your spiritual intentions. If decisions are being made that contradict your values, it's an opportunity to pause, reflect, and decide the next steps.

Example Reflection:

"We've been getting to know each other for a few months and have been spending more time alone. While it feels good in the moment to be sexually intimate, I feel guilt and shame afterward. I think we need to reflect on where this relationship is going—should we involve our families, seek premarital counseling, or move toward engagement and marriage? I'm feeling confused and need clarity."

My reflections:

_____
_____
_____

5. Seek Support If Necessary

If you're struggling to maintain boundaries or feel stuck in the relationship, seek support from trusted friends, family members, or a therapist. Guidance from someone you trust can provide perspective and tools to navigate challenges, especially if unhealthy or abusive dynamics emerge.

When to seek support and my support system:

_____
_____
_____

Embracing the Soulful Spouse-Seeking Journey

Maintaining empowered abstinence in real-life contexts is a daily commitment to your soul's growth. Some days will feel easier, while others will bring challenges and struggles. As we've explored earlier, the soul expands and contracts, reflecting the ebb and flow of life's experiences. Through compassion and self-accountability, you can gently check in with your soul, understand what it needs, and realign with your heart-centered intentions.

Remember, this journey is not about perfection—it's about sincerity and persistence in striving for alignment with Allah's guidance. By centering your values and setting boundaries, you are honoring your spiritual path and creating a foundation for a relationship that is deeply soulful and fulfilling.

"Salaam Sameera . . . My Relationship Is in Limbo"

Many Muslims find themselves in relationships that started with the intention of marriage but now feel stuck or uncertain. These situations often have deeper, soul-based reasons behind them. If you find yourself in such a relationship, approach yourself with compassion and self-accountability rather than blame. Reflecting on the deeper dynamics can help realign your heart and soul.

To gain clarity, start by reflecting on the beginning of your relationship. Consider the circumstances and past experiences that influenced your decision to engage. Evaluate whether marriage has been a goal in this relationship, and, if so, what shifted its course. Examine the relationship dynamics—are there patterns of anxiety, secrecy, or cycles of breaking and restarting? Finally, reflect on the narrative you hold about the relationship and whether it is rooted in fear or heart-centered intentions.

Relationships stuck in limbo often reveal areas of the heart that need healing or realignment. Through soulful reflection, you can gain clarity and make decisions that align with your spiritual goals, whether that leads to marriage or a compassionate parting of ways.

Soulful Premarital Sexual Health Conversations

The journey to marriage involves more than just discussions on boundaries and abstinence. It requires thoughtful conversations on sexual health, past experiences, and spiritual readiness. These discussions should be approached with sincerity, compassion, and alignment with Islamic values to foster mutual understanding and respect. The timing and depth of these conversations will vary depending on trust, cultural norms, emotional readiness, and spiritual alignment in the relationship.

For example: *"As we think about moving forward together, it's important to me that we're aligned on our values regarding intimacy, and that we communicate openly about any concerns or expectations we might have."*

Key topics include **pornography use, past relationships, sexual health education, and marital intimacy**. When discussing **pornography**, approach the topic with openness and nonjudgmental dialogue, focusing on mutual understanding and shared goals for spiritual alignment.

For example: *"I believe managing sexual desire in a healthy, soul-centered way is essential for our spiritual connection. If pornography has been part of your past, let's talk about how we can support each other in this area."*

Similarly, conversations about **past relationships** should be respectful and focused on personal growth, with attention to STI testing for mutual health and safety.

For example: *"Our pasts are personal, but I believe it's important to talk about how we can ensure our health and well-being before marriage, including considering STI testing."*

Understanding each other's **sexual health education** and comfort levels is essential for a soulful connection, and premarital counseling offers an opportunity to align values and enhance communication.

For example: *"I've been learning about the benefits of premarital education and counseling. I think it could be a wonderful opportunity for us to deepen our understanding and strengthen our marriage."*

Finally, **preparing for marital intimacy** requires open communication about hopes, concerns, and expectations, reinforcing the idea that intimacy is a shared experience that grows over time.

For example: *"Marital intimacy is a journey we'll explore together, and I want us to approach it with openness and compassion. Let's talk about what we can do to make each other feel safe, respected, and connected as we embark on this part of our lives."*

These soulful conversations lay the groundwork for a healthy, spiritually aligned marriage. By addressing these topics with care and mutual respect, couples can build a relationship based on trust, understanding, and a commitment to growth and well-being.

Reflections

_____
_____
_____
_____
_____

Premarital Focus: Sexual and Reproductive Health

Preparing for marriage involves a holistic approach—spiritually, emotionally, and physically. A key part of this is understanding your sexual and reproductive health, ensuring you're informed and ready for open discussions with your future spouse.

First, **understanding birth control and contraception** from an Islamic perspective is vital. This includes exploring options that align with your values, discussing methods with healthcare professionals, and considering how your future spouse views these decisions. Gaining this knowledge allows for open, heartfelt conversations before and during marriage. Next, **enhance your foundation in sexual health** by deepening your understanding of anatomy, physiology, sexual development, and intimacy, which will help you approach intimacy with confidence and clarity. Finally, **prioritize physical health by establishing a relationship** with a primary care doctor or OB/GYN and exploring fertility testing if needed. This preparation empowers you to engage in meaningful, soul-centered conversations about your future together.

Summary

The journey of searching for a spouse, as explored in this chapter, is deeply tied to the spiritual and soul-based framework that underpins this book. We began by recognizing the gaps in common Muslim narratives surrounding the search for a spouse—specifically, the lack of integration of spiritual and sexual health perspectives. By reframing these understandings with a focus on soul-based marriages, we shifted from surface-level approaches to deeper, heart-centered intentions. Moving beyond checklists and external qualities, we explored how aligning our search for a spouse with our soul's journey fosters relationships rooted in sincerity, compassion, and a connection to Allah.

This chapter also addressed the challenges of modern dating, both online and in-person, with a focus on managing sexualized behaviors and maintaining empowered abstinence. Practical tools and strategies were provided to help you navigate these dynamics while upholding your values and boundaries. Throughout this exploration, the emphasis has been on compassionate self-accountability and alignment with your spiritual development as a Muslim.

As we move forward in this book, the next chapter will delve into sexual intimacy in marriage, building upon the foundations laid here. May the insights, reflections, and skills from this chapter empower you in your journey, guiding you closer to your heart-centered intentions and soul-based growth.

Reflections and Action Items

_____
_____
_____
_____
_____
_____
_____
_____

Reference List

Sahih International. (1997). *The Quran: Arabic text with corresponding English meanings*. Abul-Qasim Publishing House.

Sunnah.com. (n.d.). Sahih al-Bukhari 1. Retrieved January 5, 2025, from https://sunnah.com/bukhari:1

Sunnah.com. (n.d.). Sahih al-Bukhari 5090. Retrieved January 5, 2025, from https://sunnah.com/bukhari:5090

Sunnah.com. (n.d.). Jami' at-Tirmidhi 1084. Retrieved January 5, 2025, from https://sunnah.com/tirmidhi:1084

6 Soulful Sexual Intimacy in Marriage

If there's one word that Muslims are afraid to say, it's the word "sex." I've lost count of the number of times the word "it" has been used as a substitute for "sex"—or the number of times that marital sexual intimacy is mistakenly reduced to sexual intercourse. Of course, as a Muslim myself, I completely understand why—and I hope that by the end of this chapter you have more compassion about why for yourself as well! Sex, sexual intimacy, sexual intercourse, and sexual pleasure are nothing to be ashamed of as Muslims—especially since God created all of these for us to enjoy as part of our spiritual development. As you read through this chapter—which may be the first time you're learning about sexual intimacy from these perspectives—continue to give yourself compassion. And remember that much like your soul, marital sexual intimacy is a journey for most couples, and it will be a different journey for everyone.

The Journey of the Soul

Birth · Spiritual Accountability · Spiritual Maturity · Spiritual Legacy · The Hereafter

Introduction

Here we are—perhaps the most anticipated chapter in this book, and for some, the most anticipated stage of life. Marital sexual intimacy is a profound and sacred aspect of marriage, yet it is often surrounded by myths, misunderstandings, and fears. As discussed in previous chapters, many Muslims have learned—and may now need to unlearn—what they've internalized about sexual intimacy. Unfortunately, soulful sexual health

DOI: 10.4324/9781032675862-7

education for Muslims is minimal, and much of what is learned is often inaccurate or lacks the essential spiritual contexts that Islam so beautifully provides. This gap leaves many Muslims entering marriage without the empowerment, spiritual grounding, or confidence they need to approach this aspect of their relationship with clarity and peace. Unrealistic expectations, lack of communication about desires, and anxiety rooted in misinformation or cultural taboos are common struggles. My hope is that this chapter begins to change that narrative.

Marital intimacy is a gift from Allah—a means of deepening love, fostering mercy, and fulfilling desires within a framework that nurtures the soul. As Allah beautifully reminds us: "And among His signs is that He created for you from yourselves mates that you may find tranquility in them; and He placed between you affection and mercy. Indeed, in that are signs for a people who give thought" (Quran 30:21).

This chapter redefines sexual intimacy in marriage as a collaborative journey that prioritizes process over outcomes. It's about discovering one another in deeper, more intimate ways, fostering curiosity, and building a connection grounded in Islamic frameworks of the soul. Sexual intimacy is not merely a physical act but a soulful experience that can draw you closer to each other and to Allah. The Quran emphasizes this reciprocity and mutual care, stating: "They are garments for you, and you are garments for them" (Quran 2:187).

We will explore spiritual perspectives on sexual intimacy as the foundation for discussing knowledge and skills essential for soulful marital intimacy. These include Islamic teachings, understanding sexual response, and practical approaches to gain more comfort and confidence with marital intimacy.

By the end of this chapter, my hope is that you'll feel more grounded and confident, regardless of your stage of life. For those seeking more specific guidance on the "how-to" aspects of marital intimacy, please view the additional readings and resources at the end of the book. Reflection questions at the end of this section will help you identify and compassionately unlearn any misconceptions you may hold. This journey of learning, unlearning, and deepening your understanding is a process—and a soulful one at that.

Myth Busting: Marital Sexual Intimacy

Myth: For women, sexual intercourse for the first time will be painful and bleeding is a sign of your virginity.

Fact: Sexual intercourse for the first time can be uncomfortable, neutral, and/or painful, and not every woman will bleed during intercourse for the first time. As you recall from chapter 3, the hymen is a thin piece of membrane that stretches during normal, everyday activities. Bleeding after intercourse is not a sign of virginity. We will explore nuanced reasons why pain during intercourse occurs in chapter 10.

Myth: Sexual intimacy in marriage needs to be spontaneous.

Fact: As you will learn in this chapter, there are different types of sexual desire, and this will change throughout the course of your marriage. So, while sexual intimacy at times may be spontaneous—especially during the early phase of marriage—it doesn't have to be.

Myth: Having less or different sexual desire than your spouse is an issue.

Fact: It is quite common for your spouse to differ in sexual desire—and there will be times when the reverse will also be true! There really is no such thing as "compatible" sexual desire or preferences either—sexual pleasure in marriage takes time to develop, and any such notion that spouses need to be compatible with their desire and preferences is a myth. This chapter will explore this in detail.

Reflection Questions

When you see the word "soul" next to "sexual intimacy," what comes to mind?

_____
_____
_____

Have you heard of any of these myths? Are there others that you're curious about?

_____
_____
_____

What aspects of your knowledge about sexual intimacy would you like to improve?

_____
_____
_____

> **Important Definitions**
>
> **Sexuality:** Sexuality encompasses a broad range of experiences, including feelings, thoughts, and behaviors related to sexual desire and intimacy. It integrates physical, emotional, and spiritual dimensions, reflecting how individuals understand and express their sexual selves in alignment with soulful values, as well as their connection to Allah in an Islamic context.
>
> **Sexual Intimacy:** Sexual intimacy refers to all forms of sexual and physical connection shared between spouses to foster emotional closeness and physical affection. This includes touching, kissing, cuddling, and other expressions of care that create connection and vulnerability. It is highly individualized and varies based on comfort, preferences, and shared values. Notably, sexual intimacy may or may not include sexual intercourse, recognizing the holistic and multifaceted nature of marital connection as supported by Islamic teachings on mutual care and affection (al-Kawthari, 2008).
>
> **Sexual Intercourse/Sex:** In Islamic contexts, sexual intercourse typically refers to the act of the penis entering the vaginal canal. However, the term "sex" is often used more broadly to include various sexual activities, such as oral sex (genital stimulation with the mouth). Clarifying the intended meaning of "sex" is essential, as it can range from specific acts to a broader understanding of sexual connection. This nuanced understanding promotes effective communication and ensures alignment with Islamic ethical principles (Hathout, 2006).

What's the Soul Got to Do with "It"? (Hint: Everything!)

As I mentioned in the introductory narrative, the word "it" is often used to represent sexual intercourse or sexual intimacy. In this book, we use proper terms for sexual intimacy, grounding the discussion in soul-based frameworks rooted in Islamic tradition. While marital sexual intimacy is often understood from emotional and physical perspectives, its spiritual dimension is less frequently explored. Conversations tend to focus on religious rulings—what is permissible or required post-intimacy—rather than the spiritual connection it fosters (Hathout, 2006).

Marriage, according to Islam, is a sacred union of two souls journeying toward Allah. The Quran highlights this sanctity through verses that emphasize love, closeness, and mutual protection. Such metaphors illustrate the profound intimacy and support spouses provide one another. Even the term *nikah*, traditionally referring to sexual intercourse, underscores the intrinsic connection between this sacred commitment and sexual intimacy (al-Kawthari, 2008). Sexual intimacy, therefore, is not just physical—it is a spiritual act, uniting two souls under Allah's witness. This connection may reflect a deeper bond, as Islamic perspectives suggest that souls destined to marry might have met before this worldly life.

Islamic teachings elevate marital intimacy as a sacred act of worship, symbolizing the pleasures of the Afterlife. Practices such as reciting prayers or duas (personal supplication) before intimacy integrates this physical union with spiritual devotion. Marital intimacy is, at its core, a sacred act imbued with Divine blessings, reflecting the beauty, compassion, and purpose Allah has designed for spouses. To make this more tangible, review Figure 6.1 to visualize this understanding of soulful marital sexual intimacy. With this holistic view of soulful sexual intimacy, before you transition into reflecting on this section's content the next box clarifies a few Islamic guidelines on the topic.

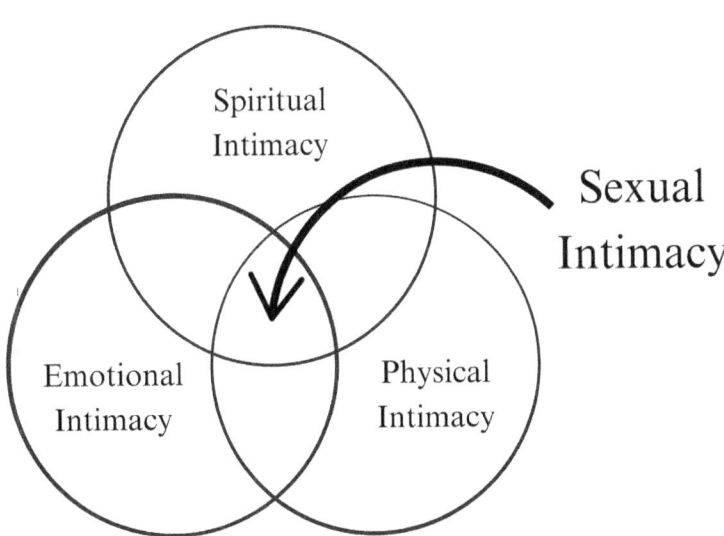

Figure 6.1 A soulful Islamic model of marital sexual intimacy

Clarifying Islamic Guidelines

Islamic guidance on marital sexual intimacy provides flexibility for couples while emphasizing mutual consent, comfort, and adherence to certain boundaries.

Sexual Intercourse: Defined as vaginal penetration, sexual intercourse allows flexibility in positions for mutual pleasure, but anal sex is prohibited. Intercourse is not permitted during menstruation or fasting in Ramadan, although other forms of intimacy are allowed.

Oral Sex: This is left to the couple's discretion, based on comfort and pleasure. Scholars differ on swallowing semen, but hygiene and comfort can be prioritized, with options like dental dams available.

Vibrators: Vibrators can enhance mutual pleasure and support sexual intimacy within marriage, especially if challenges in achieving orgasm arise. They are considered permissible when used with the intention of deepening marital connection.

The Wedding Night: Sexual intimacy on the wedding night is not obligatory. Couples should communicate expectations and comfort levels before marriage, fostering mutual understanding and adaptability.

Discussing Intimacy with Others: While marital intimacy is private, seeking professional support for challenges aligns with Islamic ethics, ensuring intimacy remains a sacred act of worship. Sharing details unnecessarily, however, contradicts the values of marital privacy and the sacredness of sexual intimacy in marriage.

Reflection Questions

Make a few notes about what comes to mind when you read the terms "emotional," "physical," and "spiritual intimacy." How do you feel about these reflections?

_____
_____
_____

When you reflect on the spiritual and sacred nature of marital sexual intimacy, what thoughts and feelings come to mind?

_____
_____
_____

> **Supplications for Couples: Before Sexual Intimacy**
>
> Given the spiritual and sacred nature of marital sexual intimacy, there are personal supplications (*duas*) that Muslim spouses are encouraged to recite before engaging in sexual intimacy to seek blessings, protection, and fulfillment. While there are no specific references in the Quran or hadith detailing prayers to be recited before sexual intimacy, the general practice of beginning any activity with the name of Allah (*Bismillah*) and seeking His protection and blessings is strongly encouraged:
>
> **Transliteration:** "Bismillah, Allahumma jannibna ash-shaytana wa jannib ash-shaytana ma razaqtana"
>
> **Translation:** "In the name of Allah, O Allah, keep Satan away from us and keep Satan away from what You have provided for us"
>
> Some couples may choose to recite certain other Quranic verses or chapters, such as those from Surah An-Nur (Chapter 24) or Ayat al-Kursi (The Verse of the Throne, Quran 2:255), seeking blessings and protection before intimacy.

Foreplay: A Crucial, Soulful Ingredient for Marital Sexual Intimacy

Having reflected on the model of soulful sexual intimacy shared above, we now delve into an essential, spiritual ingredient for marital intimacy: foreplay. As highlighted in Islamic tradition, numerous teachings emphasize the importance of foreplay in fostering meaningful and pleasurable intimacy. These teachings provide practical guidance, encouraging Muslims to approach foreplay with excellence and heart-centered intentions, aligning it with their spiritual and holistic development.

In *Islamic Guide to Sexual Relations*, al-Kawthari (2008) dedicates a chapter to foreplay, emphasizing its essential role in cultivating emotional connection and mutual satisfaction in marital intimacy. He draws from classical Islamic sources and explains how foreplay is both an act of care and a religiously encouraged practice. For instance, he cites narrations from the Prophet Muhammad (Peace and Blessings be Upon Him) that encourage tenderness, such as, "Let there be a messenger between you," referring to kisses and affectionate words. This highlights the necessity of building emotional and physical closeness before engaging in intimacy, underscoring foreplay as an act of love, care, and consideration.

Foreplay includes passionate kissing, caressing, stroking each other's genitals, and tender words—practices that create a foundation of trust, connection, and mutual pleasure. These acts are not only deeply intimate but also align with the Prophetic example of ensuring that marital intimacy is approached with kindness and attentiveness to one's spouse's needs.

Al-Kawthari also discusses how foreplay is not simply a physical act but a way to fulfill one's spouse's rights, reflecting the Quranic ideal of reciprocity in marriage. He further highlights how fulfilling these rights with care and mutual pleasure nurtures the marital bond and helps spouses grow in love, mercy, and understanding—qualities the Quran identifies as foundational to marriage: "And among His signs is that He created for you from yourselves mates that you may find tranquility in them; and He placed between you affection and mercy" (Quran 30:21).

In addition to these traditional teachings, al-Kawthari acknowledges that contemporary approaches can enhance intimacy in ways that align with Islamic values. He explains how tools such as lubricants, sex toys, and external vibrators can help ensure that both spouses experience pleasure and/or orgasm. Such tools, when used with mutual understanding and consent, align with Islam's emphasis on fostering mutual satisfaction and emotional closeness in intimacy.

This emphasis on foreplay reflects the compassionate and balanced teachings of Islam, which guide spouses to approach marital intimacy with thoughtfulness and mutual care. Foreplay is not merely a physical act but a soulful expression of love and connection, transforming intimacy into an experience that strengthens the marital bond and nurtures both the body and the soul.

With this soulful context in mind, let's explore a few key components of foreplay from Islamic perspectives.

Key Components of Foreplay in Islam

Mutual Sexual Pleasure: Islamic teachings emphasize the importance of mutual satisfaction in intimacy, underscoring that marital intimacy is not a one-sided experience but a collaborative and fulfilling act for both spouses. *Hadiths* encourage spouses to approach one another with tenderness, using kisses, kind words, caresses, and attentive foreplay to ensure both partners feel emotionally and physically ready for intimacy. This approach fosters curiosity, playfulness, and a deeper understanding of each other's needs and desires, creating an environment where intimacy becomes a shared journey rather than a mere outcome. The Prophet Muhammad (Peace and Blessings be Upon Him) exemplified this in his own relationships, highlighting the need for care and attentiveness as part of the marital bond.

Respect and Consent: Respect and consent are foundational to marital relations, forming the bedrock of ethical and loving intimacy in Islam. Coercion or forced intimacy contradicts Islamic ethics and the *sunnah* (Prophetic tradition) of marriage. The Quran emphasizes kindness, consideration, and mutual agreement, stating, "And live with them in kindness" (Quran 4:19). Spouses are encouraged to communicate openly about their needs, desires, and boundaries, ensuring that intimacy remains a source of love, connection, and mutual trust. This communication deepens the marital bond and allows couples to navigate intimacy with empathy and care.

The 4Cs of Soulful Marital Intimacy: Later in this chapter, we will explore the 4Cs—*compassion, communication, curiosity, and consent*—as essential components for building a soulful foundation for marital intimacy. These principles provide a practical framework for fostering a relationship that is grounded in mutual respect, emotional connection, and spiritual growth. By aligning the physical aspects of intimacy with these soulful principles, couples can deepen their bond and navigate their marital journey with purpose and intentionality.

With these principles of foreplay in mind, it is equally vital to address what marital sexual intimacy cannot involve or tolerate. Let's transition into examining unhealthy and abusive dynamics in the context of marriage, ensuring that marital intimacy aligns with the ethical and compassionate teachings of Islam.

When Marital Sexual Intimacy Is Unhealthy or Abusive

While this chapter emphasizes mutual pleasure, respect, and consent as integral to soulful marital intimacy, unhealthy and abusive dynamics can and do occur in some Muslim marriages. Studies indicate domestic violence rates in Muslim marriages align with U.S. national averages, with 15–20% of Muslim women experiencing domestic violence (Alkhateeb & Abugideiri, 2007). Cultural stigma often prevents survivors from seeking help, perpetuating cycles of harm (Afrouz et al., 2018).

Unhealthy Dynamics: Unhealthy dynamics disrupt the spiritual integrity of marital intimacy, such as when:

- Pain during intercourse leads one spouse to avoid intimacy without seeking help.
- One spouse secretly uses pornography, diminishing desire for their partner.
- Sexual intimacy is intentionally withheld without valid reasons or communication.

These patterns undermine the mutually equitable and pleasurable nature of marital intimacy, impacting the spiritual well-being of both spouses.

Abusive Dynamics: Abuse involves significant harm to a spouse's spiritual, physical, emotional, or sexual health. Examples include:

- Forced sexual intimacy or coercion using religious scripture.
- Emotional manipulation or shaming a spouse for withholding intimacy despite valid reasons.
- Financial control tied to sexual demands.

In abusive marriages, safety and well-being must take precedence. Islam prioritizes the preservation of life and health, and leaving the marriage may be necessary to protect one's spiritual and physical well-being.

Before transitioning into practical skills for soulful intimacy, review the box below addressing a commonly misused hadith in Muslim marriages.

The Angels Cursing Hadith: A Contextual Perspective

The *hadith* "If a husband calls his wife to his bed and she refuses and causes him to sleep in anger, the angels will curse her till morning" (Sahih al-Bukhari, Book 59, Hadith 48) is often misunderstood and misused within marriages, sometimes leading to coercion. Proper context reveals that Islamic teachings on marriage emphasize mutual respect, compassion, and collaboration. As al-Hibri and Ghazal (2018) highlight, marriage is a sacred bond rooted in ethical and spiritual values, where intimacy must reflect kindness and understanding.

Sexual intimacy, a form of worship (*ibadah*), cannot contradict these foundational principles. While sexual desire may be strong, self-restraint and spiritual guidance remind spouses to approach intimacy with mutual care. Challenges in this area often stem from deeper marital issues, requiring collaborative and compassionate resolution. Valid reasons for declining intimacy can include emotional stress, physical pain, or situational factors like fatigue or lack of privacy, all of which necessitate open communication to foster understanding and flexibility.

Fulfilling sexual "rights" is inseparable from meeting the God-given sacred responsibilities of kindness, mercy, and ethical conduct within marriage. For those weaponizing intimacy, self-reflection and compassionate self-accountability are crucial. Seeking professional support can help restore balance and uphold the interconnected values of theology, spirituality, and ethics.

Practical Skills for Soulful Sexual Intimacy

Having laid the foundations of soulful marital intimacy, this section transitions into practical skills to enhance your sexual connection. A deeper understanding of sexual response fosters mutual awareness and celebrates the ways God has designed our bodies to experience desire, arousal, and pleasure as acts of love and connection within marriage.

Sexual response involves three interconnected components: sexual desire, arousal, and pleasure. These elements are presented as distinct, yet they are deeply intertwined, and some individuals may find it challenging to separate how they feel into these categories—which is completely natural and okay!

- **Sexual Desire:** Referred to in Islamic terms as *shahwah* (passion), sexual desire reflects the natural inclination or interest in intimacy with one's spouse. It encompasses spontaneous desire, which arises without external triggers; responsive desire, activated by external stimuli; and contextual desire, influenced by situational factors. Each type is shaped by

emotional, physical, and spiritual dimensions unique to each individual and couple.
- **Sexual Arousal:** Arousal represents the "turned-on" state, involving both physical and emotional responses. This may include bodily changes like erection or vaginal lubrication, heightened sensitivity in erogenous zones, and a deeper mental and emotional connection with one's spouse. Arousal intertwines with feelings of trust, emotional safety, and mutual affection, reflecting a holistic experience of intimacy.
- **Sexual Pleasure:** The culmination of desire and arousal, pleasure spans physical, emotional, mental, and spiritual dimensions. While orgasm is often considered the peak, soulful intimacy reframes pleasure as the journey of connection and affection, found in tender moments, shared laughter, or spiritual alignment.

These three components can occur in varying sequences—either desire or arousal may be experienced first, or they may emerge simultaneously. Sexual response is also dynamic, changing from day to day and evolving over the years. Gently reflecting on and inquiring into these shifts is crucial for staying attuned to these soulful changes, as the soul is sensitive to all that it experiences.

It's important to note that female sexual response tends to be more complex and often involves additional factors, such as emotional intimacy, relational security, and life contexts, which are summarized in subsequent sections. This nuanced understanding supports couples in navigating intimacy with compassion and awareness, fostering a deeper connection aligned with their shared spiritual journey.

The Dual Control Model of Sexual Desire

Contrary to common myths, sexual desire doesn't simply "turn on" like a light switch. Instead, it operates through the dual control model, which likens sexual response to a system of brakes and gas pedals. The "gas pedal" is known as the Sexual Excitation System, and the "brake pedal" is referred to as the Sexual Inhibition System (Nagoski, 2015).

Sexual Excitation System (SES), or gas pedal, is activated by positive factors like good physical health and balanced hormones; relational elements such as trust, intimacy, and emotional safety; a romantic and comfortable environment; positive self-perception and affirming beliefs; and spiritual connection, where intimacy is seen as an act of worship and aligned with shared values.

On the other hand, the **Sexual Inhibition System (SIS)**, or brake pedal, is influenced by a range of factors, including physical issues like pain, fatigue, or hormonal imbalances; relational and emotional challenges like conflict, stress, or unresolved trauma; environmental distractions such as lack of privacy or noise; cognitive and cultural barriers like internalized shame or negative self-talk; and spiritual disconnection, such as feeling distant from Allah or guilt about sexual expression.

For many individuals—especially women—the brakes tend to be more sensitive than the gas pedal, reflecting natural protective mechanisms. For instance, unresolved emotional tension or a lack of privacy, such as staying in a guest bedroom at a parent's or in-law's home, can strongly inhibit sexual response, even when mutual desire exists. Additionally, many individuals struggle to remain present with their spouse and in their body during sexual intimacy, finding themselves pulled into intrusive thoughts. This mental distraction often diminishes arousal and pleasure. Addressing these brakes—whether by resolving conflicts, quieting inner thoughts, or creating a calm and safe environment—often yields a greater impact on intimacy than solely attempting to press the gas pedal. After all, a car cannot move forward when the brake pedal is engaged, no matter how hard the gas pedal is pressed—the same holds true for sexual desire.

When couples I work with learn about this dual control model, it often becomes a transformative tool for addressing challenges with marital sexual intimacy. Instead of framing their struggles as "something is wrong with me" or "something is wrong with my spouse," they shift their perspective to asking, "How are my gas and brake pedals doing?" This reframing fosters a sense of self-compassion and mutual understanding, enabling couples to explore and address intimacy challenges with curiosity and teamwork, rather than shame or frustration.

The Three Types of Desire

Within the framework of the dual control model, desire can be categorized into three distinct types: spontaneous, responsive, and contextual.

Spontaneous Desire: This form of desire arises without external triggers, often experienced as an intrinsic urge for intimacy. For example, a newlywed couple might frequently feel spontaneous desire during the early stages of their marriage. It is more common in men, accounting for about 75% of male experiences, compared to 15% of women (Nagoski, 2015).

Responsive Desire: Responsive desire emerges as a reaction to external stimuli, such as physical affection or emotional closeness. For instance, a wife may feel drawn to intimacy after her spouse initiates a heartfelt conversation or plans a romantic dinner. This type is prevalent in about 30% of women and 5% of men (Nagoski, 2015).

Contextual Desire: Contextual desire depends on situational factors, including emotional connection, physical environment, or life stressors. For example, a husband might feel more attuned to intimacy after resolving a disagreement or during a relaxed vacation. This type of desire is reported by about 50% of women and 20% of men, emphasizing its reliance on circumstances (Nagoski, 2015).

Understanding these types of desire validates the diversity of sexual experiences and highlights the importance of nurturing environments that foster connection. For a personalized reflection on these dynamics, refer to Table 6.1.

Table 6.1 A summary of spontaneous, responsive, and contextual sexual desires

Type of Desire	Description
Spontaneous	Arises naturally without external triggers, often felt as an intrinsic urge. Example: feeling desire simply by thinking of your partner. Common in early stages of marriage. Accounts for ~75% of men and 15% of women (Nagoski, 2015).
Responsive	Is activated by external stimuli or interaction, such as touch, words, or shared activities. Example: feeling desire after engaging in a romantic activity with your spouse. More common in ~30% of women and 5% of men (Nagoski, 2015).
Contextual	Dependent on situational factors like emotional connection, mood, or environment. Example: feeling desire after resolving a disagreement or in a stress-free setting. Prevalent in ~50% of women and 20% of men (Nagoski, 2015).

A Note on Female Sexual Response

Female sexual response is often more complex than the simplistic models typically applied to male sexual experiences, requiring a nuanced understanding of the factors that influence desire, arousal, and satisfaction. Unlike spontaneous responses, many women experience sexual motivation as a blend of physical and non-sexual reasons, such as emotional intimacy or stress relief. This layered experience highlights the importance of considering emotional and contextual factors, including spousal dynamics and environmental stressors, which significantly impact sexual receptivity and arousability.

The interplay of these factors underscores that female sexual response cannot be understood in isolation but must be viewed as a holistic process. **Arousal** often depends on a combination of physical changes, such as lubrication and sensitivity, and **emotional readiness** shaped by mood and connection. **Satisfaction**, a critical component, influences **motivation** for future encounters, emphasizing the **cyclical nature of sexual response**. Addressing these complexities allows for a more compassionate and effective approach to understanding and supporting women's sexual health and well-being, enhancing intimacy in a way that respects the multifaceted nature of female sexual experiences.

With this in mind, let's apply this information to ourselves. Remember that we're each on a journey, so approach these reflections with compassion. If needed, skip a question and revisit it when you're ready.

Reflection Questions

What new insights have you gained about your sexual response and desire?

_____
_____
_____

Are you generally aware of what hits your sexual gas pedal, and what activates your sexual brake pedal? If you are married, are you aware of this about your spouse?

_____
_____
_____

If your brake pedal feels like it's being activated more than your gas pedal, what can you start to address so that it's no longer hitting your brakes? These factors can be internal or external to you.

_____

_____

_____

"My Spouse Doesn't Want to be Intimate as Much as I Do"

Differences in sexual desire are a common concern among Muslim married couples seeking therapy—and it's important to know that these differences are normal and can be navigated with understanding and care. Often, one spouse—typically the husband, though not always—expresses worry that their partner seems less interested in intimacy, leading to feelings of insecurity about physical or sexual connection. However, these concerns frequently stem from a misunderstanding of the natural variations in sexual desire, as well as the influence of stressors, self-confidence, and emotional readiness.

Rather than reflecting a problem in marriage, these differences often highlight the importance of understanding the three types of sexual desire—spontaneous, responsive, and contextual—and the interplay of brakes and gas pedals in sexual response. Many couples labeled as "mismatched" may simply lack awareness of their own and their spouse's sexual desire type or the factors influencing them. Couples are encouraged to reflect on these dynamics individually and then use the next section to communicate and collaboratively plan their sexual intimacy.

Soulful Marital Sexual Intimacy in Action: The 4Cs

With a deeper understanding of sexual response and its nuances, we now transition to the practical implementation of the information shared in this chapter. Soulful marital sexual intimacy requires intentional effort and alignment with key principles that nurture a fulfilling and spiritually

Soulful Sexual Intimacy in Marriage   139

grounded relationship. These principles, known as the 4Cs, are foundational to maintaining intimacy and overcoming challenges that may arise.

Open, honest, and empathetic **communication** is essential for building a safe space to discuss needs, desires, and challenges in marital intimacy. If discussing intimacy feels difficult, it signals the need to address individual and relational barriers to meaningful dialogue. When communication flows naturally, **consent**—rooted in mutual respect and pleasure—becomes an organic part of intimacy, ensuring it reflects love and sacred connection rather than force or coercion.

With communication and consent as a foundation, **collaboration** allows spouses to actively work together to enhance sexual intimacy, fostering deeper connection and transforming intimacy into an act of worship (*ibadah*). **Compromise** is equally vital, especially when differences in desire arise. Through mutual understanding and effort, couples can find ways to honor each other's needs, maintaining balance and harmony.

These 4Cs—Communication, Consent, Collaboration, and Compromise—form the bedrock of soulful marital intimacy. Explore Figure 6.2 for a visual overview before delving deeper into how to practice and nurture these principles in your relationship.

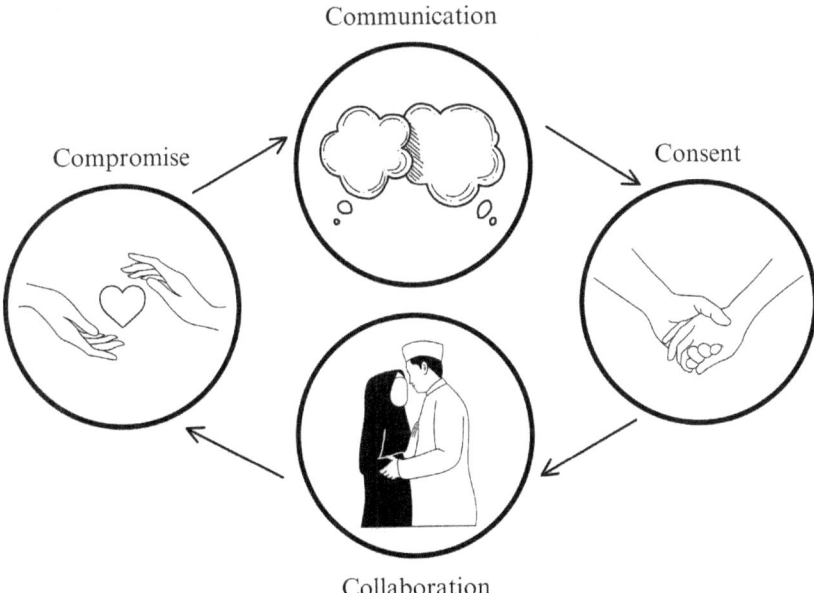

Figure 6.2 A visual representation of the cyclical nature of the 4Cs

Communication: Heart-Centered Conversations about Sexual Intimacy

Since we've just explored sexual response in detail, and you have a foundational understanding of sexual desire, we're going to transition into how to hold conversations about sexual intimacy—both before and after marriage. And yes, it is Islamically permissible to talk about sexual health and intimacy before marriage. As long as it's heart-centered.

What does heart-centered mean? If you recall from chapter 5, we explored the concept of heart-centered intentions during the search for a spouse. These intentions are ideally from the depths of our soul, originating from the heart where God's presence resides. This contrasts with lower-self intentions, which tend to be self-gratifying and take us away from our spiritual development. Let's explore this distinction in greater detail, using Table 6.2.

Table 6.2 A summary of the definitions, soulful impacts, and self-reflection prompts for lower-soul sexualized versus heart-centered behaviors

	Lower-Soul, Sexualized Behavior	Heart-Centered Behavior
Definition	Sexualized behavior comes from the lower soul (nafs al-ammarah) and is self-gratifying. It is driven by unbalanced and mismanaged sexual desire (shahwah).	Heart-centered conversations about sexual health in marriage align us with our spiritual development. They are held with God in our hearts and minds.
Impacts on Our Soul	Talking sexually to someone takes us away from our spiritual development; gives in to the lower-soul and is self-gratifying; and goes against Islamic ethics of treating everyone we encounter as a sacred person, not as a physical or sexual being. Examples of sexualized behavior include sending sexually explicit messages or pictures; or initiating sexually explicit conversations.	Heart-centered conversations about sexual health before marriage have beneficial purposes and are in line with our spiritual development. These conversations are held with God's presence in mind, for the sake of a future and/or present marriage. For example, holding conversations about setting boundaries with empowered abstinence; being open about learning from past sexual activity; and preparing for marital sexual intimacy.

(*Continued*)

Table 6.2 (Continued)

	Lower-Soul, Sexualized Behavior	Heart-Centered Behavior
Self-Reflection	What is my awareness about why I'm showing up this way? Do I continue to blame others for my behaviors? What narrative do I tell myself to justify these behaviors? For example, that I "can't control myself"? Why am I not expecting more of myself and how I show up? What inner wounds could be leading to these behaviors?	As I approach engagement and marriage, which conversations about sexual health are important to hold? What are my intentions? What concerns do I have about sexual intimacy in marriage? What is my understanding of spirituality and sexual intimacy in Muslim marriages?

Now that we've explored the significance of heart-centered conversations, let's dive into how to hold them and which topics to address. These conversations unfold in two key phases: before marriage, to establish shared values and boundaries, and after marriage, to nurture intimacy and mutual understanding.

Before Marriage

Sharing Your Values and Boundaries

As we explored in the previous chapter, discussing your values and boundaries about physical and sexual intimacy is a crucial step before marriage. While relationships may begin online, they will eventually transition to real-life interactions, regardless of whether they are long-distance or not.

When to hold this conversation: Ideally, this conversation should occur when you are committed to getting to know someone for the sake of marriage. This might happen early in the process or a few weeks later, as exclusivity develops.

How to hold this conversation: Plan this discussion intentionally, giving the other person advance notice so they can prepare. For example:

"Since we've decided to get to know each other exclusively, I'd like to set aside time to talk about physical and sexual boundaries. Are you free to chat about this soon?"

When discussing specific topics, use "I" statements to center your feelings and needs:

> "I feel strongly about maintaining physical boundaries before marriage and would like to share my perspective. I'd also like to hear your thoughts."

Reflections

Consider writing your thoughts here. What emotions come up for you when preparing for this conversation? What would make you feel more confident about approaching it?

_____

_____

_____

Conversations about Current or Past Sexual Activity

This topic often causes stress and confusion within Muslim relationships. The extremes of disclosing everything or hiding entirely can be overwhelming. Islam encourages a balance: protecting oneself and aligning values with your partner, without delving into unnecessary details that are meant to remain between each of us and Allah. For instance, details of past relationships are less important than ensuring there are no risks of transmitting STIs in marriage.

When to hold this conversation: The timing depends on the specific topic. For example:

- Discussing pornography use (past or current) may be helpful early in the relationship, alongside values and boundaries.
- Conversations about past sexual activity might be more appropriate closer to engagement, ensuring clarity before committing fully.

How to hold this conversation: Given the sensitivity of these topics, schedule the discussion to allow time for reflection. Practicing your words in advance or writing them down can help you feel more prepared.

Conversation starter:

"This is difficult to share, but I feel it's important because we're moving toward marriage. I've had previous sexual activity and have taken steps to *forgive myself and ensure I'm healthy. I plan to undergo STI testing before marriage to confirm this."*

Reflections

_____
_____
_____
_____

Preparing for Marital Sexual Intimacy

This topic is one many Muslims recognize as important to address before marriage, yet they're often unsure how to approach it or what to discuss. The purpose of these conversations is *not* to delve into the specifics of what will happen in bed after marriage. Instead, the focus should be on sharing your questions, perspectives, needs, and concerns about marital sexual intimacy. Once married, these conversations will naturally become more detailed as you begin to explore and understand each other's needs and preferences in real time.

When to hold this conversation: Plan to have these conversations after your engagement and before the *nikah* (Islamic marriage ceremony). Prioritize creating space for these discussions to ensure you're both aligned and prepared for this significant aspect of married life.

How to hold this conversation: This phase of communication involves addressing a few key topics to ensure mutual understanding and alignment before marriage. Approaching these topics with care, empathy, and openness will help foster trust and set the tone for a healthy marital relationship.

Fears and Worries about Intimacy in Marriage: It's normal to have concerns or anxieties about marital intimacy, and sharing these with your partner can help ease some of those fears. Begin with "I" statements to express your feelings without placing blame or pressure.

Conversation starter:

"I feel a bit nervous about intimacy after marriage because it's such a new experience for me. Have you had any similar thoughts or worries?"

Past Trauma That May Impact Sexual Intimacy

If you or your partner have experienced trauma that could affect intimacy, it's important to share this gently and at a level of detail you're comfortable with. The focus should be on understanding and support, not on reliving the trauma.

Conversation starter:

"There's something important I'd like to share because it might affect our intimacy after marriage. I've experienced some challenges in the past that I'm working through, and I'd like your support as we navigate this together."

Birth Control and Contraception

Discussing birth control is an essential part of planning for marital intimacy, particularly if you have specific preferences or concerns. These conversations can help align expectations and ensure mutual comfort with family planning decisions.

Conversation starter:

"I think it's important to discuss birth control options before marriage. Have you thought about what might work best for us?"

The Wedding Night

While the wedding night is often portrayed with certain expectations (and misunderstood to have Islamic "milestones" such as consummating with sexual intercourse), it's important to approach it with realism and compassion. Discussing your hopes and preferences beforehand can alleviate pressure and ensure a more soulfully aligned experience.

Conversation starter:

"I think it's important for us to talk about the wedding night and take any pressure off. I'd prefer for us to focus on being comfortable and connecting emotionally first. How do you feel about this?"

Reflections

_____
_____
_____

After Marriage

Couples who struggle to *talk* about sexual intimacy often find it difficult to experience *pleasurable* sexual intimacy. The foundation of fulfilling intimacy in marriage is emotional communication—an area where many couples, especially men, face challenges. Sexual intimacy thrives when spouses are emotionally attuned to one another, creating a safe and loving space to explore physical connection as an extension of their emotional bond.

Soulful Contexts for Communication

Effective communication about sexual intimacy requires emotional connection, vulnerability, and an understanding of the sacred nature of marital intimacy. The following soulful contexts can guide and nurture these conversations:

1. Cultivate Gratitude: Sexual intimacy is a Divine blessing, fostering emotional, physical, and spiritual connection. Frame conversations with gratitude to keep the focus on love and appreciation:

"I'm so grateful for the closeness we share. I'd love to talk about how we can nurture that even more."

2. Create Sacred Spaces: Marital intimacy reflects the love and mercy Allah places between spouses. Establish physical and emotional spaces where both partners feel safe and valued.

"I want us to create a space where we can share openly about what makes us feel loved and cherished."

3. View Intimacy as Worship: Approach conversations about intimacy as an act of worship, rooted in mutual care and the intention to fulfill each other's needs.

"I want us to approach intimacy as a way to show love and compassion for one another, in line with what Allah has intended for marriage."

4. Suspend Problem-Solving, Analysis, and Defensiveness: Conversations about sexual intimacy require safety and validation. Avoid trying to "fix" or analyze what your spouse shares and focus on understanding their feelings.

"I feel like you're analyzing the situation without understanding how I feel. Which emotions do you think I might be experiencing from what I shared?"

5. Use Emotional Communication as the Foundation: Center conversations on feelings using "I" statements. This helps foster a non-confrontational environment:

"I feel disconnected when we don't spend time talking before bed."

"I've been wondering how we can explore intimacy in a way that feels more fulfilling for both of us."

6. Give Specific Feedback Related to Sexual Needs: Feedback is most effective when specific, actionable, and shared with love. Focus on what works well and how to enhance intimacy further.

"Do you remember when you did [specific action]? That really made me feel special."

"I know that for you, getting in the mood is easier than for me. Here's what can help me feel more ready: [specific suggestions]."

Approaches to Enhance Communication

To foster emotional intimacy and improve communication about sexual intimacy, couples can adopt the following practical approaches:

1. Set Aside Time for Daily Check-Ins: Establish a habit of spending a few minutes together at the end of each day to reconnect. This is not a time for problem-solving but for sharing feelings and reflections about your day.

"I felt really appreciated today when you . . ."

"I've been feeling a bit disconnected lately and want to spend more time together."

2. Schedule Weekly "Team Meetings": Dedicate time each week to discuss deeper topics, including your emotional and sexual needs, without interruptions. Approach these meetings as teammates working together rather than adversaries solving problems.

Begin with gratitude: *"I want to start by saying how much I appreciate the way you . . ."*

Address topics calmly: *"I'd like us to talk about how we're feeling about intimacy this week."*

Be intentional: *"Let's set aside some time to share feedback about how we're connecting emotionally and physically."*

Summary of Communication: Before and After Marriage

Effective communication is the cornerstone of soulful marital intimacy. Before marriage, it is essential to establish open and honest conversations about values, boundaries, and expectations for physical and sexual intimacy. These discussions create a foundation of trust and mutual understanding. After marriage, communication deepens to include emotional connection, specific feedback, and collaborative dialogue about intimacy. Setting aside time for regular check-ins and team meetings can help couples navigate challenges and foster a fulfilling intimate relationship.

Now that we've explored communication, let's move to the next essential component of soulful marital sexual intimacy: **consent**.

Reflections

_____
_____
_____
_____
_____
_____

Consent

In a marriage rooted in soulful connection, consent is far more than a technical agreement—it is the expression of love, respect, and care that allows intimacy to thrive. The Prophet Muhammad (Peace and Blessings be Upon Him) exemplified gentleness and mutual care in all aspects of his relationships, particularly within marriage. He emphasized kindness and attentiveness, teaching that intimacy should never involve coercion, harm, or disregard for a partner's comfort.

Defining Marital Rape

Marital rape, defined as any non-consensual sexual act performed by one spouse upon the other, is a grave violation of Islamic principles and the soul's dignity. It involves force, coercion, or manipulation to achieve intimacy, which directly contradicts the sunnah of marriage and the ethics of Islamic teachings. Marital rape disregards a partner's autonomy and emotional well-being, undermining the very essence of a loving and respectful marital bond.

The Quran and Prophetic traditions emphasize the importance of mutual kindness, compassion, and understanding in marriage. Any form of intimacy achieved through force, manipulation, or neglect of a partner's comfort and consent is impermissible and against Islamic guidelines. The use of force or manipulation in intimacy neglects the soulful context of consent and transforms what should be an act of love into an act of harm. This not only contradicts Islamic ethics but also damages the emotional and spiritual connection between spouses.

Creating a Soulful Environment for Consent

Consent flourishes when both spouses feel safe, respected, and valued. This requires open communication about feelings and needs, attentive listening to verbal and non-verbal cues, and practicing empathy and patience to ensure intimacy is never pressured but mutually embraced.

Examples of Soulful Consent in Action:

A spouse asks: *"I'd love to be close with you tonight. How do you feel about that?"*

When one partner is hesitant: *"I understand you're not ready right now, and that's okay. Let's spend time together in other ways."*

Expressing care: *"Your comfort and happiness matter to me. Please let me know what feels right for you."*

Let's next explore **collaboration**, where both spouses actively work together to deepen their connection and enhance intimacy as a shared spiritual journey.

Collaboration

Collaboration in marital intimacy involves both spouses actively contributing to a fulfilling and soulful connection. It is not about one partner leading and the other following, but rather about creating a shared journey of love, pleasure, and growth. Collaboration transforms intimacy into a shared act of worship (*ibadah*), where both partners are engaged in deepening their bond as part of their spiritual path.

Soulful Context: Intimacy in marriage is an opportunity for both spouses to work together, supporting each other's needs and desires while aligning with the Prophetic example of gentleness and reciprocity. Collaboration requires patience, adaptability, and a shared commitment to nurturing the relationship.

Examples:

- *"I've noticed we've both been busy lately. How about we plan a special evening to focus on reconnecting?"*
- *"What would make intimacy feel more meaningful for you this week?"*
- *"I realize that you're feeling stressed, and I'd like to help you relax first. What would feel good for you?"*
- *"When you shared [specific feedback], I appreciated it. I'd love to explore that more together."*

Collaboration is about both spouses actively contributing to their intimate connection, approaching intimacy with a soulful mindset. However, there will inevitably be times when desires or levels of interest differ. In these moments, the ability to practice **compromise** becomes essential, ensuring that both partners feel valued, and that balance and harmony are maintained in their marital bond.

Compromise

Compromise acknowledges that marital intimacy requires balancing the needs and desires of both spouses. There will be times when energy levels, emotional states, or physical health differ. Compromise involves meeting each other halfway, ensuring that both partners feel seen, heard, and cared for. It reflects the Quranic principle of living together with kindness (*ma'roof*).

Soulful Context: The spirit of compromise is rooted in the idea that marriage is a partnership of mutual support. When differences arise, couples are encouraged to communicate openly and seek solutions that respect both partners' needs. The Prophet Muhammad (Peace and Blessings be Upon Him) demonstrated this in his relationships, always prioritizing his wives' comfort and well-being.

Examples:

- *"I'm not feeling up for intimacy tonight, but I want to make time for you soon. Can we plan for another day this week?"*
- *"I noticed you enjoy [specific activity], and I'd like to try incorporating it into our time together. How do you feel about that?"*
- *"I'm not feeling particularly in the mood tonight, but I'd still like to be close to you and share this moment together."*

- *"Your pleasure and happiness mean a lot to me, and I'd like to be there for you even if I'm not feeling as connected to the physical aspect tonight."*

These moments of loving compromise can deepen emotional and physical connection, reinforcing the bond of care and mutual respect. They reflect the essence of partnership in marriage, where both spouses prioritize each other's well-being and strive to nurture intimacy as an act of love and mercy.

Bringing the 4Cs Together

By practicing communication, consent, collaboration, and compromise, you create a foundation for marital intimacy that is deeply rooted in love, mutual respect, and spirituality. These principles align your intimate connection with the soulful and spiritual dimensions of marriage, fostering a relationship that reflects the Prophetic example of compassion, gentleness, and care.

Before we transition to the final section of this chapter on gaining confidence with marital sexual intimacy, take a few moments to reflect on the 4Cs, and make note of any action items or feelings that arose as you reviewed this section.

Reflections

_____
_____
_____
_____

Gaining Confidence with Marital Sexual Intimacy

Building comfort with marital sexual intimacy is a gradual process that reflects Allah's compassion and wisdom, allowing couples to approach intimacy at their own pace. By grounding intimacy in God-consciousness (*taqwa*) and setting intentions through practices like *dhikr* (remembrance of God) or *dua* (personal supplication), couples can align their connection with the sacred nature of marriage. Scheduling time for intimacy fosters emotional and physical preparation, while remaining present during these moments deepens the bond between spouses. The next section explores soulful approaches to pleasure mapping and foreplay, essential practices for mutual understanding, care, and connection in marital intimacy.

Soulful Marital Intimacy: Navigating Diverse Needs with Compassion

Marital intimacy is a sacred bond, deeply rooted in mutual love, understanding, and connection. For spouses with varying needs—whether physical, neurological, or intellectual—nurturing this bond requires compassion, sensitivity, and a commitment to meeting each other where they are. Disabilities or health conditions may shape how intimacy is experienced, but they do not diminish its spiritual and emotional significance.

For couples navigating these challenges, seeking guidance from trained professionals can be transformative. Physical therapists (PTs) can offer strategies to address physical limitations, improve mobility, or alleviate pain that may impact intimacy. Occupational therapists (OTs) can help adapt intimate activities to accommodate individual needs, ensuring comfort and accessibility. Speech-language pathologists (SLPs) can assist in fostering open and meaningful communication between partners, particularly when neurological conditions affect expression or comprehension. Additionally, therapists or counselors trained in sexuality and sexual health can provide faith-sensitive support to address emotional and relational aspects of intimacy.

Compassionate communication between spouses is vital in understanding each other's needs, preferences, and boundaries. Adapting intimacy to align with each partner's abilities and comfort fosters a sense of safety and connection. Tools such as assistive devices, sensory accommodations, and individualized techniques can also enhance intimacy in ways that honor the unique dynamics of your relationship.

Remember, intimacy is not defined solely by physical acts but by the love, effort, and presence that spouses bring to their connection. With patience, creativity, and professional support, couples can cultivate a soulful, fulfilling intimacy that strengthens their bond and deepens their shared journey toward Allah.

Soulful Approaches to Pleasure Mapping and Foreplay

1. Use Gentle Communication: Pleasure mapping requires openness and vulnerability. Approach the process with kindness and curiosity, ensuring that both partners feel safe and valued. Use "I" statements to share your preferences and questions, and check in regularly:

"I'd like to learn more about what makes you feel connected during intimacy."
"Does this feel good for you?"
"What else would you like to try?"

2. Explore Through Touch and the Five Senses: Use varied touches—such as soft strokes or gentle pressure—and incorporate tools like warm oils or feathers for variety. Engage all five senses to enhance the experience:

- **Sight:** Dim lights or use candles for a soothing environment.
- **Sound:** Play calming or sensual music.
- **Smell:** Introduce scents like lavender or sandalwood.
- **Taste:** Experiment with flavored oils or foods.
- **Touch:** Explore textures, temperatures, and sensations that evoke comfort and pleasure.

3. Focus on Non-Sexual Intimacy: Pleasure mapping and foreplay do not always need to lead to sexual activity. Non-sexual intimacy, such as holding or caressing, builds trust and emotional connection, forming a foundation for deeper physical closeness.

4. Embrace Foreplay as a Journey: Foreplay is more than a precursor to sexual intercourse—it can be a fulfilling destination on its own. It encompasses physical touch, flirtation, sensual massage, and verbal affirmation. Stay attuned to your spouse's reactions and use trial and error to learn what feels pleasurable for both of you. Foreplay helps build arousal, desire, and emotional connection, ensuring that intimacy is a mutual and enjoyable experience.

Intercourse as a Possible Destination

Sexual intercourse can be a goal, but it doesn't always need to be. The focus should be on mutual pleasure and connection. If intercourse is the aim, ensure both spouses feel prepared through open communication:

- *"Are you feeling ready for this step?"*
- *"What can I do to help us feel more comfortable?"*

Practical considerations, such as having lubrication, condoms, massage oil, or pillows for positioning nearby, can help create a smoother and more enjoyable experience.

Post-Intimacy Moments

Aftercare is an essential aspect of intimacy, nurturing the bond created during the act. The release of oxytocin (the bonding hormone) encourages attachment between spouses. Spend time together after intimacy to strengthen this connection:

- Cuddle, laugh, or hold each other in silence.
- Share affirmations like, *"I love how close I feel to you right now."*
- Offer gratitude to Allah for the gift of your marital connection.

Remember to avoid debriefing immediately after intimacy; instead, allow yourselves to stay present and in the moment. Post-intimacy rituals will evolve over time as you learn what brings comfort and joy to each other.

Confidence with marital sexual intimacy grows through intentionality, communication, and patience. By grounding your actions in soulful practices, staying present, and prioritizing mutual pleasure and connection, you can foster a deeply fulfilling and spiritually aligned intimate relationship. Let your journey together reflect the mercy, love, and compassion that are the hallmarks of an Islamic marriage.

Summary

This chapter explored sexual intimacy in marriage as a collaborative and soulful journey, emphasizing the process over specific outcomes. It highlighted the beauty of deepening emotional, spiritual, and physical bonds, reflecting Allah's mercy and love between spouses. Framed within an Islamic perspective, sexual intimacy was presented as both an act of worship and a profound expression of marital unity.

Building on this soulful foundation, the chapter provided insights into sexual response, including the dynamics of desire, arousal, and pleasure. It introduced the dual control model, exploring the balance between excitation and inhibition systems, and examined three types of sexual desire: spontaneous, responsive, and contextual. Unique aspects of female sexual response were also discussed, encouraging empathy and mutual awareness.

Practical tools rooted in the 4Cs—Communication, Consent, Collaboration, and Compromise—offered a framework for fostering fulfilling intimacy. Strategies such as pleasure mapping, intention-setting, and sensory mindfulness encouraged God-consciousness, curiosity, and connection. Aftercare was emphasized to strengthen emotional and spiritual bonds.

Looking ahead, chapters 10 through 12 will delve deeper into sexual health challenges within marriage, while chapter 7 will equip parents to guide their children through sexual health education, integrating emotional, physical, and spiritual growth.

Reflections and Action Items

Reference List

Afrouz, R., Crisp, B. R., & Taket, A. (2018). Seeking help in domestic violence among Muslim women in Muslim-majority and non-Muslim-majority countries: A literature review. *Trauma, Violence, & Abuse*. Advance online publication. https://doi.org/10.1177/1524838018781102

Ahmed, S. (2020). The holistic approach to marital intimacy in Islam: Exploring emotional and physical connection. *Islamic Perspectives Journal, 15*(3), 123–135.

Alkhateeb, L., & Abugideiri, S. E. (2007). *Change from within: Diverse perspectives on domestic violence in Muslim communities*. Peaceful Families Project.

Hathout, H. (2006). *Reading the Muslim mind*. American Trust Publications.

Hibri, A., al-, & Ghazal, G. (2018). Debunking the myth: Angels cursing hadith. KARAMAH: Muslim Women Lawyers for Human Rights. Retrieved December 26, 2024 from https://karamah.org/debunking-the-myth-angels-cursing-hadith/

Kawthari, M. I. A., al- (2008). *Islamic guide to sexual relations*. Huma Press.

Nagoski, E. (2015). *Come as you are: The surprising new science that will transform your sex life*. Simon & Schuster.

Sahih International. (1997). *The Quran: Arabic text with corresponding English meanings*. Abul-Qasim Publishing House.

7 Soulful Parenting Approaches for Sexual Health

This topic marks one of my earliest experiences in the field of sexual health for Muslims. At the time, I was working with Islamic schools, and we had received board approval to implement a curriculum for grades five and above. A critical part of this curriculum was a parent workshop designed to explain the program, address questions, and secure parental consent. That experience solidified my belief that parents must be educated about sexual health, Islam, and soul-based perspectives before they begin these conversations with their children. Why is this so important? If parents are not empowered, have unresolved shame, or misunderstand key aspects of this topic, those issues will inevitably be projected onto their children. This chapter is built on the premise that empowering parents with the knowledge, tools, and confidence they need is essential for fostering soul-based sexual health conversations with their children throughout their development. As you'll see, there's no such thing as a single, all-encompassing "talk." Instead, these discussions are a series of smaller, ongoing conversations that take place gradually, each one building on the last. This chapter provides the guidance to help parents navigate these moments with confidence and soul-centered intention.

The Journey of the Soul

Birth — Spiritual Accountability — Spiritual Maturity — Spiritual Legacy — The Hereafter

DOI: 10.4324/9781032675862-8

Introduction

Parents have held a special place in my heart throughout my career. Leading training sessions and coaching parents on soulful sexual health parenting has shown me the transformative impact of integrating spiritual, emotional, and physical dimensions into parenting. This chapter condenses years of experience into a practical framework, designed to guide parents in nurturing their children's sexual health with compassion and depth.

For many Muslim parents, addressing sexual health with their children feels daunting—like "opening up a can of worms." It's natural to feel hesitant, especially when these conversations are shaped by cultural taboos or personal insecurities. Parents often carry their own experiences of shame or misunderstandings, which can make knowing where to start challenging. This chapter acknowledges these hesitations with compassion and offers tools to help navigate this delicate yet vital aspect of parenting, grounded in Islamic, soul-based frameworks.

As you read, remember that you are your child's foremost expert. Parenting approaches should be as unique as the child, and the framework provided here is flexible, allowing you to adapt it to your child's personality and developmental stage. By focusing on foundational elements—physical, emotional, and spiritual development—this chapter aims to create a bedrock for future conversations about sexual health, taking a gradual and sensitive approach to help you navigate with confidence.

This is not a prescriptive checklist but a compassionate guide, encouraging you to extend grace to yourself as you make decisions rooted in your family's unique dynamics. The chapter includes specific topics and conversation starters tailored to developmental stages, empowering you to approach these discussions with comfort and clarity. Together, we'll explore Islamic perspectives on soulful parenting, unlearn shame often tied to these topics, and cultivate an approach that embodies compassion and accountability. Before we begin, pause to reflect on your feelings, expectations, and hopes as you embark on this meaningful journey.

> **Reflection Questions**
>
> How do I feel when I read the words "soulful parenting approaches for sexual health education"?
> _____
> _____
> _____

What are my soulful hopes for my child/children in relation to their sexual health and overall development as Muslims?

_____

_____

What are some of my fears or doubts about embarking on this soulful sexual health journey with my children?

_____

_____

Soulful Parenting Approaches for Sexual Health: Islamic Perspectives

As we explore the role of parents in soulful sexual health education, it's crucial to recognize a common misconception: reducing sexual health to permissible and impermissible behaviors. While well-intentioned, this reactive approach often overlooks the soul and holistic foundations of sexual health, leaving children without the tools to navigate their development effectively.

As discussed earlier, the soul enters the body at 120 days of gestation and remains with us throughout life, evolving alongside our physical, emotional, and sexual development. Parenting within the Islamic tradition reflects this holistic integration, emphasizing mercy, compassion, and justice while nurturing all aspects of a child's being. The parent–child relationship becomes a deeply spiritual interaction, where the parent's presence and behaviors leave an imprint on the child's soul. For this reason, parents must embark on their own soulful journey to guide their children positively and compassionately.

Islam does not shy away from addressing sexual health; instead, it views this as part of a parent's spiritual obligation. For this reason, parents must acquire the knowledge and skills to engage in soul-centered sexual health education, despite any doubts or discomfort.

A proverbial saying that is often misunderstood as a *hadith*, and is in with the *sunnah* (Prophet tradition) serves as the guidepost for soulful parenting approaches: "Play with them for seven years, discipline them for seven years, and befriend them for seven years." Let's apply this toward soulful parenting approaches across these developmental stages.

1. **Play (0–7 years):** A time for nurturing love, care, and trust through playful interaction. Foundational teachings during this stage focus on physical, emotional, and spiritual development.
2. **Discipline (7–14 years):** With children capable of understanding responsibilities, this stage emphasizes instilling good manners, religious practices, and discipline. Soulful sexual health education builds on earlier foundations, introducing nuanced contexts about puberty (*bulūgh*) and spiritual accountability.
3. **Friendship (14+ years):** As children transition to adulthood, parents foster independence through guidance and support. Soulful sexual health education continues, layering knowledge that supports maturation and moral decision-making.

These developmental stages—encompassing physical, emotional, sexual, and spiritual milestones—serve as the foundation for soulful parenting approaches. Before delving into these stages in detail, let's first reflect on our own relationship with sexual health and how parents can prepare for this soulful journey.

Soulful Parenting: Compassionately Unlearning Internalized Shame

Hamed, an inquisitive 8-year-old, excitedly hands his mom a permission slip for a school field trip and asks, "Mama, what does sex mean?" Startled, his mom's reaction is immediate—she takes the form and angrily responds, "Don't say that word again, it's a bad word!" Confused and hurt, Hamed's cheerful demeanor fades, replaced by tears, as his mom, caught in shock, fails to notice his sadness.

Leila, a 13-year-old who recently began menstruating, overhears a teammate in the locker room say, "This bathroom door lock is broken, but don't come in—I'm inserting a tampon!" Confused by the giggles that follow, Leila asks her mom at home, "What's a tampon?" Her mom retorts, "Where did you learn about this, and why are you asking me? You use pads like other Muslim girls," before walking away. Leila, left frozen and uncertain, feels her stomach drop as her question remains unanswered.

Take a moment to compassionately check in with how you feel after reading these narratives. What thoughts are arising? How about your emotions? Do you see yourself in these responses?

These narratives were shared with me by parents who have attended my educational workshops. The parents were deeply compassionate with themselves and reflected on how they showed up when their children asked them questions about their sexual health. Similar experiences have been shared with me by other parents who were unsure how to respond when their children came face-to-face unexpectedly with content related to sex and sexual health, such as when a parent's child was exposed to a kissing scene on television; when a child saw a large picture of a woman in her underwear at a mall store; when a child accidentally encountered a pornographic image while completing an online search for a homework project; and many more.

The reason I am sharing these examples to begin the section on unlearning internalized shame is simple: the emotions, thoughts, and behaviors that arise from us when we come across sexual health situations with our children are signs of our internalized shame. So, let's begin by defining shame. Although it is a common word, many Muslims parents are unaware of what it actually means.

Shame as a Barrier to Soulful Parenting

As mentioned in chapter 4, shame is a deep emotional response to the perception of violating social, moral, or religious norms, often leading parents to feelings of inadequacy or disconnection. Shame targets the self and frequently stems from unmet expectations, external criticism, or internalized beliefs (Tangney & Dearing, 2002). For parents, this emotional state can profoundly impact how they engage with their children, especially on sensitive topics like sexual health. Chronic shame may manifest as anxiety, emotional withdrawal, or reactive behavior, constricting the heart and pulling parents into a lower-soul state marked by fear and defensiveness (Gilbert, 2003). This dynamic can hinder open communication and prevent parents from fostering a soulful, compassionate connection with their children.

When parents respond to their children from a place of internalized shame, conversations about sexual health often shut down before they begin. For example, Hamed's innocent question about the word "sex" on a permission slip and Leila's curiosity about a classmate's use of a tampon were met with dismissive and reactive responses. These reactions, rooted in the parents' shame, suppressed the children's natural curiosity and inadvertently reinforced feelings of discomfort or secrecy around their bodies and sexuality. This cycle of shame can create barriers to a child's soulful connection to Allah and hinder their understanding of God-given sexual health.

To unlearn this cycle, parents must first address their own internal experiences of shame. By reflecting on its emotional and physical presence and understanding how it impacts their behaviors, parents can begin to unlearn shame-based responses. Developing self-awareness and aligning as a parenting unit—whether as a married couple, divorced co-parents, or single parents with a support network—fosters an environment of compassion and openness, encouraging children to explore these topics without fear.

Parents are therefore encouraged to reflect individually on their experiences with shame and its impact. The "Getting on the Same Soulful Page" questions provided in this section offer a framework for alignment, allowing parents to approach these conversations with unity, clarity, and soulful intention.

Compassionately Unlearning Shame: Individual Reflective Exercise

Reflecting over the content of this book and its earlier chapters, check in with any feelings of shame that may still be present. Compassionately note how shame is still present.

_____

_____

_____

Using a soulful sexual health approach, how do you envision approaching sexual health topics with your child/children? How do you hope to make them feel and think about sexual health as a Muslim?

_____

_____

_____

How do you plan to further enhance your soulful knowledge of sexual health? How can you continue to check in and address any shame-based responses which arise?

_____

_____

_____

Getting On the Same Soulful Page: Aligning as a Caregiving Unit

Now that you've had some time to reflect on any presence of shame toward sexual health, it's important to connect with someone who can empathize with you. Research highlights the significance of a compassionate witness—whether it's your spouse, co-parent, friend, or a relative—who can hold space for you as you process how shame has impacted you and how you are reframing sexual health from a soulful, empowered perspective.

A compassionate witness helps to reduce the intensity of shame by fostering connection and empathy, which are essential for emotional healing (Brown, 2006; Gilbert, 2003; Tangney & Dearing, 2002).

For this aspect of the unlearning shame process, it's important that you choose someone who truly can hold space for you—who will listen, show you empathy, and be a support without any judgment. You will know intuitively who this person is, so trust your gut instinct.

As a note for those who are married or co-parenting a child, it is equally important for both parents to center their own journey with sexual health, and to relate to where the other person is at with their journey. And by coming together to discuss this, hopefully on an ongoing basis, parents can work together to provide compassionate, soulful sexual health learning moments with their child/children.

Once you've selected this person, take a few moments with the following reflection questions to prepare for the conversation:

Who would you like to have this conversation with? Why are you choosing this person?

_____
_____
_____

What would you like to share with this person with regards to your awareness about any shame with sexual health? What do you feel is important for them to compassionately witness?

_____
_____
_____

With regards to your soulful perspectives of sexual health, and how you're unlearning shame, what would you like to share with this person?

_____
_____
_____

How would you like this person to continue to be involved in your unlearning shame journey? How can they be a support and resource for you?

_____
_____
_____

How do you feel after having the conversation? Do you notice any changes in your body and mind?

_____

_____

_____

Now that we have focused internally on our own shame and how this can impact us soulfully when parenting and educating our children, let's set the record straight on some misconceptions when we are teaching our children about sexual health.

> **Myth Busting: Teaching Children about Sexual Health**
>
> **Myth:** Teaching children about sexual health means talking to them about sex, which might make them overly curious about it.
>
> **Fact:** Sexual health goes beyond sexual intimacy and encompasses emotional, physical, and spiritual foundations, particularly for pre-pubertal children who are not yet sexual beings. Soul-based education empowers children with values-aligned knowledge, fostering informed decisions and alignment with Islamic principles without promoting undue curiosity.
>
> **Myth:** Sexual health education should wait until children are teenagers.
>
> **Fact:** Beginning conversations early builds trust and open communication. Teenagers require foundational knowledge about emotional, physical, and spiritual health developed over time. Starting young ensures they're prepared for more complex topics, such as sexual intimacy, which align with a developmental framework like that of this book.
>
> **Myth:** Focusing on what is *halal* versus *haraam* related to sexual health is sufficient for children.
>
> **Fact:** A solely *halal* versus *haraam* framework overlooks the compassionate, soul-based perspectives integral to Islamic tradition. This also narrows the holistic Islamic tradition to theology and ignores the central importance of ethics and spirituality, as was explored in chapter 2. Children need heart-centered guidance that deepens their understanding of Allah's wisdom and fosters a loving, not fear-based, connection to Him. Revisiting chapters on abstinence and the soulful search for a spouse can support more nuanced conversations.

Soulful Sexual Health Education for Children: A Developmental Approach

I'm guessing that this is the section you've been waiting to arrive at—and I'm going to hold you in suspense a little bit longer. Before we jump into the "what" to teach and "when," we need to start with the important "how" and "why" contexts.

As I've shared above, soulful sexual health education for children requires crucial foundational information in three areas of development: physical, emotional, and spiritual health. In fact, it is these three aspects of our lives as Muslims that serve as the foundation for our sexual health—so much in fact that we cannot skip over them. Figure 7.1—which may look familiar from chapter 2—shows the relationship between these three areas of our health and how they relate to sexual health. Definitions of these areas are also provided for context.

Physical Health Foundations: Teaching children about their bodies begins with helping them understand that God created them with purpose. Use correct terminology for body parts, including genital (external) and reproductive (internal) organs, while emphasizing their functions. Personal hygiene connects physical and spiritual health, reinforcing practices essential to Muslim self-care, such as cleanliness for prayer. As children near puberty, prepare them for physical changes like menstruation or voice deepening to ensure they feel informed and confident.

Emotional Health Foundations: Fostering self-worth and emotional awareness helps children recognize and express their feelings healthily.

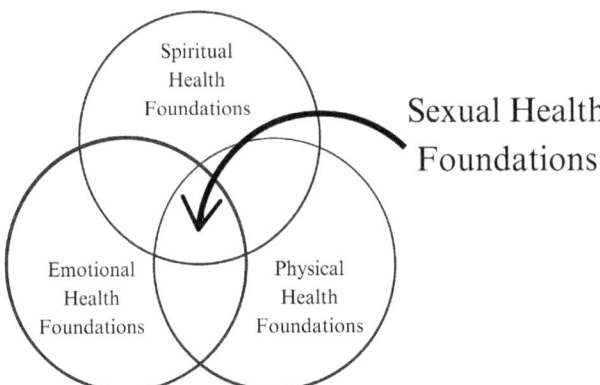

Figure 7.1 A Venn diagram of emotional, physical, spiritual, and sexual health foundations for children

Teach them personal boundaries, empowering them to respect their emotions and those of others. Discuss consent early, such as choosing how to greet extended family, to foster agency and confidence. Equip children to recognize inappropriate behavior and seek help when needed by promoting open communication about emotional safety and well-being.

Spiritual Health Foundations: Help children develop a meaningful relationship with God by introducing foundational aspects of faith, including prayers and religious rituals. Model consistent practices, guiding them to integrate worship into daily life. Teach values like compassion and self-accountability, encouraging reflection and alignment with spiritual goals. Nurture their personal growth with self-compassion, emphasizing the lifelong journey of bettering the soul and building spiritual resilience.

Sexual Health Foundations: Sexual health integrates with physical, emotional, and spiritual development. Tailor conversations to a child's stage, covering topics like:

- The human life cycle, including Quranic perspectives on creation and maturity.
- The sacred relationship between husband and wife in Islam, highlighting its spiritual and physical dimensions.
- Puberty changes, such as new feelings and bodily developments, explaining these are natural and God-given.
- Normalizing "liking" someone as part of growing up, while emphasizing that God judges actions, not feelings.
- Addressing exposure to pornography proactively, encouraging open communication to ensure children feel safe discussing concerns without fear of punishment.

Take a few moments to reflect on these foundations of sexual health. Which foundational areas do you feel more comfortable with? Which ones do you anticipate needing more support and research on? Use the following space to write some notes about how you're feeling and what you're thinking after reviewing this past section.

_____
_____
_____

Ongoing Small Conversations versus "The Talk"

So far in this chapter, we've covered the "why" of soulful sexual health education for children, and also have started to explore the "what." And we need to go into the "how" before we take a deeper dive into soulful developmental approaches to these conversations.

Speaking of conversations, that's what we need to understand about educating children. As parents, you will be having many small conversations about sexual health over the duration of your child's life and development. Some of these conversations will arise from questions your child may ask (more on that soon), from situations they encounter, or you as a parent initiating a conversation during a natural learning moment. Let's focus on the final type of conversation first, since they are ideally what happens the most frequently.

Soulful Parenting Approaches: Supporting Children with Unique Needs

As a school-based occupational therapist, I've had the privilege of working with children and youth with special needs and disabilities, helping them grow in ways that honor their individual capacities. Part of this work included adapting sexual health curricula to support children and youth with special needs. Through these experiences, I've seen firsthand how every child is unique, created by Allah with a specific capacity that will, *inshaAllah*, grow and develop according to His plan. This capacity is not determined solely by chronological age but by their developmental age, which reflects their readiness to engage with the world.

For parents of children with special needs, adapting natural learning moments around sexual health is essential. Meeting your child where they are means recognizing their unique abilities and using approaches that make information accessible and meaningful. Simplify language to ensure clarity, use visual systems to support understanding, and integrate assistive technology when appropriate to enhance communication and engagement.

Collaboration is key to success. Partnering with school and community professionals—such as occupational therapists (OTs), speech-language pathologists (SLPs), child psychologists, special education teachers, and educational assistants—can provide valuable insights.

Sexual health education for children with special needs is not a one-size-fits-all journey. With patience, creativity, and collaboration, parents can provide compassionate, faith-centered support, fostering their child's growth and equipping them with knowledge and skills aligned with their abilities.

Natural Learning Moments

Parenting carries the Divine responsibility to prepare children for the world, and Islam's comprehensive guidance leaves no aspect of life untouched, including sexual health. Conversations on this topic can be normalized through "natural learning moments," seamlessly integrated into daily life with compassion and wisdom. Natural learning moments align with the Islamic principle that God is present in every aspect of life (*ihsaan*). These opportunities arise organically, offering a soul-centered approach to sexual health education that fosters curiosity, understanding, and faith. Key elements include:

Attuning to Curiosity: Respond thoughtfully to your child's questions, offering age-appropriate, faith-based explanations. For example, when asked where babies come from, frame the response as life being a gift from God.

Embracing the Right Timing: Everyday activities—like bath time, dressing, or watching TV—can prompt discussions. Use these moments to introduce topics naturally, reminding children of God's presence and guidance.

Providing Age-Appropriate Insights: Tailor information to your child's level of understanding, using correct anatomical terms for younger children and more nuanced discussions for older ones. Reinforce the sacredness of their bodies as a trust from God.

Drawing from Everyday Life: Use real-world observations, like noticing a pregnant woman or reflecting on nature, to connect physical realities with spiritual teachings, presenting them as signs (*ayat*) of God.

Cultivating Ongoing Discussions: Sexual health education should be an ongoing dialogue that evolves with your child's understanding, creating a supportive environment that intertwines spiritual and sexual well-being.

Weaving in Spirituality and Ethics: Align discussions with Islamic teachings that emphasize the soul's journey and connection to God. Move beyond rules to instill a holistic view of sexual health—including spirituality and ethics as discussed in chapter 2—as part of their overall spiritual development.

By embracing these moments, parents present sexual health as a natural and sacred aspect of life, fostering a deeper connection to faith and understanding. Soulful sexual health education not only supports holistic health as children grow, but also serves as prevention of harm, such as child sexual abuse. With these foundations in mind, we can now explore how these frameworks apply across the three developmental stages outlined earlier.

Preventing Child Sexual Abuse Through Soulful Sexual Health Education

Soulful sexual health education is vital for preventing child sexual abuse, emphasizing both empowering children with knowledge and ensuring parents remain vigilant protectors. Children are inherently vulnerable, and it is the responsibility of parents and trusted adults to create safe environments, monitor interactions, and be proactive in safeguarding their well-being.

Key practices for prevention include:

Teach Body Awareness: Help children see their bodies as sacred blessings from Allah. Use correct anatomical terms, teach privacy, and explain the importance of caring for and protecting their bodies in age-appropriate ways.

Empower Children to Speak Up: Encourage children to voice discomfort and practice saying "No" in role-play scenarios. Reassure them they can share anything without fear of blame or punishment.

Create a Safe Space for Conversations: Foster open communication, letting children know their feelings matter and they will never face judgment for expressing concerns.

Explain Safe and Unsafe Touch: Clearly differentiate between safe (e.g. a parent helping with hygiene) and unsafe touch (e.g. inappropriate contact), using simple, relatable examples.

Encourage Situational Awareness: Teach children to trust their instincts and speak up if something feels wrong, even if they're unsure why.

Stay Vigilant as a Parent: Ultimately, a child's safety depends on the attentiveness of adults. Monitor their interactions, enforce safeguards in communal and online settings, and prioritize their safety over societal discomfort in addressing concerns.

By integrating these practices, soulful sexual health education builds children's confidence, nurtures self-awareness, and empowers them to seek help when needed—all while ensuring their safety remains a priority.

A Soul-Based Development Framework for Sexual Health Education

This section presents the "what" to teach and discuss with your child as it relates to sexual health education and its three foundations: physical, emotional, and spiritual health. Based on the Islamic guidance outlined earlier in the chapter—"Play with them for the first seven years, discipline them for the next seven years, and befriend them for the following seven years"—each developmental stage will be explored in terms of what to teach. Suggestions to incorporate these teachings into natural learning moments are made, alongside a case study for practice and suggested conversation openers as well. *Bismillah* (In the Name of God), let's begin!

Stage 1: 0–7 Years—"Play with Them"

During this stage, parents nurture their children through love, care, and playful interaction, establishing a foundation of trust and security. These early years are crucial for developing a child's sense of belonging and confidence, setting the stage for healthy emotional, physical, and spiritual growth.

The goal of soulful parenting approaches for sexual health during this stage is to teach children foundational information about their bodies, emotions, and the importance of self-awareness, all within an age-appropriate, soul-centered framework.

Natural Learning Moments

Self-Care

- Toilet training: Teach your child the proper names for private body parts in a matter-of-fact way. For example: *"We clean our private parts after using the toilet because this helps us stay healthy."*
- Bathing: Model appropriate boundaries by teaching your child about privacy during bath time. For instance: *"Our bodies are special, and we keep certain parts private except when Mommy or Daddy is helping you stay clean."*
- Dressing: Encourage independence by allowing your child to dress themselves and reinforcing modesty, such as: *"We wear clothes to cover our private parts because our bodies are a gift from Allah."*

Bedtime

- Use bedtime stories or reflections to introduce simple concepts of self-awareness and gratitude. For example: *"Allah made every part of* your body, and it helps you do amazing things like run, hug, and play. Let's thank Allah for our bodies before we sleep."

Before Visiting Extended Family Members

- Teach your child about bodily autonomy by emphasizing that they have control over their bodies, especially if you notice discomfort when greeting adults they are not comfortable with. For instance: *"You can give a hug if you want, but it's okay to say no if you'd rather wave or say salaam instead."*

Preparation for Being Around Other Children

- Use playdates or daycare interactions as opportunities to discuss boundaries. For example: *"If someone touches you in a way you don't like, it's okay to say 'Stop' and tell a teacher or me."*

When They See Pictures Online

- If your child sees an image online that prompts questions, respond with calm curiosity. For example: *"Let's talk about that picture. Sometimes we see things online that aren't for kids. If you're ever unsure, ask me, and we can talk about it together."*

Before They Access a Device

- Establish clear guidelines and boundaries for device use. For example: *"Your tablet is for learning and playing fun games in the living room, with mama or baba around. If you ever see something confusing or upsetting, come and tell me right away."*

Before a Playdate or Sleepover

- Reinforce safety and boundaries. For example: *"If you feel uncomfortable or need help, let the adult in charge know. And remember, it's always okay to call me if you want to come home. You can use our code word to tell me that you want to leave."*

By embedding soulful sexual health education into natural learning moments, parents can lay a foundation of trust, confidence, and understanding in their children. These early interactions teach children to value their bodies, understand boundaries, and develop emotional awareness, all in alignment with Islamic values.

Table 7.1 An overview of physical, emotional, and spiritual health foundations for ages 0–7

Physical Health	**Body Knowledge, Care, and Safety:** Teach children the anatomical names for all body parts, including external genitals, and guidelines on when and with whom these names can be used. Introduce self-care practices for different body parts, including the importance of washing private areas with water and proper showering routines. Educate about privacy, boundaries, and modesty, such as knocking before entering bedrooms, identifying trusted adults, and knowing what to do if they feel unsafe. Encourage open discussions about private parts and hygiene, reassuring children that their curiosity is valued and rooted in caring for the body God has entrusted to them.
Emotional Health	**Emotional Foundations:** Teach children to recognize and express their feelings while respecting others' emotions. Reassure them that their feelings are valid and important. Explain "good touch" as touches that make them feel safe, like hugs from family, and "uncomfortable touch" as anything that causes unease or fear, emphasizing the need to tell a trusted adult if this happens. Encourage children to trust their feelings about touch, reminding them that God gave us feelings to guide us. Discuss affection, such as hugging or cuddling, as expressions of love within the family, appropriate with parents, siblings, and grandparents. Highlight the importance of respecting personal boundaries, modeling consent for physical affection, and navigating cultural expectations around touch within extended families.
Spiritual Health	**Islamic Foundations:** Introduce basic Islamic concepts, such as Islam, Muslim, God, and prayer, including why we pray and its connection to gratitude and worship. Teach the value of cleanliness (*tahara*) and self-care as integral to both worship and daily life. Emphasize that our bodies are a trust from God, and we have a responsibility to care for them. Explain the life cycle of all living creatures, from being with God to returning to Him, and introduce the soul as a part of us that carries our life experiences to the next world in God's presence.

Suggestions for Conversation Starters:

- *"Each body part has its own name, so while washing up, let's learn the names of these parts."*
- *"We close our bedroom door to change because taking off clothes for pajamas is a private thing."*
- *"Mama and baba share special touches like kissing on the lips because we're married, but we kiss your cheeks and hug you because we love you as our child. Friends show care differently, like with high-fives or fist bumps."*

- *"If you see pictures or videos of people wearing little clothing, let us know. You're not in trouble; we just want to keep you safe. And remember, the iPad stays in the living room and charges at 7pm, okay?"*

Case Study:

Read the following situation shared earlier in the chapter and reflect on how you would respond if this question was posed by your child.

Hamed, an inquisitive 8-year-old, excitedly hands his mom a permission slip for a school field trip and asks, "Mama, what does sex mean?"

(**Hint:** Always ask your child where they heard this word or piece of information from, and from whom, before you start thinking about how to respond!)

Notes

_____
_____
_____
_____
_____
_____

Stage 2: 7–14 years—"Teach Them"

During this second developmental stage, the focus shifts to discipline and education as children become more capable of understanding responsibilities. Parents are encouraged to instill ethical behaviors, religious practices with deeper spiritual meanings, and a sense of self-responsibility. The child's relationship with God begins to move beyond acts of worship, becoming more abstract and integrated into their understanding of life.

Soulful parenting during this stage builds on earlier foundations by introducing nuanced discussions about sexual development and preparing children for puberty (*bulūgh*), the age of spiritual accountability. Parents should intentionally address topics like bodily changes, new feelings, menstruation, or nocturnal emissions, recognizing that puberty typically begins between ages 8 and 13 for girls and 10 and 18 for boys. By layering this information thoughtfully, parents can guide their children toward both spiritual and emotional maturity.

Natural Learning Moments

Hygiene and Privacy

- Reinforce the importance of personal hygiene, especially as their bodies begin to change. For example: *"As you grow, your body will need more care, like using deodorant and washing regularly. These are ways we take care of the body Allah has gifted us."*

Understanding Boundaries

- Teach them about respecting others' privacy and their own. For instance: *"It's important to knock before entering someone's room, just like they should for you. This helps us respect each other's space."*

Teaching Them How to Pray and Make *Wudu*

- Connect physical cleanliness with spiritual preparation. For example: *"We make wudu to purify our bodies and hearts for prayer. It's a way of showing gratitude to Allah for the blessings of our bodies."*

Explaining Why a Woman Sometimes Can't Pray

- Use natural moments, like when your child notices a female relative not praying, to introduce menstruation in an age-appropriate way: *"Sometimes, women don't pray because they're on their monthly cycle. It's a special time when Allah gives them a break from certain acts of worship."*

Before School-Based Sexual Health Education

- Prepare your child by framing the school's teachings within an Islamic soulful context. *"You'll learn about how the body changes during puberty at school. It's good to know this, and we can talk more about it together to understand what Allah says about these changes."*

Soul-Centered Use of Social Media

- Guide your child's social media use by aligning it with spiritual values: *"Not everything online is meant for you. If something feels confusing or upsetting, it's okay to stop and tell me. Allah loves when we protect our hearts and minds."*
- Encourage respectful interactions: *"Talk to people online with the same kindness and respect you practice in real life. Don't share personal information like your full name, address, or school, even if they ask."*

- Teach boundaries and soulful respect for one's life and body: *"Our private lives are special and don't need to be shared online, including family photos, personal struggles, or where we live."*

When They Have Questions about Friends or School

- If your child comes to you with questions about friends or what they've learned in school, use it as an opportunity for open dialogue. *"It's great that you're asking these questions! Let's talk about what your friend said and how we understand it from an Islamic perspective."*

Table 7.2 An overview of physical, emotional, and spiritual health foundations for ages 7–14

Physical Health	**Prepare for Puberty:** Foster independence in self-care while reinforcing Islamic values of cleanliness and accountability. Build self-esteem through character and skills rather than physical appearance and develop critical thinking by encouraging reflection on media and online content. Discuss pre-puberty physical changes, such as hair growth, breast buds, voice changes, and vaginal discharge. Educate on body safety, recognizing and preventing sexual abuse, and how to express discomfort during sleepovers or away from home. Amplify hygiene practices, introducing hair removal, deodorant use, and menstrual care. Explain nocturnal emissions, proper self-care, and *ghusl* for post-puberty rituals.
Emotional Health	**Teach Emotional Development:** Gently explain that as children grow, they may experience new feelings toward others, accompanied by physical reactions like tingling or warmth. Normalize these feelings as natural and God-given, creating a safe space for open conversations on understanding and managing emotions with kindness. Highlight Islamic values of modesty, respect, and meaningful relationships, encouraging respectful interactions and focusing on shared goals like community or volunteer projects. Reinforce the importance of family and trusted adults as sources of support and guidance.
Spiritual Health	**Enhance Spiritual Contexts:** Encourage children to enhance their God-consciousness in daily activities by teaching them how to pray, make *dua* (personal supplication), have conversations with God, and seek forgiveness with compassion. Emphasize God's presence within them and focus on self-accountability framed in kindness. Discuss sexual intimacy with age-appropriate clarity, presenting it as a spiritual experience rooted in the soul and framed by the sanctity of marriage. Highlight modesty as an inner, soul-driven practice tied to self-respect, faith, and personal values, fostering a sense of inner dignity and respectful interactions.

Suggestions for Conversation Starters:

- "Did you know the Quran talks about how a baby is created? Surah Al-Mu'minun (23:12–14) describes the stages of creation, from a drop of fluid to a fully formed human. Isn't it amazing how Allah designs our bodies?"
- "The Quran also mentions life's stages in Surah Ar-Rum (30:54): 'Allah created you from weakness, then strength, then weakness again.' It's a reminder of how we grow and change throughout life."
- "I wanted to talk about the changes we go through as we become teenagers. It might feel uncomfortable, and that's okay. Since Allah created our bodies, it's important to learn about them together. I even found a book we can read together!"
- "I made a special self-care kit for you with things like deodorant, pads, lotion, or a razor. Let's go through it and learn how and when to use these items."

Case Study:

You have heard from your 13-year-old that their friends have "boyfriends" and "girlfriends." You are aware that your child being in middle school means that his/her peers have started to date—and are quite open about it around others. It's important for you to educate your child about dating and relationships in middle school, so they feel empowered and knowledgeable about living their Muslim values out around others who have different values.

How would you start having smaller conversations about dating with your child? What are you concerned about? How would you approach this beyond "*halal* and *haraam*," or instilling psychological fear of God? How would you encourage them to ask questions and normalize any feelings of "liking someone"?

Notes

_____
_____
_____
_____
_____
_____

Stage 3: 14+ years—"Befriend Them"

In this final developmental stage, parents transition to a "befriending" role, focusing on fostering compassionate self-accountability and responsibility toward God. Adolescents experience significant brain changes, making it harder for them to consider long-term consequences, and they naturally turn to peers for guidance while testing boundaries to gain independence. By shifting their approach, parents can create space for teens to reflect on decisions and consequences while offering unconditional support and serving as trusted advisors, even when mistakes occur.

Soulful parenting for sexual health during this stage builds on earlier foundations while preparing teens for adulthood. With exposure to topics like dating, finding a spouse, abstinence, and marriage—both online and socially—it's vital for Muslim teens to understand not just the "what" but also the "why" and "how." As teens develop abstract thinking, parents should provide deeper context on Islamic perspectives of the soul, spiritual growth, and making decisions.

Natural Learning Moments

Use Open-Ended Questions to Foster Reflection:

- Ask your teen thought-provoking questions to introduce topics naturally and encourage critical thinking. For example:
  - *"What do you think about the way dating is portrayed in movies or online? How does that align with what we've talked about regarding relationships in Islam?"*
  - *"Have you noticed how social media influences what people think about relationships and intimacy? How do you feel about that?"*

Leverage Current Events or Trends:

- Use news stories, social media trends, or viral videos as conversation starters. For instance:
  - *"I saw a post online about someone struggling with boundaries in a relationship. What do you think is important when it comes to setting boundaries?"*
  - *"There's been a lot of talk about online influencers promoting certain lifestyles. How do you think their values align with what we believe?"*

Share Personal Experiences:

- Offer your own stories to normalize challenges and empathize with their struggles. For example:
  - *"When I was your age, I remember feeling confused about certain topics too. It wasn't easy, but learning to make decisions based on my faith really helped me."*

- *"I know it's a lot harder for teens now with everything online. How can I support you in making decisions that feel right for you?"*

Discuss Situations from Real Life or Online:

- Bring up scenarios from daily life to discuss sexual health topics. For example:
  - *"If you're ever in a situation where someone crosses a boundary, what do you think you could say or do?"*
  - *"What would you do if a friend came to you for advice about a relationship?"*

Raise Topics Proactively:

- Initiate discussions about topics that may not come up naturally, while being mindful of their emotional readiness. For instance:
  - *"I wanted to talk about how we soulfully approach finding a spouse in Islam. What qualities do you think are most important in a partner?"*
  - *"Let's discuss what empowered abstinence means and how it can align with your personal goals and values."*

Encourage Participation in Learning Opportunities:

- Suggest in-person events, online videos, workshops, or courses to broaden their understanding. For example:
  - *"There's a workshop on relationships and self-awareness for teens. I think it could be helpful—what do you think?"*
  - *"Would you be open to watching a video together about how to make values-based decisions in difficult situations?"*

Suggestions for Conversation Starters:

- *"The Quran talks about relationships in Surah Ar-Rum (30:21), where Allah says He created mates for peace, affection, and mercy. Relationships should bring care, not confusion or harm."*
- *"It's normal to feel attraction—God created these feelings for a purpose, connected to soulful marriage. Let's also talk about how identity and feelings relate to our soul in meaningful ways."*
- *"Social media makes relationships look glamorous, but it's not always real. Thinking critically about what we see helps us navigate online spaces with integrity."*
- *"As you take on responsibilities and make decisions, it's okay to take your time. I'm here to support you and help you figure things out when needed."*

Table 7.3 An overview of physical, emotional, and spiritual health foundations for ages 14+

Physical Health	Provide nuanced guidance on empowered abstinence and sexual decision-making, referencing soulful insights from chapter 5. Encourage teens to seek accurate information about marital sexual intimacy, including topics like contraception, sexual response, and soulful perspectives (chapter 6). Deepen their understanding of menstruation by introducing cycle syncing and hormone-balancing practices, such as nutrition, exercise, sleep, and meditation rooted in spiritual practices. Support managing sexual desire through physical activity and creative outlets. Guide them in finding a trusted medical provider for reliable physical and sexual health guidance.
Emotional Health	Normalize the challenges of peer pressure and societal influences, supporting teens in confidently living their Islamic values. Enhance their emotional intelligence by teaching nuanced language to acknowledge and accept their feelings in the moment. Normalize feelings of attraction and encourage healthy outlets for these emotions. Advocate for seeking professional support when emotions feel overwhelming, connecting them to trusted professionals for guidance. Foster critical thinking skills to challenge cultural or community pressures around life milestones, such as career, finances, marriage, or parenthood.
Spiritual Health	Encourage your teen to explore soulful Islamic resources, such as Imam al-Ghazali's works or online scholars and professionals, to deepen their spiritual growth. Support self-accountability in religious practices by brainstorming personalized methods that resonate with them. Shift their perspective on challenges by framing them as part of the soul's journey, moving away from interpretations like "God is punishing me." Broaden their understanding of God's wisdom beyond human limitations, emphasizing trust in Divine timing and the unique unfolding of life events according to Allah's plan.

Case Study:

Your 22-year-old child is showing frustration and sadness as their peers are starting to get engaged and married. They are in the middle of an intense graduate degree program and feel pressured to focus more on getting married than on their education and career. Your child shares that they've heard that having children in your 20s is "better" than in your thirties, and that as you age and try to get married, there are fewer choices for a spouse, and you're made to compromise. They're feeling behind in life and are concerned that they're falling even more behind. How do you empathize with their concerns while broadening their physical, emotional, and spiritual health perspectives?

Notes

_____
_____
_____
_____
_____

Soulfully Responding to Your Child's Sexual Health Questions

Children often ask unexpected questions about sexual health, leaving parents feeling unprepared or uncertain. These moments are valuable opportunities to build trust and guide your child's understanding with compassion and intention. Staying calm and centered is key, as it reassures your child that their curiosity is safe and welcome.

Pause and seek clarity. Take a deep breath before responding and gently ask your child for more context to understand their perspective. For example: *"That's an interesting question! Can you tell me what made you think about this or where you heard about it?"* This allows you to gauge their developmental understanding and gives you time to collect your thoughts.

Provide a thoughtful response or defer with honesty. Offer an answer that aligns with their developmental stage and Islamic values. If you're unsure, it's okay to say: *"I'm glad you asked, and I want to give you a thoughtful answer. Let me research this/let's explore this together, and we'll talk tonight."* Following up is essential, as failing to revisit their question may discourage future openness.

These interactions, while sometimes surprising, are opportunities to nurture trust, model honesty, and show that curiosity is a natural and welcome part of their growth. They allow you to align your parenting with soulful values, fostering connection and meaningful guidance.

Holding Soul-Based Conversations about the LGBTQ+ Spectrum

The Islamic tradition defines marriage as a sacred union between a man and a woman, with sexual intimacy occurring within its sanctity. While same-sex attraction is a feeling some may experience, normative Islamic teachings emphasize managing desires and aligning actions with spiritual goals through empowered abstinence. Some contemporary Muslim groups reinterpret these frameworks, but traditional perspectives rooted in classical scholarship remain widely accepted.

Islam emphasizes privacy and personal accountability, encouraging individuals to focus on their spiritual journeys without imposing beliefs on others. Decisions about one's body, sexual decisions, and the soul remain personal unless they cause harm to others. Respecting others' choices while upholding one's values demonstrates the balance Islam encourages between personal boundaries and collective respect.

Discussing LGBTQ+ topics can be challenging for Muslim parents, often leading to avoidance or fear-based approaches focused solely on religious rulings. These methods risk creating an "us versus them" dynamic, missing the compassion and nuance necessary for meaningful dialogue. A soul-based approach enables parents to guide their children with understanding, aligning with Islamic values while fostering open, supportive conversations that empower growth and confidence.

Conversations about Feelings, Actions, and Identity

Islam differentiates between feelings, actions, and identity, offering a nuanced framework:

- **Feelings:** Internal experiences, including same-sex attraction, are seen as having been created by God and provide insight into one's inner reality. Feelings, in and of themselves, are not sinful but are opportunities for introspection and spiritual growth.
- **Actions:** Same-sex sexual behavior, such as all sexual behaviors outside marriage, is prohibited in normative teachings, with emphasis placed on aligning actions with spiritual values and accountability.
- **Identity:** A Muslim's core identity is rooted in servitude to God and the soul's purpose, transcending labels tied solely to sexuality. This perspective encourages understanding of one's self through a spiritual lens, integrating feelings and actions into a holistic journey toward Allah.

This framework allows parents to navigate sensitive topics with compassion, helping children understand the distinction between feelings and actions while emphasizing the soul's overarching journey.

Public LGBTQ+ conversations often lack space for Islamic perspectives, leaving Muslims who uphold traditional beliefs vulnerable to accusations of intolerance. However, respecting others' choices while maintaining personal spiritual commitments is possible, especially when balancing privacy and focusing on one's family and community values.

Navigating LGBTQ+ topics requires parents to approach discussions with clarity, compassion, and a deep understanding of their child's developmental stage and emotional needs. Here are practical steps, enriched with context, to guide parents in fostering meaningful, soul-based conversations:

Reflect on Personal Feelings: Before engaging in conversations, take time to explore your own emotions, shame, or misunderstandings about LGBTQ+ topics. Consider how your upbringing, cultural influences, or personal experiences may shape your perspective. Reflecting on these feelings ensures that your approach is grounded in clarity and compassion. Acknowledge any fears or discomfort you may have and remind yourself that approaching the topic with care is part of your role in nurturing your child's spiritual and emotional growth.

Plan Developmentally Appropriate Conversations: Tailoring LGBTQ+ conversations to your child's developmental stage ensures that discussions are age-appropriate, compassionate, and aligned with their level of understanding. Here are examples of conversation starters for the three stages summarized in this chapter:

Early Childhood (Ages 4–7): At this stage, children are naturally curious but may not yet grasp complex topics. Focus on foundational values like kindness, respect, and privacy.

"Sometimes you might see people who look or dress differently. Everyone is unique, and we treat others with kindness because that's what Allah loves."

"In our family, we believe that marriage is between a man and a woman, like how mama and baba got married. What questions do you have about this?"

Middle Childhood (Ages 8–14): During this stage, children are more aware of societal and cultural influences. Use their curiosity to provide context and reinforce Islamic values.

"You might hear friends or see things online about people identifying as LGBTQ+. Have you heard this term before? Let's talk about what it means and how we can understand it through our faith."

"In Islam, we believe that everyone has feelings, and sometimes those feelings can be confusing. It's okay to talk about feelings and understand how they guide us in making good choices."

Adolescence and Young Adulthood (Ages 15+): Teens and young adults often have more exposure to diverse perspectives and may have deeper questions. Engage them with respect, encouraging critical thinking and dialogue.

"You might have friends or classmates who identify as LGBTQ+. How do you feel about these topics, and how do you think we can approach them in a way that reflects our faith and values?"

"Let's discuss how Islam views feelings, actions, and identity, and how these align with our relationship with Allah. What questions or thoughts do you have about this?"

"As you grow, you'll encounter different perspectives. What helps you stay grounded in your faith while understanding others' experiences?"

Review Previous Foundations: Build on earlier lessons about sexual health and personal values. Connect concepts like identity, feelings, and actions to Islamic teachings on self-accountability and the soul's journey. Reinforce earlier discussions about consent, self-awareness, and emotional boundaries, highlighting how these principles apply to relationships and interactions. By framing LGBTQ+ topics within the broader context of sexual health education, you provide your child with a cohesive, faith-centered understanding.

Acknowledge Concerns with Compassion: Be honest about your hesitations or discomfort but frame them as opportunities for mutual learning and growth. For example, you might say, *"This is a topic I'm still learning about too, but I want us to have an open and honest conversation."* This approach fosters trust and shows your child that it's okay to navigate complex topics together. Remember that acknowledging your uncertainties demonstrates humility and models a willingness to grow.

Recognize that discussing LGBTQ+ topics is not a one-time conversation but an ongoing dialogue that evolves as your child grows. By creating an environment of openness and mutual respect, you invite your child to share their thoughts, ask questions, and express concerns without fear of judgment. Remember that your role as a parent is to guide and support, not to control or impose, allowing your child to develop a nuanced understanding that aligns with their faith and personal journey.

By framing these discussions within a soul-based context, parents can help their children navigate LGBTQ+ topics with self-awareness, spiritual alignment, and confidence.

Summary

As this chapter concludes, several key points are crucial to continue centering and uplifting in your child's soulful sexual health education journey. First and foremost, as parents, you are the true experts of your children and are uniquely positioned to understand your child's personality and developmental needs. With this understanding, parents are encouraged to adapt the provided soulful parenting framework to align with their child's individuality, trusting in their instincts and knowledge.

Parenting Adult Muslim Children: A Soulful Role in Their Marital Journey

Parenting evolves as your child transitions into adulthood, especially during significant life events like marriage. This shift involves offering soulful guidance, compassionate support, and a steady presence rooted in humility and trust in Allah's plan. Your role is not to control but to guide with a focus on values like compassion, self-accountability, and the soul's journey.

Encourage your child to approach courtship with authenticity and intention, letting go of rigid checklists or biases and prioritizing their well-being and spiritual growth. Create a supportive environment for open conversations without undue pressure. During challenges such as heartbreak or divorce, be a nonjudgmental source of strength, offering steady love and reminding them of their connection to Allah. Adapt your approach by seeking feedback, asking questions like, *"Am I supporting you in a way that feels helpful? Is there anything I could do differently?"*

When preparing for marriage, center your child's and their spouse's values and preferences over societal or extended family expectations. Balance cultural traditions with soulful intentionality, keeping their union as the priority. By embracing this role, you empower your adult child to navigate their marital journey with confidence, trust, and spiritual alignment.

Additionally, I hope that parents feel reassured and reminded that soulful sexual health education is about more than just teaching children about sex. Instead, this journey begins with nurturing the child's physical, emotional, and spiritual development, laying the groundwork for a more comprehensive understanding of sexual health as they mature. This gradual approach is designed to ease any parental anxiety surrounding the topic and to be aligned with Islamic perspectives of soulful parenting according to developmental needs.

Finally, the chapter has highlighted the importance of flexibility and compassion in parenting. Rather than offering a rigid script, the soulful framework presented here is meant to be adaptable, allowing parents to respond to their child's unique developmental stage, maturity, and needs. By extending the same compassion to themselves that they offer their children, parents can confidently and comfortably integrate soulful sexual health education into their parenting journey.

Reflections and Action Items

Reference List

Ali, K. (2006). *Sexual ethics and Islam: Feminist reflections on Qur'an, hadith, and jurisprudence*. Oneworld Publications.

Brown, B. (2006). Shame resilience theory: A grounded theory study on women and shame. *Families in Society, 87*(1), 43–52.

Gilbert, P. (2003). Evolution, social roles, and the differences in shame and guilt. *Social Research: An International Quarterly, 70*(4), 1205–1230.

Kugle, S. S. (2010). *Homosexuality in Islam: Critical reflection on gay, lesbian, and transgender Muslims*. Oneworld Publications.

Lewis, H. B. (2003). The role of shame in symptom formation. *Psychological Bulletin, 112*(3), 385–389.
Tangney, J. P., & Dearing, R. L. (2002). *Shame and guilt*. Guilford Press.
Tangney, J. P., Stuewig, J., & Mashek, D. J. (2007). Moral emotions and moral behavior. *Annual Review of Psychology, 58*, 345–372.
Yip, A. K. T. (2016). "Coming out" within Islam: Interpretations and challenges. *Sexualities, 19*(5–6), 564–578.

8 Soulful Sexual Health and Spiritual Maturity

I remember turning 40 and sensing that something meaningful had settled within me. Only later did I come to understand that this shift wasn't random—it aligned with what Islam designates as the age of spiritual maturity. There was a quiet but powerful clarity that began to take root, as though I had finally arrived at a fuller understanding of myself—mind, body, and soul. This spiritual maturity contrasts sharply with mainstream narratives that reduce aging to a decline in vitality and purpose. Sexual health is often confined to the reproductive years, especially for women, while men's sexual health is assumed static or irrelevant beyond midlife. These reductive views strip aging of its beauty and depth, ignoring the wisdom and spiritual refinement that come with it. Islam offers a transformative perspective, designating 40 as a milestone of spiritual maturity—a time to embrace growth, gratitude, and a deeper connection with Allah. This chapter encourages rejecting limiting cultural narratives and embracing sexual health as a sacred and evolving aspect of holistic well-being. With spiritual maturity as our foundation, we can approach this life stage with dignity, resilience, and purpose, seeing changes not as endings, but as transitions that strengthen our connection to ourselves, our Creator, and those we love.

The Journey of the Soul

Birth — Spiritual Accountability — Spiritual Maturity — Spiritual Legacy — The Hereafter

DOI: 10.4324/9781032675862-9

Introduction

Middle adulthood, typically beginning around age 40, is a transformative life stage that brings shifts in identity, relationships, and health. For Muslims, this period is a milestone of spiritual maturity, marking a progression toward wisdom, integration, and deeper self-awareness. The Islamic tradition encourages viewing aging not as a decline but as a path to spiritual refinement, heightened self-accountability, and alignment with Divine purpose. This soulful perspective emphasizes caring for oneself, including sexual health, as part of our responsibility to Allah, offering a holistic foundation for navigating this stage of life.

As the body undergoes changes such as hormonal shifts, menopause, or fluctuations in sexual desire, these transformations can be approached with patience, compassion, and spiritual insight. Middle adulthood presents an opportunity to reframe these changes as avenues for growth and intimacy, aligning physical health with a deepened spiritual connection. For men, challenges like reduced testosterone or shifts in sexual performance may prompt adjustments in lifestyle and mindset. For women, menopause and hormonal changes introduce new dimensions to vitality and sexual health. Both call for integrating accurate health knowledge with soulful resilience.

This chapter explores how sexual health evolves during middle adulthood within the framework of Islamic tradition and spiritual maturity. It highlights the intersection of faith and health, offering practical guidance to address physical changes, nurture intimacy, and maintain preventative care. By embracing a balanced approach to aging, Muslims can navigate these years with dignity, fostering personal well-being and marital harmony as an extension of their spiritual journey.

With this context in mind, take a moment to reflect on your feelings about your soulful sexual health as you enter middle adulthood. Let's explore how Islamic perspectives can guide us through this life stage with grace and purpose.

Reflection Questions

How has your understanding of intimacy and sexual health evolved as you've grown older, and in what ways has your spiritual maturity influenced this perspective?

_____
_____
_____

What societal or cultural narratives about aging and sexual health have influenced your views, and how can you align your approach to this stage of life with Islamic teachings and values?

_____

_____

What aspects of your sexual health and soulful maturity are you curious to explore further, and how might gaining this knowledge enhance your well-being and relationships?

_____

_____

Islam, the Soul, and Spiritual Maturity

In Islamic tradition, the age of 40 marks a profound milestone in spiritual maturity, signaling a pivotal stage of personal and soulful growth. Far from the societal narrative of decline after 40, Islam views this age as a culmination of experiences preparing us for a deeper connection with Allah and a clearer understanding of our soul's purpose.

The Quran highlights this in Surah Al-Ahqaf (Quran 46:15), describing 40 as the age of gratitude, repentance, and striving for righteous deeds, aligning one's life with Divine will. Prophet Muhammad (Peace and Blessings be Upon Him) also exemplifies this significance, receiving his first revelation at 40, underscoring readiness for greater responsibilities.

This period invites reflection on our life journey, acknowledging past missteps with compassion and embracing transformation through renewed devotion. It serves as a reminder of life's preciousness and our limited time to draw closer to Allah. With a softened heart and deeper purpose, we are encouraged to align our actions with our soul's journey, integrating spiritual maturity with physical, emotional, and sexual well-being.

Each soul's path is unique, and comparison holds no place in this Divine tapestry. Challenges in middle adulthood, including sexual health changes, are not shortcomings but opportunities for growth and connection to Allah. As we explore soulful approaches to sexual health in later stages of life, let the age of 40 be a reminder of our holistic existence, deepening our understanding of ourselves and nurturing the souls of those we love.

Life Beyond Linear Milestones: Soulful Contexts

Middle adulthood often brings significant transitions in career, relationships, and family dynamics, such as children leaving home. While societal and social media narratives emphasize rigid milestones for success and fulfillment, Islam teaches that life is a Divinely guided, non-linear journey where every experience—expected or unexpected—is an opportunity for growth.

Soulful sexual health evolves during this stage, encompassing emotional, spiritual, and relational dimensions beyond physical intimacy. It invites self-acceptance, deeper connections, and alignment with our values. Life transitions—whether career shifts, relationship changes, or empty-nest adjustments—challenge us to nurture both individual well-being and shared bonds.

- **Career Transitions:** Professional shifts can impact confidence and energy, requiring self-care and spiritual grounding to restore self-worth and foster emotional connection.
- **Relationship Changes:** Divorce, remarriage, having children or widowhood each bring unique challenges and opportunities for growth, highlighting the importance of vulnerability, respect, and healing.
- **Rediscovering Connection:** For couples whose children have left home, this phase offers renewal and deeper intimacy through patience, communication, and adaptation.

Amid these transitions, societal pressures around aging and linear milestones can create feelings of inadequacy. Social media often amplifies these narratives, but Islam reminds us to embrace our unique paths with faith, gratitude, and self-compassion, releasing comparisons.

Soulful sexual health aligns intimacy with values of love, mercy, and resilience, viewing it as a sacred connection that grows with life's changes. By deepening our connection with Allah, prioritizing well-being, and fostering open communication, we cultivate intimacy as an ongoing expression of spiritual growth and fulfillment, honoring every stage of life as an opportunity for renewal and soulful connection.

Using Figure 8.1, reflect on key aspects of your life between the ages of 15 (spiritual accountability) and 40 (spiritual maturity). On a piece of paper, note down spiritual milestones and learnings, focusing on inner awareness and development over societal milestones and expectations.

Soulful Sexual Health and Spiritual Maturity 189

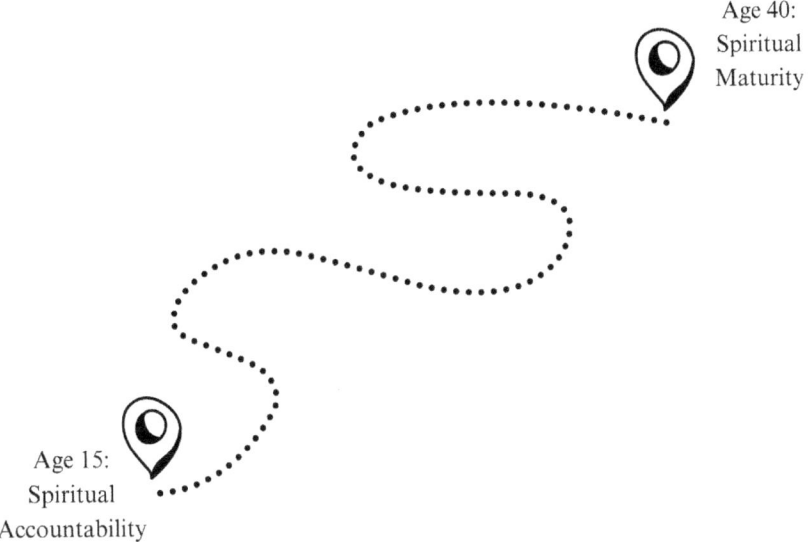

Figure 8.1 A reflection activity from spiritual accountability to spiritual maturity

Exploring Soulful Sexual Health Changes for Women: Context and Barriers

As Muslim women journey through middle adulthood, from age 40 onwards, understanding the changes in their sexual health can provide clarity, compassion, and support for this transformative phase of life. This period brings both physical and emotional shifts that can impact intimacy and self-connection and approaching it with soulful insight allows us to view these changes as part of our holistic health journey. It is a time marked by unique transitions, beginning with perimenopause (the phase leading up to menopause) and culminating in menopause itself—a period in which menstruation ceases, signaling the end of the reproductive years.

As Muslim women transition into perimenopause and menopause, they may encounter a range of unique challenges, myths, and misunderstandings shaped by cultural, social, and religious contexts. Let's learn about both the perimenopause and menopause in turn, defining what they are and how we can approach these changes soulfully.

Perimenopause: Navigating the First Stages of Hormonal Transition

Perimenopause, meaning "around menopause," is the transitional stage when hormonal changes, especially in estrogen and progesterone, begin.

Unlike menopause, which marks the cessation of menstruation, perimenopause is characterized by unpredictability. Typically starting in a woman's 40s, it brings symptoms like irregular periods, hot flashes, fatigue, and mood shifts, lasting several years and varying greatly between individuals. For some, these changes are mild, while for others, they may significantly impact daily life and emotional well-being (Mayo Clinic, n.d.-b).

This phase can be challenging, compounded by societal and cultural stigmas that discourage open discussion. Narratives emphasizing youthfulness often leave women feeling isolated or unprepared. For Muslim women, cultural misunderstandings around menstruation and aging may add further barriers, despite Islam's emphasis on caring for physical and emotional health.

However, perimenopause is also an opportunity for self-reflection and growth. Islam encourages viewing life transitions as part of Allah's design, calling for patience, gratitude, and self-care. By embracing this stage with awareness and intentionality, women can transform it into a period of empowerment, realigning with their values, nurturing their well-being, and deepening their spiritual connection.

Menopause: Soulful Contexts of Ongoing Changes

Menopause, marking 12 months without menstruation, typically occurs in the late 40s to early 50s and signifies the end of reproductive years. This hormonal shift brings physical changes such as hot flashes, sleep disturbances, and decreased vaginal lubrication, which can affect intimacy and self-perception. While natural, these changes often challenge a woman's confidence and sense of identity (Mayo Clinic, n.d.-a).

Societal and cultural narratives frequently frame menopause as a loss of youth and desirability, reinforcing stigmas and isolation. In some Muslim communities, taboos around aging, sexual health, and intimacy add further silence, with cultural misconceptions sometimes misinterpreting religious teachings about worship and family roles.

However, menopause is an opportunity to reimagine sexual health and intimacy as dynamic and evolving. Practical adjustments, like using lubricants during sexual intimacy or exploring lifestyle adjustments, paired with a focus on emotional and spiritual closeness, can empower women to navigate this stage with self-compassion. By embracing this transition, women and their spouses can deepen their connection, transcending societal expectations to foster a bond rooted in mutual understanding and support.

Additionally, by viewing aging positively, women can use the Islamic concept of spiritual maturity as a framework to approach menopause not as a loss but as an opportunity to realign with their values and deepen their connection to Allah. By embracing this stage of life with intentional self-care and openness, women can navigate its changes with dignity and resilience.

Seeking Medical and Professional Support: The Menopause Journey

Menopause is a personal and transformative journey, and professional support—both medical and holistic—can enhance well-being. **Regular check-ups** with a physician or gynecologist help monitor hormonal shifts, bone density, and cardiovascular health, while providing guidance on treatments like hormone replacement therapy (HRT) or non-hormonal options for managing symptoms such as hot flashes, vaginal dryness, and mood swings. Interim appointments can address emerging concerns and adjust care as needed.

Holistic approaches, including acupuncture, yoga, mindfulness, and herbal supplements, complement medical care by supporting the body, mind, and soul. Working with a functional nutritionist or naturopathic doctor can provide tailored dietary and lifestyle strategies to promote hormonal balance. Regular sessions with holistic practitioners further enhance physical and emotional well-being.

Seeking support reflects the values of self-accountability and compassion, aligning care for the body with its role as a trust from Allah. By combining medical and holistic resources, women can navigate menopause as an opportunity for growth, renewal, and soulful connection. For further insights, chapter 10 explores holistic and spiritual approaches to women's sexual health, offering practical tools for this life stage.

Table 8.1 summarizes key features of perimenopause and menopause. Reflection questions are provided to reflect on how this information relates to your soulful sexual health.

Table 8.1 A summary of the differences between the perimenopause and menopause stages

Aspect	Perimenopause	Menopause
Definition	Transition period leading up to menopause, usually starts in a woman's 40s but can begin earlier.	Defined as 12 consecutive months without a menstrual period, marking the end of reproductive years.
Duration	Can last from four to ten years.	Permanent; marks the end of menstruation.

(Continued)

Table 8.1 (Continued)

Aspect	Perimenopause	Menopause
Average Age	Begins around ages 40–45, but can vary.	Average age is 51, but varies globally.
Hormonal Changes	Fluctuations in estrogen and progesterone, with declining levels as the ovaries gradually reduce function.	Drastic decline in estrogen and progesterone as ovarian function ceases.
Menstrual Cycle	Irregular periods, heavier or lighter than usual, skipped cycles common.	No menstrual periods for 12 consecutive months.
Symptoms	Hot flashes, mood swings, sleep disturbances, irregular periods, breast tenderness, fatigue, anxiety, and PMS-like symptoms.	Hot flashes, night sweats, vaginal dryness, reduced libido, mood changes, sleep disturbances, weight gain.
Physical Changes	Skin dryness, possible increase in hair shedding, joint pain, weight changes.	Vaginal and skin dryness, thinning hair, reduced bone density, weight gain.
Impact on Bone Health	Gradual bone density decrease begins with declining estrogen levels.	Increased risk of osteoporosis due to low estrogen.
Impact on Cardiovascular Health	Increased risk as estrogen levels fluctuate and decrease.	Higher risk of heart disease post-menopause.
Fertility	Declines but pregnancy is still possible.	Fertility ceases; pregnancy is no longer possible.

Reflection Questions

What stands out to you from this summary of perimenopause and menopause?
_____
_____
_____

If you are currently in either stage or are approaching them, what questions do you have? What information would be helpful for you to know?
_____
_____
_____

What barriers or misconceptions about this soulful life transition have you come across?

_____

_____

_____

Soulful Navigation: Perimenopause and Menopause

Muslim women can embrace perimenopause and menopause as opportunities for personal and spiritual growth by cultivating self-compassion, seeking knowledge, and building supportive connections. The following are key approaches to navigate these transitions:

- **Embrace Divine Purpose:** Recognize these changes as part of Allah's design, reframing menopause as a sacred transition rather than something to fear. This perspective fosters peace and acceptance.
- **Seek Knowledge:** Educate yourself about physiological and emotional changes to demystify the experience and make informed self-care choices. Clarify Islamic teachings on menstruation, worship, and obligations to gain spiritual renewal and freedom.
- **Build Community:** Connect with other women to share experiences, wisdom, and encouragement. Safe spaces for open conversations help break isolation and nurture a sense of belonging.
- **Practice Self-Compassion:** Embrace kindness toward your body and heart. Acts of self-care—prayer, *dhikr* (remembrance of God), or rest—reinforce your worth, rooted in your relationship with Allah, beyond physical changes.
- **Reflect and Renew:** View this phase as a time to reassess priorities, refine goals, and deepen spiritual practices. Menopause can be a transformative journey of introspection and renewal.

By reframing menopause as a natural, meaningful stage of life, dismantling cultural taboos, and engaging in open dialogue, women can navigate this transition with confidence, honoring its beauty and the wisdom it brings.

Reflection Activity

Using Figure 8.2, reflect on and make a few notes about the support and information that would help you navigate your journey into and through middle adulthood.

194 *Soulful Sexual Health for Muslims*

Figure 8.2 Reflection activity exploring soulful support and resources for women navigating changes during their journey to spiritual maturity

Exploring Soulful Sexual Health Changes for Men: Context and Barriers

As Muslim men enter middle adulthood, they often face myths, societal pressures, and cultural barriers that shape their self-perception and relationships. A prevalent myth is that men remain unaffected by aging, leading to unrealistic expectations about physical and sexual health. Natural changes in strength, stamina, or libido can create feelings of inadequacy when compared to these ideals.

Societal pressures around career success and financial security further amplify stress. The expectation to "have it all figured out" as a provider often discourages men from sharing struggles or seeking support, fearing judgment or disappointment. This silence can lead to emotional strain, affecting personal well-being and relationships.

The belief that men don't need emotional or spiritual support reinforces a culture of isolation, where seeking help is viewed as weakness rather than a step toward holistic well-being. By addressing these myths and barriers, Muslim men can embrace this phase with self-compassion, open communication, and a renewed focus on spiritual and emotional growth, paving the way for resilience and self-discovery.

Soulful Foundations: Male Physical, Emotional, and Spiritual Changes

For men over 40, sexual health evolves through gradual physical, hormonal, emotional, and psychological shifts, collectively known as andropause or "male menopause." Unlike menopause, this transition lacks a definitive marker but is equally significant, inviting men to approach it with self-compassion and spiritual awareness.

Cultural constructs of masculinity—emphasizing strength and invulnerability—often discourage men from discussing vulnerabilities, fostering shame and isolation instead of emotional growth. These barriers hinder authentic connections with oneself and others.

A soulful perspective reframes these changes as opportunities for spiritual and emotional development. Just as the body evolves, so does the soul, offering a chance to deepen self-awareness, gratitude, and connection to Allah. Embracing these shifts aligns men with compassion, self-accountability, and their soul's journey.

Aging brings changes in cardiovascular health, hormonal balance, and physical vitality, profoundly affecting men's energy, emotional well-being, and intimacy. These shifts, if unaddressed, can lead to frustration, anxiety, and strain in relationships (Mount Carmel Health System, 2024). However, they also present opportunities for soulful growth and connection.

Cardiovascular Health: Cardiovascular health directly influences energy, endurance, and intimate relationships. As men age, reduced blood flow can lead to fatigue, lower stamina, and challenges in physical intimacy. These changes may result in feelings of frustration or inadequacy, potentially straining personal confidence and marital connections. Declining heart health can also lead to reduced engagement in physical activities, further exacerbating a sense of detachment from one's vitality.

Hormonal Changes: Declining testosterone levels, commonly associated with andropause, affect energy, sexual desire and mood. These hormonal shifts often challenge traditional notions of masculinity tied to physical vitality, leaving men feeling disoriented or inadequate. Changes in muscle mass, fat distribution, and emotional stability may also contribute to feelings of loss or reduced confidence in personal and relational dynamics.

Emotional and Psychological Well-Being: Middle adulthood often brings increased emotional introspection and vulnerability, which can clash with societal ideals of stoicism and invulnerability. Unacknowledged emotions, such as anxiety, irritability, or sadness, may manifest as strained relationships with family or spiritual detachment. Left unaddressed, these feelings can deepen isolation, impacting both mental health and the capacity for meaningful connections.

Sexual Performance: Men may experience slower arousal, reduced stamina, or challenges in sustaining intimacy, which can affect self-esteem and their sense of role within a partnership. These changes, often viewed through a lens of performance, can create emotional distance in relationships and prompt a reevaluation of one's identity and capacity for connection.

Physical Vitality and Appearance: Aging brings visible changes such as weight gain, reduced muscle tone, or graying hair, which can affect self-perception and feelings of worth. These shifts may lead men to avoid social interactions or spiritual responsibilities, fostering a sense of detachment from their community or spiritual path. Without reframing these changes, self-esteem may erode, and men may struggle to align their evolving identity with their roles within their family and community.

Cumulative Impact: These interconnected changes—physical, emotional, and relational—can influence how men perceive themselves and engage with the world. If left unaddressed, they may lead to a cycle of withdrawal, reduced confidence, and strained relationships. However, understanding these shifts as part of a natural progression can foster acceptance and help men navigate middle adulthood with clarity and purpose.

> **Reflection Questions**
>
> What stands out to you from this summary of sexual health changes for men?
> _____
> _____
> _____
>
> If you are currently in either stage or are approaching them, what questions do you have? What information would be helpful for you to know?
> _____
> _____
> _____
>
> What barriers or misconceptions about this soulful life transition have you come across?
> _____
> _____
> _____

Soulful Navigation for Men

Muslim men can navigate the sexual health changes of middle adulthood as an opportunity for self-discovery, connection, and spiritual growth. Embracing this stage with intention, resilience, and trust in Allah reframes it as a natural progression. Here are soulful ways to approach this journey.

Grounding in Faith and Gratitude: Recognize life changes as part of Allah's wisdom, fostering acceptance and gratitude. Acts of worship, *dhikr*, and reflection provide peace and resilience, helping men view challenges as opportunities for growth in patience and humility.

Embracing Self-Care as a Spiritual Responsibility: Caring for the body through exercise, nutrition, and sleep honors the trust Allah has given. Small, consistent habits, such as walking or eating mindfully, enhance vitality, confidence, and meaningful connections.

Cultivating Emotional Awareness and Connection: Acknowledge emotional shifts as natural and enriching. Sharing feelings with trusted friends, family, or counselors fosters emotional resilience and deepens connections with oneself and loved ones, supporting soulful intimacy.

Redefining Intimacy Beyond the Physical: Explore intimacy as a blend of companionship, understanding, and shared goals. Open communication with a spouse about needs and changes nurtures closeness. Focus on emotional intimacy through shared worship, listening, and thoughtful gestures to strengthen love and connection.

Seeking Knowledge and Wisdom: Learn about physical, emotional, and spiritual health to demystify changes and reduce frustration. Seeking support from healthcare providers, mentors, or counselors is a path to deeper self-understanding, not a sign of weakness.

Reflecting on Purpose and Legacy: Reassess life purpose and contributions, aligning daily actions with spiritual values. Focus on leaving a legacy through family, community service, or personal growth, cultivating fulfillment and spiritual growth.

By blending faith, self-care, emotional connection, and purpose, men can soulfully navigate this stage as a deeply enriching chapter. This journey brings them closer to Allah, strengthens relationships, and fosters spiritual maturity, honoring middle adulthood as a sacred step toward fulfillment and legacy.

Soulful Support for Men: Social Groups

Many men experience loneliness and a lack of close friendships as they age, negatively impacting mental, emotional, and physical health. Building meaningful social connections is not only a psychological necessity but also a soulful act rooted in the Islamic principles of brotherhood (*ukhuwwah*) and collective support.

Creating friendships with like-minded men fosters belonging, accountability, and shared growth, providing vital support for navigating the complexities of middle adulthood.

Soulful Ways to Build Connections

Spiritual Fellowship: Participate in *halaqas* (religious study circle) or prayer groups at the mosque to bond with others while deepening your connection to Allah.

Physical Activities: Join sports leagues, hiking groups, or walking clubs to combine physical health with camaraderie.

Mentorship and Volunteering: Mentor younger men or volunteer in your community to foster purpose and connection through acts of service.

Book Clubs or Discussion Groups: Engage in discussions on Islamic teachings or shared interests to build friendships through intellectual and spiritual exploration.

Community Events: Attend workshops, lectures, or social gatherings at local mosques or community centers to meet value-aligned individuals.

Close friendships nurture the soul, as emphasized by the Prophet Muhammad (Peace and Blessings be Upon Him): "A man follows the religion of his close friend; so each of you should be careful whom he takes as a friend" (Sunnah.com, n.d., Abu Dawud 4833). Meaningful relationships alleviate loneliness, improve mental health, and reduce risks like heart disease.

By fostering soulful connections, men can transform loneliness into growth, embrace middle adulthood as a time of wisdom and companionship, and enrich their spiritual journey.

Reflection Activity

Using Figure 8.3, reflect on the support and information that would help you navigate your journey into and through middle adulthood.

Figure 8.3 Reflection activity exploring soulful support and resources for men navigating changes during their journey to spiritual maturity

Soulfully Navigating Preventative Exams: An Overview for 40 and Beyond

Before we move forward to discussing soulful sexual health as a couple when we reach spiritual maturity, it is important to highlight the individual self-care we must all do as part of our Divine responsibility to our health and well-being. This includes medical check-ups to ensure we are happy and healthy as we age.

Preventative health exams are essential tools for identifying potential issues early, ensuring long-term health, and enhancing overall quality of life. These exams align with the Islamic value of caring for one's body as an *amanah* (trust) from Allah.

Preventative Health Checks: Women

Pelvic Exam and Pap Smear: Pelvic exams and Pap smears are essential for screening cervical cancer and assessing overall pelvic health. Women should typically undergo this exam every three to five years, depending on their medical history and doctor's recommendations. Early detection of abnormalities through these tests can prevent more serious conditions and ensure prompt treatment.

Mammogram: Mammograms detect early signs of breast cancer and are recommended every one to two years for women over 40, depending on individual risk factors. As one of the most common cancers in women, early detection through regular mammograms significantly improves treatment outcomes.

Bone Density Test: Screening for osteoporosis becomes crucial, especially after menopause. Bone density tests are typically recommended starting at age 50 or earlier if risk factors are present. Hormonal changes during menopause increase the likelihood of bone loss, and early screening helps prevent fractures.

Hormone Level Testing: Hormone level tests help monitor estrogen and progesterone levels, especially during perimenopause and menopause. These tests are often recommended if symptoms like hot flashes, fatigue, or mood swings arise. Understanding hormonal shifts can empower women to manage symptoms effectively.

Preventative Health Checks: Men

Prostate Exam: Prostate exams screen for prostate cancer and other prostate-related conditions. These exams are generally recommended starting at age 50, or earlier for those with a family history of prostate cancer. Prostate cancer is common in men over 50, and early detection greatly improves treatment outcomes.

Testosterone Level Testing: Monitoring testosterone levels is vital for assessing libido, energy, and mood. Men experiencing symptoms such as fatigue or changes in sexual health should consult their doctor about testing. Addressing hormonal imbalances can support overall well-being.

Sexually Transmitted Infection (STI) Screening: Like women, men in cases of remarriage or new intimate relationships should prioritize STI screenings. Discussing this with a healthcare provider helps ensure health for both the individual and their spouse.

Cardiovascular Health Screening: Assessing heart health, including cholesterol and blood pressure checks, is crucial for men over 40. Good cardiovascular health supports physical stamina and sexual function. Regular screenings can prevent major health issues.

Preventative Health Checks: Men and Women

Diabetes Screening: Diabetes screening is essential for identifying risk factors or managing existing conditions, especially for individuals who are overweight or have a family history of diabetes. Unmanaged diabetes can affect nerve function and blood flow, influencing intimacy and overall health.

Mental Health Support: Mood changes, anxiety, and depression may arise during midlife transitions. Mental health support (i.e. therapy, group therapy, support groups, etc.), when needed, provides support for emotional well-being, which is closely linked to physical health and intimacy.

Thyroid Function Test: Testing for hypothyroidism or hyperthyroidism is important, as these conditions can affect energy levels, mood, and sexual desire. Addressing thyroid health contributes to overall hormonal balance and vitality.

> **General Health Check-Up:** Annual general check-ups provide a comprehensive view of health, including weight, diet, and lifestyle factors. These assessments help address underlying issues that may influence sexual and overall well-being.

As we move forward to our next phase in life, it's essential that we continue viewing these preventative health measures as acts of worship, reinforcing their spiritual significance through the soulful care of our body. Additionally, taking proactive steps to maintain our sexual health is not only an individual responsibility, but also a means of nurturing marital intimacy and ensuring the strength needed to fulfill personal and communal roles.

In the final part of this chapter, we will explore how you can connect deeply with your spouse while reaching spiritual maturity, offering soulful guidance on how to navigate the next part of your life journey together as a couple.

Soulfully Navigating Changes with Marital Sexual Intimacy

As couples enter middle adulthood, marital intimacy often evolves due to hormonal changes like menopause or reduced testosterone, as well as life events such as children leaving home, career shifts, or caregiving responsibilities. These factors can influence sexual desire, energy, and comfort, requiring spouses to adapt how they connect and support each other.

During this stage, intimacy deepens beyond physical connection, becoming a space for emotional vulnerability, mutual respect, and spiritual bonding. Challenges may arise from societal or personal expectations of what intimacy "should" look like, leading to frustration or inadequacy. By reframing intimacy as dynamic and evolving, couples can embrace this phase with compassion and openness.

Intentionality is key to maintaining or reigniting intimacy. Through honest self-reflection and empathetic communication, couples can better understand and respond to each other's needs. This period offers a chance to redefine connection, aligning intimacy with shared values and goals. By approaching changes with patience and collaboration, couples can nurture a relationship that grows in depth and meaning. Here's a step-by-step guide to how you can do this.

Soulful Steps for Navigating Changes in Marital Intimacy

1. **Individual Reflection:** Each spouse begins by reflecting on their feelings and changes related to health, intimacy, and connection. Focus on how physical, emotional, or spiritual shifts have impacted well-being and the relationship. Consider emotions tied to these changes and personal hopes for fostering connection.
2. **Set Intentions:** After reflection, set intentions for the discussion, prioritizing open-mindedness, empathy, and respect. Commit to listening, understanding, and exploring ways to nurture intimacy together.
3. **Create a Comfortable Space:** Choose a calm, private setting for the conversation, free of distractions, where both partners feel safe and at ease.
4. **Share Personal Experiences:** Each spouse shares reflections using "I" statements, focusing on their experiences without assigning blame. This creates a compassionate space for honest expression and understanding.
5. **Listen and Validate:** Actively listen to each other's experiences with empathy and patience. Acknowledge emotions and perspectives, building trust and mutual understanding.
6. **Explore New Ways to Connect:** Discuss ways to nurture intimacy beyond physical connection, such as shared hobbies, quality time, acts of affection, or spiritual bonding. Explore what intimacy means and adapt approaches to deepen connection.
7. **Commit to Ongoing Communication:** Agree to revisit the conversation periodically, adjusting approaches as needs evolve. Emphasize the dynamic nature of marriage and support each other through ongoing dialogue, healthcare consultations, or counseling when needed.

By reflecting individually and engaging in open, empathetic communication, couples can embrace changes in marital intimacy as an opportunity for growth and deeper connection.

Reflection Activity

Using Figure 8.4, reflect as a couple on what can support marital sexual intimacy through spiritual maturity.

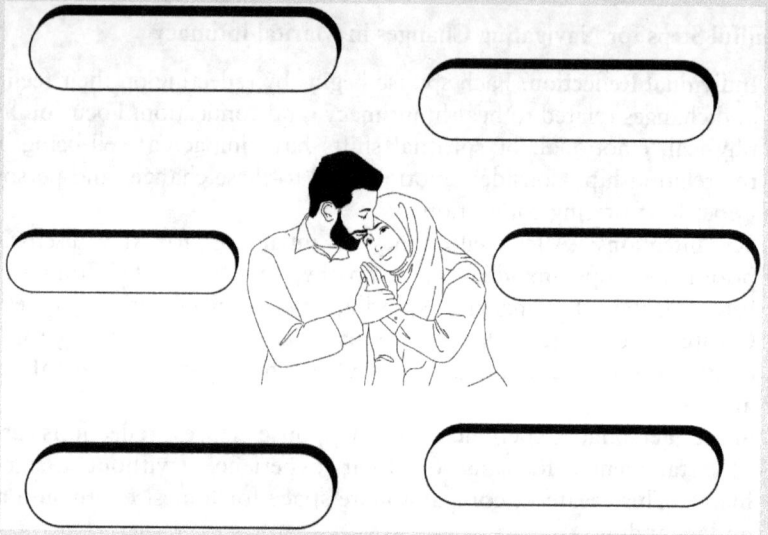

Figure 8.4 Reflection activity exploring soulful support and resources for married couples navigating changes during their journey to spiritual maturity

Enhancing Spiritual Intimacy Through Reminiscing

Muslim couples in middle adulthood can deepen their spiritual intimacy by reflecting on their shared journey through life, framed by Islamic values. Reminiscing about moments of praying together, performing acts of worship like *hajj* (major pilgrimage to Mecca) or *umrah* (minor pilgrimage to Mecca), or overcoming challenges with Allah's guidance can rekindle the spiritual foundation of their relationship. Celebrating milestones and expressing gratitude for each other's qualities not only reinforces their bond but also highlights the blessings that have strengthened their faith and connection over the years.

Engaging in meaningful activities can make reminiscing a soulful experience. Couples might create a memory journal to compile reflections and photos of significant spiritual experiences, revisit mosques or other special locations, or share moments of gratitude over tea or coffee, recounting Allah's blessings. Reflecting on Quranic verses that have shaped their marriage or composing a shared *dua* (personal supplication) expressing gratitude and hopes for the future can also be enriching. Reviewing old photos, planning a community project, or taking a reflective walk in nature are other ways to nurture connection and faith. These practices transform reminiscing into a deliberate act of spiritual growth, strengthening the marital bond while deepening their shared devotion to Allah.

Notes and Ideas

_____
_____
_____
_____

Summary

As individuals approach the age of 40 and beyond, spiritual maturity becomes a guiding context through which to understand and embrace changes in identity, relationships, and physical health. Hormonal shifts, menopause, or decreased libido, while challenging, can be reframed as opportunities for growth, deeper intimacy, and self-care. A spiritually mature perspective fosters patience, compassion, and a renewed focus on aligning these changes with the values of faith and holistic well-being.

This chapter has explored how societal and cultural narratives about aging can shape perceptions of sexual health and intimacy, sometimes creating barriers to self-acceptance or fulfillment. By grounding these experiences in an Islamic framework that values life's transitions as opportunities for growth, Muslims can approach this stage with resilience, self-awareness, and spiritual clarity.

Chapter 9 explores a spiritual legacy of soulful sexual health, setting the stage for the next two chapters, which delve deeper into sexual health challenges that Muslims may encounter, and soulful approaches for these issues. Chapter 10 focuses on challenges specific to women, while chapter 11 addresses those faced by men. Both chapters provide a compassionate prelude to seeking professional support, which will be explored in chapter 12. Together, these chapters offer a roadmap for addressing sexual health with wisdom, faith, and the resources needed to nurture holistic well-being throughout our soulful development, including middle adulthood and beyond.

Reflections and Action Items

_____
_____
_____
_____
_____
_____
_____
_____
_____
_____

Reference List

American Survey Center. (2021). *The state of American friendship: Change, challenges, and loss.* https://www.americansurveycenter.org/

Holt-Lunstad, J., Smith, T. B., & Layton, J. B. (2010). Social relationships and mortality risk: A meta-analytic review. *PLoS Medicine*, 7(7), e1000316. https://doi.org/10.1371/journal.pmed.1000316

Mayo Clinic. (n.d.-a). *Menopause—Symptoms and causes.* Retrieved January 4, 2025, from https://www.mayoclinic.org/diseases-conditions/menopause/symptoms-causes/syc-20353397

Mayo Clinic. (n.d.-b). *Perimenopause—Symptoms and causes.* Retrieved January 4, 2025, from https://www.mayoclinic.org/diseases-conditions/perimenopause/symptoms-causes/syc-20354666

Mount Carmel Health System. (2024, June 17). *Men's health and aging: Navigating midlife changes.* Retrieved from https://www.mountcarmelhealth.com/newsroom/blog-articles/mens-health-and-aging-navigating-midlife-changes

Sahih International. (1997). *The Quran: Arabic text with corresponding English meanings.* Abul-Qasim Publishing House.

Sunnah.com. (n.d.). *Sunan Abi Dawud 4833.* Retrieved January 5, 2025, from https://sunnah.com/abudawud:4833

9 A Spiritual Legacy of Soulful Sexual Health

This chapter emerged after writing chapter 8, where I came to realize how often sexual health in older adulthood is overlooked or dismissed entirely. Reflecting on the journey of the soul that this book has sought to illuminate, I understood the importance of addressing sexual health as a meaningful continuation of our spiritual legacy. I thought deeply about my relationships with older adults—my parents, in-laws, and the elders in my community. Through these interactions, I have witnessed a profound wellspring of wisdom, resilience, and lived experience. Yet, what stands out most is the soulful openness many elders possess to keep learning and growing. This openness isn't just inspiring; it's a reminder that the soul's journey is ongoing, evolving until our very last breath. Sexual health in older adulthood may look and feel different for everyone, shaped by physical changes, relational dynamics, and personal histories. Yet, it remains a vital dimension of holistic well-being. For older adults, reflecting on their spiritual legacy provides an opportunity to align their intimate relationships with the values of compassion, self-accountability, and connection to Allah. This chapter invites older adults to reflect on the legacy they wish to leave—one rooted in dignity, soulful connection, and an enduring commitment to living intentionally. By embracing this stage of life with openness and gratitude, we honor the remarkable journey of the soul and continue to align our actions with our ultimate purpose.

The Journey of the Soul

Birth — Spiritual Accountability — Spiritual Maturity — Spiritual Legacy — The Hereafter

DOI: 10.4324/9781032675862-10

Introduction

Society often undervalues older adults, framing aging as a decline. In contrast, Islam honors this stage as a time to share wisdom, deepen faith, and support the next generation. The Quran and Prophetic traditions emphasize respect for elders, viewing them as sources of guidance and advocates for intergenerational growth, including understanding the soulful nature of sexual health.

In older adulthood, physical, emotional, and sexual health evolve, bringing changes such as erectile dysfunction, vaginal dryness, or decreased desire. While challenging, these shifts are opportunities to cultivate creativity, adaptability, and deeper intimacy. Emotional transitions—like an empty nest, loss of a spouse, or shifting priorities—invite vulnerability and renewed connections, transforming these experiences into sacred paths for growth and gratitude.

Sexual health at this stage is also about spiritual legacy—reflecting on values, lessons, and practices that will resonate with future generations. Older adults can model faith-centered approaches to intimacy, support family members, and break stigmas surrounding intimacy and aging. Grounded in spiritual maturity, they offer compassionate guidance, integrating physical, emotional, and spiritual realities.

This chapter explores how older adulthood transforms sexual health into a soulful practice, honoring physical changes, fostering emotional bonds, and nurturing a spiritual legacy. It highlights the beauty of this stage, where reflecting on the past and embracing the future align with faith, purpose, and intergenerational connection.

Reflection Questions

How have your life experiences, values, and faith shaped the wisdom you can share with others in your family and community? What aspects of your journey do you feel are most meaningful to pass on?

_____

_____

_____

In what ways can you reframe the physical, emotional, or relational changes of older adulthood as sacred opportunities for growth, gratitude, and deeper connection to the Divine?

_____

_____

_____

A Spiritual Legacy of Soulful Sexual Health 209

How does your current approach to sexual health align with your spiritual goals and legacy? What steps can you take to embody a soulful perspective that nurtures both yourself and those around you?

_____

_____

_____

Soulful Reflections on Older Adulthood: A Sacred Stage of Life

In Islam, older adulthood is revered as a time of dignity, wisdom, and spiritual depth. The Quran and Prophetic traditions affirm this stage as an opportunity for reflection, growth, and meaningful contributions to family and community. Aging, including changes in physical and sexual health, is framed as a natural part of Allah's Divine design, inviting gratitude, patience, and deeper intimacy.

The Quran highlights life's progression as a sign of Allah's wisdom: "It is Allah who created you in weakness, then made strength after weakness, then made weakness and gray hair after strength. He creates what He wills, and He is the All-Knowing, the All-Powerful" (Quran 30:54). This verse reminds older adults to embrace transitions with humility, recognizing these changes as sacred opportunities for spiritual and relational growth.

The Journey Toward the Next World

Older adulthood is not only a time to reflect on the past but also to prepare for the eternal Hereafter. The Quran reminds believers: "And We have certainly created man, and We know what his soul whispers to him, and We are closer to him than [his] jugular vein" (Quran 50:16). This verse underscores the nearness of Allah, especially as one contemplates life's finite nature. As the soul approaches the culmination of its earthly journey, older adults are uniquely positioned to focus on aligning their actions and priorities with the goal of closeness to Allah.

Islamic scholars such as Imam al-Haddad, in *The Five Lives of Man*, emphasize that life in this world (*dunya*) is but one stage in the soul's journey, which begins in the preconception stage ('Alam al-Arwah) and continues through stages like the Intermediate Realm (Barzakh) and ultimately the Hereafter (Dar al-Akhirah). Older adulthood becomes a sacred phase of preparation, shifting focus from outward achievements to inner reflection and spiritual readiness.

Integrating Soulful Sexual Health and Spiritual Legacy

Sexual health in older adulthood becomes part of this preparation. By aligning intimacy and relationships with faith, older adults nurture the love and mercy Allah has placed between spouses. These experiences contribute to refining the soul, cultivating virtues like patience, gratitude, and compassion. The Prophetic saying "The best of you are those who live long and excel in their deeds" (Sunnah.com, n.d., Tirmidhi 2330) encourages older adults to excel not only in worship but also in modeling healthy, faith-centered relationships for younger generations.

This stage also invites reflection on legacy: What values, lessons, and practices will resonate beyond oneself? Older adults are uniquely equipped to guide families and communities by sharing their wisdom on integrating physical, emotional, and spiritual aspects of life. By embodying a soulful perspective, they demonstrate how challenges in aging, including physical and relational transitions, can become sacred opportunities for growth and resilience.

Using Figure 9.1, take a moment to reflect on your soulful sexual health journey thus far, centering compassion as you note down key moments in your life.

Figure 9.1 A reflection on your soulful sexual health legacy into older adulthood

Embracing the Eternal Journey

The challenges of aging—physical changes, emotional shifts, and transitions in relationships—are sacred reminders of the fleeting nature of this world and the need to prioritize what truly matters. Soulful sexual health and meaningful connections become part of the broader journey of returning to Allah, preparing the soul for the Hereafter with intention, faith, and hope.

Older adulthood, enriched by wisdom and spiritual maturity, is not merely a time of decline but a profound stage of life that integrates past experiences with the promise of the eternal journey ahead. By embracing this sacred phase with humility and gratitude, older adults can leave a legacy of faith, love, and resilience for future generations.

Soulful Sexual Health Contexts for Oneself

Older adults often face the misconception that intimacy and sexual health are irrelevant or inappropriate in later life. In reality, sexual health—encompassing physical, emotional, and spiritual dimensions—remains a meaningful part of older adulthood, offering opportunities for connection, growth, and fulfillment.

Physical Changes: Aging brings physical changes like reduced hormone levels, such as lower estrogen in women post-menopause, leading to vaginal dryness and discomfort, or decreased testosterone in men, contributing to lower desire and erectile dysfunction. Chronic health conditions, such as diabetes or cardiovascular disease, and side effects from medications can further impact sexual function, requiring adjustments to maintain comfort and connection.

Emotional Changes: Emotional shifts, including grief over a spouse's loss, caregiving roles, or retirement, influence intimacy and closeness. Increased anxiety or depression from health struggles or life transitions may further affect sexual health, necessitating intentional effort to maintain emotional bonds.

Sexual Changes: Shifts in desire, whether decreased libido or changes in intensity, require couples to renegotiate expressions of intimacy. These adaptations often shift focus from performance to emotional and spiritual connection, fostering deeper bonds.

A Soulful Perspective

When approached through a soulful lens, these transitions invite older adults to embrace growth and resilience. Seeking professional support, such as from healthcare providers or therapists specializing in sexual health, empowers individuals to address challenges with confidence and dignity. Islam's teachings frame physical closeness as an act of worship, fostering love and mercy between spouses, regardless of the form intimacy takes: "And among His signs is that He created for you mates from among yourselves, that you may dwell in tranquility with them, and He has put love and mercy between your hearts" (Quran 30:21).

In addition, meaningful connections with others in similar stages of life—through faith-based gatherings or discussion groups—offers mutual support, understanding, and brave spaces to explore soulful sexual health. By honoring their bodies, adapting with self-compassion, and remaining rooted in faith, older adults can integrate physical, emotional, and spiritual dimensions of intimacy, enriching their relationships and spiritual journey.

For Others: Soulful Wisdom and Presence

Older adults play a vital role in fostering connection and purpose, significantly contributing to their emotional, social, and spiritual well-being. Research highlights that strong social ties and spiritual engagement enhance longevity and quality of life, providing resilience and a sense of belonging (Holt-Lunstad et al., 2010; Koenig, 2012). This stage offers older adults the opportunity to channel their wisdom into purposeful contributions to their families and communities.

By sharing insights and serving as role models, they fulfill the soulful purpose of passing on lessons that extend beyond personal experiences. This might include guiding younger generations through milestones like marriage or parenthood, addressing struggles such as social media pressures, or offering faith-centered reassurance. These contributions sustain a sense of purpose and legacy while enriching relationships, reflecting the Islamic value of intentional living and service as worship.

Sharing guidance doesn't require oversharing personal details. Older adults can focus on lessons from their soulful journeys, emphasizing spiritual and emotional growth. For example, they might share how they cultivated patience during transitions or strengthened their relationship with Allah through vulnerability. These modest acts of sharing provide reassurance and encouragement, nurturing the next generation while reinforcing their own sense of purpose.

Balancing personal growth with acts of service is key. Older adults can mentor newlyweds, guide young adults on aligning sexual health with faith, or contribute to community discussions on intimacy and aging. These efforts align personal soulful focus with outward care, creating a legacy of wisdom and compassion that transcends their immediate circles and fulfills the Islamic principle of service as worship.

> **A Legacy of Compassion: Soulful Conversation Ideas with Younger Muslims**
>
> Older adults have a unique role in fostering intergenerational bonds, sharing wisdom, and helping younger Muslims navigate the integration of faith, sexual health, and intimacy. Through meaningful dialogue, they can inspire confidence, compassion, and a deeper understanding of how Islamic values shape these aspects of life.
>
> To spark such conversations, older adults might reflect on their own journey by exploring questions like: *What key lessons have I learned about balancing faith and sexual health? How has my understanding of intimacy and spirituality evolved over time? What values or practices do I hope to pass on? How do I maintain a soulful connection to my body and mind as I age?*
>
> For younger Muslims, discussions could center around their soulful journey, such as: *How do your spiritual values shape your understanding of sexual health and its connection to faith? What challenges do you encounter—whether from society, culture, or technology—that make it difficult to nurture a soulful connection with your body and faith? What kind of guidance or support from older Muslims would feel most meaningful and non-judgmental as you navigate these experiences?*
>
> By approaching these conversations with curiosity and compassion, older adults can create a supportive, judgment-free space for younger Muslims to share their perspectives. This exchange fosters a legacy of wisdom, faith, and mutual growth, ensuring that soulful guidance continues to inspire future generations.

Ultimately, older adulthood offers the opportunity to integrate personal experiences with communal contributions, modeling how soulful sexual health is not only an individual practice but also a gift to share with others. This stage of life becomes a powerful testament to the interconnectedness of social and spiritual engagement, with older adults leaving behind a legacy of spiritual resilience and holistic well-being.

Given this crucial context of balancing self and others with regards to your ongoing soulful sexual health journey, let's take a few moments to reflect on what's standing out to you before we explore practical methods to share your wisdom.

Sharing Soulful Sexual Health Wisdom

Older adults have a wealth of wisdom and life experience that can inspire and guide others in their journeys, particularly in the realm of soulful sexual health. Sharing this wisdom can take many forms, depending on personal interests, skills, and opportunities. The first step is for you to reflect on what you hope to impart and share with others, using the following reflection questions as a guide:

Reflection Questions

What values and lessons about soulful sexual health have shaped my journey? Which parts of my life stand out to me the most?

_____
_____
_____

How can I pass on these values to the next generation in ways that align with Islamic soulful faith traditions and wisdom?

_____
_____
_____

In what ways can I support others (family, friends, community) in addressing sexual health with a compassionate, soul-centered focus?

_____
_____
_____

With these reflections in mind, the following practical ideas and creative activities offer ways for older adults to pass on their insights, foster meaningful connections, and contribute to the well-being of their family and communities.

Written Contributions: Older adults can reflect on their life experiences and insights by writing journals, memoirs, or books on topics like intimacy and faith. Personal letters to younger family members offer heartfelt guidance and advice for navigating life transitions.

In-Person Engagements: Organizing or participating in *halaqas* (religious study circles), mentorship programs, and workshops allows older adults to share their wisdom and foster meaningful relationships. These gatherings create supportive spaces to discuss faith-centered relationships and soulful sexual health.

Art-Based Activities: Creative storytelling, photo projects, and multimedia presentations provide unique ways to share lessons on love, intimacy, and growth. These artistic expressions inspire meaningful conversations and connections within families and communities.

Digital Outreach: Using blogs, social media, or podcasts, older adults can engage a wider audience by sharing insights on soulful intimacy and aging from an Islamic perspective. Online groups and webinars create safe spaces for dialogue and learning.

Intergenerational Activities: Family storytelling nights and collaborative projects, such as creating scrapbooks or life skills mentoring, strengthen bonds across generations. These activities emphasize the values of connection, gratitude, and faith.

Community Leadership: Advocating for soulful sexual health awareness and creating educational materials helps older adults support their communities. Training programs empower others to take on mentorship and leadership roles, spreading their wisdom and compassion.

By engaging in these and other activities, older adults can contribute to the spiritual and relational growth of their families and communities while reinforcing their own sense of purpose and legacy. These efforts exemplify how soulful sexual health extends beyond the self, becoming a powerful tool for fostering connection, understanding, and holistic well-being across generations.

Use Table 9.1 to identify which activities and approaches resonate the most with your soul. You may want to make note of people, organizations, and resources that can support your soulful imparting of wisdom. As a reminder, this book can also serve as a resource for your soulful sharing journey.

Table 9.1 Soulful action planning steps for sharing your spiritual legacy with others

Soulful Action Planning Step	Notes
Activities and Approaches that Resonate with My Soul	
People I Want to Support or Mentor	
Organizations or Communities I Can Engage With	
Resources (Books, Courses, Tools) to Support My Journey	
Next Steps I Can Take to Share My Wisdom Soulfully	

Summary

Older adulthood is a stage of life marked by grace, reflection, and connection, offering a unique opportunity to embrace transitions and changes with patience and gratitude. Rather than viewing this stage as a time of decline, Islam encourages seeing it as a time of renewal—a chance to align every aspect of life, including sexual health, with spiritual values and a soulful sense of purpose. It is also a sacred period to reconnect with the eternal journey of the soul, reflecting on life's transitions as preparation for the Hereafter. By embracing physical, emotional, and relational changes, older adults can align their actions and intentions with their ultimate purpose: seeking closeness to Allah, nurturing a legacy of faith and resilience, and fostering spiritual growth and hope for the eternal promise of the Hereafter.

As this chapter has explored, navigating physical, emotional, and sexual health changes in older adulthood provides an opportunity to deepen one's relationship with Allah, foster intimacy as an act of worship, and approach challenges with creativity and adaptability. This stage also presents a profound responsibility: to impart wisdom and support to others. By sharing life lessons with family and community, older adults can become stewards of soulful sexual health, modeling the integration of faith, emotional resilience, and holistic well-being.

Readers are encouraged to fully embrace their role as nurturers and mentors, contributing their insights and experiences in ways that reflect the beauty of their faith. Whether through mentoring, writing, leading discussions, or simply being present for meaningful conversations, older adults have the power to leave behind a legacy of spiritual resilience and compassionate guidance. By doing so, they enrich not only their own lives but also the lives of those around them, fostering a culture of soulful sexual health rooted in the timeless values of Islam.

Reflections and Action Items

_____
_____
_____
_____
_____

Reference List

Fiske, A., Wetherell, J. L., & Gatz, M. (2009). Depression in older adults. *Annual Review of Clinical Psychology, 5*(1), 363–389.

Ghazali, A., al- (1989). *Ihya' Ulum al-Din [The revival of the religious sciences]* (N. Haqq trans.). Islamic Texts Society.

Holt-Lunstad, J., Smith, T. B., & Layton, J. B. (2010). Social relationships and mortality risk: A meta-analytic review. *PLOS Medicine, 7*(7), e1000316.

Koenig, H. G. (2012). Religion, spirituality, and health: The research and clinical implications. *ISRN Psychiatry, 2012*, Article 278730. https://doi.org/10.5402/2012/278730

McCabe, M. P., & Althof, S. E. (2014). A systematic review of the psychosocial outcomes associated with erectile dysfunction: Does the impact of erectile dysfunction extend beyond a man's inability to have sex? *The Journal of Sexual Medicine, 11*(2), 347–363.

Santoro, N., Epperson, C. N., & Mathews, S. B. (2015). Menopausal symptoms and their management. *Endocrinology and Metabolism Clinics of North America, 44*(3), 497–515.

Sahih International. (1997). *The Quran: Arabic text with corresponding English meanings*. Abul-Qasim Publishing House.

Sunnah.com. (n.d.). Jami' at-Tirmidhi 2330. Retrieved January 5, 2025, from https://sunnah.com/tirmidhi:2330

Trompeter, S. E., Bettencourt, R., & Barrett-Connor, E. (2012). Sexual activity and satisfaction in healthy community-dwelling older women and men: The Rancho Bernardo Study. *Journal of the American Geriatrics Society, 60*(2), 240–246.

10 The Soulful Navigation of Female Sexual Health Challenges

Sexual health challenges often carry an immense and deeply personal weight—especially for women. From my own journey, both personal and professional, I've come to see that the ways we are conditioned to understand and navigate these challenges often fall short of the soulful compassion and guidance we truly need. Many of these pressures—marrying at a certain age, having (multiple) children, hiding struggles behind a veneer of strength—don't stem from Islam. Instead, they are rooted in colonized and cultural misunderstandings of what it means to be a woman and a Muslim. I've witnessed, time and time again, how the lack of compassionate, knowledgeable, and brave spaces for women to address their sexual health challenges stifles healing and growth. It leaves us questioning our worth and our connection to Allah. If I could speak to my younger self, I would tell her this: "Sexual health challenges—like physical, mental, and spiritual health struggles—are a normal part of life. They are not your fault, nor are they a reflection of Allah's love for you. They do not diminish your femininity, your worth as a Muslim, or your ability to live a fulfilling and soulful life. Sexual health challenges will arise, and they are meant to be soulfully navigated as part of your spiritual journey." I hope this chapter serves as a reminder of this truth and offers you the tools and perspectives to embrace your challenges with courage, faith, and compassion.

The Journey of the Soul

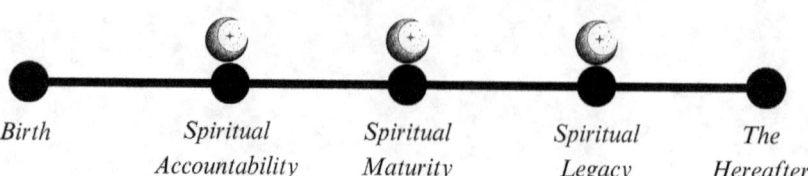

Birth   Spiritual Accountability   Spiritual Maturity   Spiritual Legacy   The Hereafter

DOI: 10.4324/9781032675862-11

The Soulful Navigation of Female Sexual Health Challenges

Introduction

Soulful sexual health spans the entirety of our lives, yet for many Muslims, access to holistic education on this topic is limited. Often, we confront our sexual health only when faced with challenges, viewing struggles as punishments or reflections of sin rather than integral aspects of the soul's journey. For women especially, these difficulties are frequently internalized, leading to feelings of shame or inadequacy. Whether healing from past trauma, navigating guilt tied to pornography use, struggling with intimacy in marriage, or feeling unable to meet the expectations of being a "good" Muslim spouse, these experiences can create profound disconnection—from one's body, partner, and even Allah.

This chapter reframes these struggles as opportunities for spiritual growth rather than failures. By exploring common sexual health challenges faced by women and layering them with Islamic reflections, this chapter offers compassionate guidance and soulful tools to process and address these issues in ways that honor both body and spirit.

The goal is to empower you to approach your sexual health with confidence, compassion, and self-accountability, reminding you that even in moments of struggle, your body is a sacred trust from Allah—deserving of care, understanding, and connection.

> **Reflection Questions**
>
> Gently bring your awareness to any sexual health challenges you've experienced. How have you made sense of these issues through your soulful identity?
>
> _____
> _____
> _____
>
> Which sexual health challenges are you interested to learn more about?
>
> _____
> _____
> _____

Soulful Contexts of Female Sexual Health Challenges

For Muslims, the journey to grow closer to Allah often involves making sense of life's trials through faith. However, women facing sexual health challenges—such as pain during intimacy, hormonal imbalances, or fertility issues—may internalize these struggles as punishments or inadequacies, distorted by shame-based perspectives. This lens not only burdens the heart but also creates barriers to healing and spiritual growth.

Adopting a soulful perspective rooted in compassion and self-accountability reframes these challenges as opportunities for growth and connection with Allah. Sexual health struggles are not failures but calls to care for the body as a trust from Allah, guiding us toward spiritual and physical alignment. Trials, temporary in nature, invite us to honor our bodies and nurture our souls, embracing al-Ghazali's reminder that understanding the soul leads to understanding Allah.

Each woman's journey is unique, reflecting personal tests from Allah that foster resilience and growth. Addressing challenges with compassionate self-accountability shifts the focus from blame to healing, integrating physical, emotional, and spiritual care. Trauma, which often impacts sexual health, must also be approached with gentleness and holistic healing.

As we move forward, the next section explores the connection between trauma and sexual health, offering soulful approaches to healing while encouraging self-compassion and deeper faith.

Myth Busting: Muslims and Sexual Health Issues

Muslims, like anyone else, may experience trauma and sexual health challenges, often seeking meaning through such questions as, "Why did this happen to me?" or "Am I being punished?" Misunderstandings rooted in shame-based teachings or incomplete knowledge can complicate the healing process, making it harder to approach these struggles with self-compassion and spiritual purpose.

Myth: God is punishing me for my sins through this sexual health issue

Fact: Allah's trials are not punishments but opportunities for growth and connection with Him. Sexual health struggles invite self-care and spiritual refinement, as part of the soul's natural journey.

Myth: Being a victim of sexual violence reflects my morality as a Muslim

Fact: Experiencing harm is never a reflection of one's worth or faith. Allah is Just and honors the resilience of victims while holding perpetrators accountable. Healing is an act of courage and self-compassion. Victim blaming, which unfairly shifts responsibility for harm onto the victim, contradicts the soulful value of compassionate self-accountability, which calls for those who harm others to take ownership of their actions and seek alignment with Allah's justice and mercy.

Myth: My sexual health struggles define my womanhood and femininity

Fact: A woman's worth is not tied to her physical health or societal standards. Our bodies are a trust from Allah, and caring for them reflects submission to His will. Our *ruh*, the essence of our soul, remains incorruptible and central to our identity.

Sexual Trauma

Noor, a Muslim woman in her late 20s, is engaged to Bilal, whom she has been getting to know for the past six months. As their conversations about marriage deepen, the topic of sexual intimacy begins to surface more frequently. However, instead of feeling excited, Noor finds herself becoming increasingly anxious. She often steers the conversation away from intimacy, overwhelmed by a sense of panic. This distress is rooted in memories of being touched inappropriately by an extended family member during her childhood. As these conversations trigger her trauma, Noor feels confused and unsure where to begin.

It has been rare for me to not meet a Muslim woman who isn't living with some form of sexual trauma. And like many other religious and non-religious communities, sexual trauma is unfortunately far too prevalent. Given that many of us as women don't have ongoing compassionate and nuanced spaces to learn about our soulful sexual health, it may result in us not understanding or realizing that we've experienced trauma until later in life. Just as the narrative about Noor shared, it may be when we visit the OB/GYN, talk about sexual intimacy with our future spouse, or engage in marital sexual intimacy that we realize we're struggling and have experienced trauma.

Compassion is crucial to extend to ourselves when we first realize that we've experienced trauma and move forward through our healing journey. As we explored in the previous section, it is common for Muslims to internalize their trauma as reflective of God's love for them, or how successful of a Muslim they are. And with trauma often comes shame, which can further disconnect us from our soulful sexual health. As we notice and bring awareness to our sexual trauma and resulting struggles, it is paramount that we see our soul as being on an ongoing journey of healing and spiritual development, rather than being a "broken problem" that needs to be fixed.

What Is Sexual Trauma?

Before we explore how sexual trauma can impact our soulful sexual health, it is important to give ourselves more language and foundational information about it. Sexual trauma is often thought to be the sexual events that happened to us that were unwanted, out of our control, and without our consent. However, when we look more closely at the term "sexual trauma," we see that it has a different meaning. **Trauma itself refers to the psychological, spiritual, and physiological internal responses that we feel because of what we've experienced.** Sexual violence is the umbrella term used to describe various forms of unwanted sexual acts that may have happened to us. The primary forms of sexual violence that contribute to trauma include:

Sexual Harassment: Sexual harassment involves unwelcome sexual advances, requests for sexual favors, and other verbal or physical conduct of a sexual nature. For Muslim women, harassment might have occurred during puberty while at school or even on marriage apps when seeking a spouse, through receiving unwanted sexual messages or requests.

Sexual Abuse: Sexual abuse refers to non-consensual sexual activity, often within relationships of trust or authority, such as child sexual abuse or abuse in premarital relationships. This form of abuse can be ongoing and involve manipulation, grooming, and exploitation, profoundly impacting a victim's psychological and emotional well-being. Many Muslim women may have experienced sexual abuse during childhood by an adult known to them, such as an extended family member, or by a religious leader or teacher in the community.

Sexual Assault: Sexual assault includes any non-consensual sexual act, such as rape, forced sexual acts, or unwanted sexual contact. Given the prevalence of sexual assault in society, Muslim women may have experienced this while getting to know a potential spouse or within marriage, where sexual intimacy becomes a tool for control.

Sexual trauma, therefore, is the result of these types of sexual violence that cause lasting emotional, spiritual, and sexual impacts. In the aftermath of trauma, the body's natural stress response system is activated when something around or within us triggers our past trauma, causing the brain's nervous system to activate a "fight, flight, freeze, or fawn" response. This releases stress hormones like adrenaline and cortisol, preparing the body to deal with perceived danger. Ultimately, the brain has not learned that we are safe in the present moment, so it continues to scan for perceived dangers and activates the brain's protective trauma response.

The impacts of sexual trauma are ultimately multifaceted and deeply complex. To gain compassionate awareness of how trauma manifests in the present moment, it can be helpful to explore the four common trauma responses. Most women will experience a blend of trauma responses, and there are often one or two which predominantly appear.

- **Fight Response:** The fight response involves confronting perceived threats through anger, aggression, or a need for control. This can manifest as restlessness or harmful behaviors toward others when unrecognized. In relationships, it may look like pushing a spouse away or becoming confrontational when sensitive topics arise.
- **Flight Response:** The flight response seeks to escape danger, often through overworking, perfectionism, or avoidance. It can manifest as anxiety or a compulsion to avoid conflict. In relationships, this may involve deflecting intimacy or avoiding difficult conversations perceived as threatening.
- **Freeze Response:** The freeze response leads to paralysis, dissociation, or withdrawal in the face of perceived threats. Individuals may feel numb or struggle to engage socially or emotionally. In marriage, it may appear as emotional absence or an inability to respond during challenging interactions.
- **Fawn Response:** The fawn response centers on people-pleasing to secure safety and avoid conflict. This often results in neglecting personal needs, codependency, and weak boundaries. Assertiveness may be avoided, with uncomfortable discussions labeled as confrontations to be evaded (Walker, 2013).

Take a moment to reflect on this information and consider how your trauma may be manifesting in your current life. Think back to a few situations when you felt triggered from your trauma and compassionately explore what was felt in your body and how you responded as a result.

_____
_____
_____
_____
_____
_____

224 Soulful Sexual Health for Muslims

Impacts of Sexual Trauma

Understanding trauma, including sexual trauma, through an Islamic soulful lens requires a compassionate approach that acknowledges its profound emotional, physical, spiritual, and sexual impacts. Trauma is not a punishment from Allah but a test that invites healing and a deeper connection with Him. While each person's experience is unique, many Muslim women face challenges navigating the complexities of their healing journey. These impacts are not reflections of one's faith or worth but natural responses to the trauma endured, underscoring the importance of approaching oneself with compassion.

Trauma, including sexual trauma, leaves wounds on the heart, as discussed in chapter 2. These wounds cause the soul to constrict for protection and operate in survival mode, disrupting a woman's ability to engage with the world in a healthy, balanced way. This constriction, while a natural response, can hinder the soul's ability to connect deeply with Allah and others. Feelings of guilt, shame, and spiritual disconnection often weigh heavily on the heart, mind, and body. Refer to Figure 10.1 for a visual representation of how trauma affects the heart and soul, which may serve as an aid for the upcoming reflection questions.

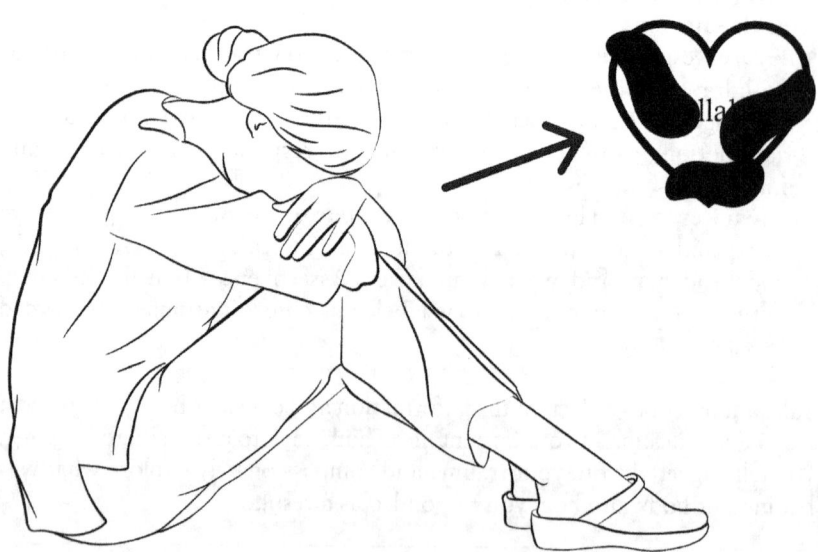

Figure 10.1 A visual representation of sexual trauma causing wounds on the heart and the soul to constrict in protection

To foster deeper insight and compassion, Table 10.1 outlines the emotional, physical, spiritual, and sexual health impacts of trauma, highlighting how it shapes overall well-being. Healing from an Islamic perspective involves nurturing the soul alongside the body and mind. Using Table 10.1, take a moment to reflect on how trauma may be manifesting in your life and note areas for care and growth as you pursue healing.

Table 10.1 A summary of the impacts of trauma on emotional, physical, spiritual, and sexual health

Physical Health Impacts	Emotional Health Impacts
• Chronic pain (e.g. headaches, back pain) • Sleep disturbances such as insomnia or nightmares • Gastrointestinal issues like stomach pain or nausea • Fatigue or chronic exhaustion • Heightened startle response • Increased susceptibility to illness due to stress • Physical symptoms without a clear medical cause (somatization)	• Anxiety and/or panic attacks • Persistent sadness • Guilt • Shame and self-blame • Difficulty trusting others • Emotional numbness • Challenges regulating emotions such as anger or frustration • Difficulty forming or maintaining relationships • Fear of rejection or abandonment
Spiritual Health Impacts	**Sexual Health Impacts**
• Questioning one's faith or relationship with Allah • Feelings of being spiritually "unclean" or distant from God • Difficulty engaging in worship (e.g. prayer or Quran recitation) • Fear of punishment or believing trauma is a punishment from Allah • Loss of spiritual connection or disconnection from the religious community • Internal conflict between religious teachings and the trauma experience • Difficulty finding peace or solace in spiritual practices	• Fear of or aversion to sexual intimacy • Loss of interest in sexual activity • Pain during intercourse (dyspareunia) • Difficulty experiencing pleasure or arousal • Dissociation during intimacy • Hypervigilance or feeling unsafe in intimate settings • Challenges with physical closeness or vulnerability with a spouse • Avoidance of sexual or reproductive wellness visits • Intrusive thoughts or flashbacks during sexual activity • Struggles with body image or self-confidence in intimate moments

Reflections

_____
_____
_____

Soulful Reflections on Sexual Trauma

Healing from sexual trauma is a multifaceted journey requiring a holistic approach that honors the mind, body, and soul. Chapter 1 introduced the Islamic understanding of the soul as a multidimensional entity—*nafs* (behaviors), *qalb* (heart), *aql* (intellect), and *ruh* (spirit)—each playing an essential role in our health and well-being. From this perspective, healing draws on Allah's mercy and guidance, reminding us that restoration is possible through His presence in our struggles. Trauma disrupts the harmony of these interconnected aspects, and healing requires addressing emotional, physical, spiritual, and sexual well-being to foster self-compassion and a closer connection to Allah.

Healing is not about "getting over" trauma but about recognizing its layers within the soul and gradually expanding our capacity to navigate triggers and difficult emotions. Trauma responses are stuck reactions within the *nafs* and *qalb*, creating tension that disconnects the *ruh* from a state of peace. Avoiding these responses can hinder the healing process, as unprocessed pain weighs heavily on the soul's journey. Soulful healing involves feeling and processing these responses in the presence of God, allowing the body and soul to release pain, restore balance, and nurture alignment with one's spiritual purpose. By anchoring the healing process in the holistic understanding of the soul, individuals can find resilience and renewal through Allah's mercy.

Examples of Healing Approaches Across Dimensions:

- **Emotional Health:** Practices like journaling to process feelings, engaging in somatic experiencing therapy to process trauma responses, or practicing compassionate presence with difficult emotions rather than analyzing them.
- **Physical Health:** Incorporating somatic therapies like yoga or deep breathing exercises to release tension and reconnect with the body; regular physical activity for grounding and restoring balance.
- **Spiritual Health:** Deepening connection with Allah through consistent prayer, Quran recitation, or engaging in acts of charity to restore faith and purpose.
- **Sexual Health:** Gradual reengagement with intimacy through open communication with a spouse, guided exercises for body awareness, or working with a sex therapist specializing in trauma recovery.

The Soulful Navigation of Female Sexual Health Challenges 227

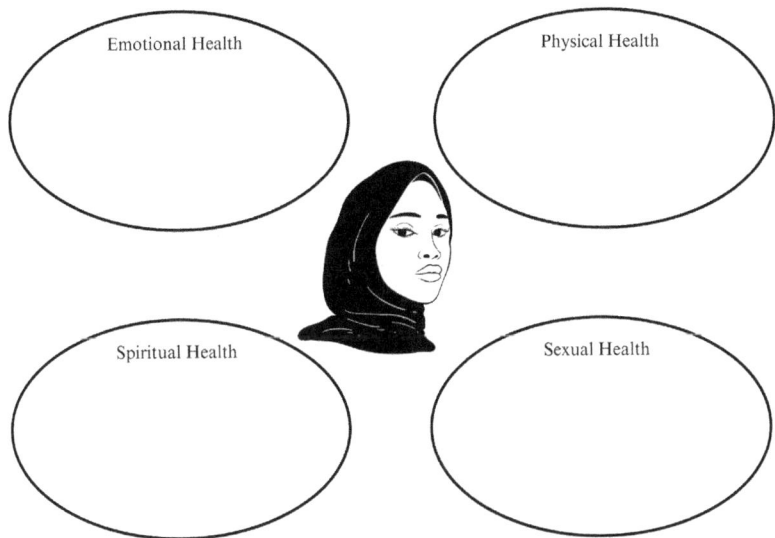

Figure 10.2 A reflection on holistic healing approaches from trauma

As trauma and healing are deeply personal and complex, the following section provides a reflection activity with Figure 10.2, which can be explored with the suggested questions to help you better understand how your trauma is manifesting and healing approaches. Combined with chapter 12 on seeking soulful support, these insights aim to guide your healing journey, whether self-led or supported by professionals.

Reflection Questions

As you reflect on the content, how is sexual trauma impacting your individual emotional, physical, spiritual, and/or sexual health?
_____
_____
_____

With regards to your relationships (i.e. partner, spouse, familial, etc.), how is sexual trauma impacting them? What seems to be challenging and/or triggering?
_____
_____
_____

> Reflecting on the four types of trauma responses, which ones are you aware of being present in your day-to-day life? Note down a few examples of when and how they show up.
>
> _____
> _____
> _____
>
> Based on the previous two questions, which aspects of your emotional, physical, spiritual, and sexual health would you like to compassionately work on?
>
> _____
> _____
> _____
>
> What would you benefit from learning more about with regards to sexual trauma? Are there types of professional support you might need?
>
> _____
> _____
> _____

As we transition to the following sexual health challenges that Muslim women face, it's important to remember that trauma—and often, sexual trauma—may be one of the factors or is the root cause. Continue to show compassion toward the many complex ways in which sexual trauma impacts our soul and remember that you're not alone.

Menstrual Challenges

For Muslim women, menstruation marks both the beginning of sexual health and spiritual accountability to Allah. While a natural part of life, many women face challenges with their menstrual cycles, as these cycles are intricately connected to overall health and can reflect physical, emotional, and environmental shifts. Common issues include irregular cycles, painful periods, heavy bleeding, PMS (premenstrual syndrome), absent periods, and spotting, often stemming from hormonal imbalances, underlying conditions like PCOS (polycystic ovary syndrome) or endometriosis, or lifestyle factors. These challenges highlight the importance of understanding menstrual health as a key component of well-being.

Let's explore each of these common challenges in more detail, with impacts to fertility being discussed later in this chapter.

The Soulful Navigation of Female Sexual Health Challenges 229

Irregular Cycles: Irregular menstrual cycles can mean that a woman's cycle is shorter or longer than the typical range of 21 to 35 days, or that she experiences unpredictable changes in cycle length. Hormonal imbalances, such as those involving estrogen or progesterone, often contribute to irregularity, as do lifestyle factors like stress or diet. PCOS is a common underlying condition that can cause irregular cycles due to an imbalance in reproductive hormones, often leading to anovulation (a lack of ovulation), which affects cycle predictability. Thyroid disorders also impact menstrual regularity by altering hormone levels (Mayo Clinic, n.d.-c).

Painful Periods (Dysmenorrhea): Painful periods, medically known as dysmenorrhea, affect many women and are typically characterized by cramping or intense lower abdominal pain. This pain is caused by uterine contractions that help shed the uterine lining. For some, these contractions are severe, often indicating deeper issues like endometriosis, fibroids, or pelvic inflammatory disease (PID). Dysmenorrhea can interfere with daily activities, sleep, and overall quality of life, making it crucial to address and manage (Mayo Clinic, n.d.-c).

Heavy Bleeding (Menorrhagia): Menorrhagia, or excessive menstrual bleeding, is another common issue that can affect quality of life. Heavy bleeding may result in fatigue or anemia due to substantial blood loss each cycle, which underscores the importance of addressing it. Causes of menorrhagia often include hormonal imbalances, fibroids, or reproductive health conditions like adenomyosis, where the uterine lining grows into the uterine muscle, resulting in heavy bleeding and cramping (Mayo Clinic, n.d.-c.).

Premenstrual Syndrome (PMS) and Premenstrual Dysphoric Disorder (PMDD): PMS includes a range of symptoms like bloating, mood swings, fatigue, and headaches that many women experience in the days leading up to menstruation. For some, these symptoms are mild, while others experience PMDD, a more severe form that includes intense emotional symptoms such as depression or irritability, significantly disrupting daily life. Both conditions are often influenced by hormone levels, stress, and dietary habits (Mayo Clinic, n.d.-c).

Absent Periods (Amenorrhea): Amenorrhea, the absence of menstruation outside of pregnancy, breastfeeding, or menopause, can indicate underlying health issues. Primary amenorrhea occurs when a woman hasn't had her first period by age 15, while secondary amenorrhea is when periods stop for three or more months after regular cycles. Common causes include hormonal imbalances due to PCOS or thyroid issues, stress, extreme exercise, or insufficient body weight(Mayo Clinic, n.d.-c).

> **Myth: Painful periods are just a normal part of being a woman**
>
> **Fact:** While mild discomfort or cramping during menstruation is common, severe or debilitating pain is not normal and can indicate an underlying health issue. Conditions like endometriosis, fibroids, or hormonal imbalances often contribute to excessive pain, which can interfere with daily activities and overall well-being. Additionally, lifestyle factors such as stress, diet, and exercise can impact hormonal balance, exacerbating menstrual pain and irregularities. If you consistently experience severe pain, it's a signal worth discussing with a healthcare provider, as there are many ways to manage or reduce menstrual pain effectively.

Understanding common menstrual issues leads us to two significant conditions that often underlie and intensify these symptoms: polycystic ovary syndrome (PCOS) and endometriosis. Both conditions are widely prevalent and can profoundly affect a woman's menstrual health and overall well-being.

Polycystic Ovary Syndrome (PCOS): PCOS is a hormonal disorder that affects ovarian function, leading to symptoms such as irregular menstrual cycles, cyst formation on the ovaries, and elevated levels of androgens (male hormones). This hormonal imbalance can cause issues beyond menstruation, including weight gain, insulin resistance, acne, and excess hair growth. Women with PCOS may struggle with fertility due to irregular ovulation, and managing PCOS often requires a combination of lifestyle changes, hormonal therapies, and medications to regulate menstrual cycles and address insulin resistance (Mayo Clinic, n.d.-a).

Endometriosis: Endometriosis is a condition where tissue similar to the lining of the uterus grows outside the uterus, often on the ovaries, fallopian tubes, and surrounding pelvic area. This misplaced tissue reacts to menstrual hormones, causing painful cramping, inflammation, and sometimes

The Soulful Navigation of Female Sexual Health Challenges   231

heavy bleeding. Endometriosis can also lead to scar tissue and adhesions, which can impact fertility and cause chronic pelvic pain. Treatment for endometriosis typically involves pain management, hormonal therapy to slow tissue growth, and, in some cases, surgical intervention to remove endometrial growths (Mayo Clinic, n.d.-b).

Reflection Questions

With these common menstrual issues in mind, let's take a few moments to reflect on your menstrual cycle. Do you notice any challenges or issues with your menstrual cycle? If so, note them down and reflect on questions you have about these challenges.

_____
_____
_____

What emotional and spiritual impacts do you notice your menstrual challenges having?

_____
_____
_____

In the following section, we transition to learning about pelvic floor dysfunction, with menstrual issues possibly contributing.

Pelvic Floor Dysfunction

Ayesha and John just celebrated their two-year anniversary. They met in graduate school and consider each other to be best friends and deeply in love. Since getting married, however, the couple has struggled with sexual intimacy. While they are comfortable with and enjoy sexual intimacy such as foreplay, Ayesha becomes quite tense and expresses vaginal pain during attempted intercourse. The couple is confused about what's happening but don't know how to talk about this and what to do. This has led John to stop initiating sexual intimacy, for fear of hurting Ayesha further, and Ayesha to feel intense shame about her body.

Pain during sexual intercourse is one of the most common concerns of Muslim women. It's a topic I hear from both single Muslim women thinking ahead to marriage, and from those experiencing pain during sexual intercourse with their spouses. As we've discussed throughout the book, Muslims lack access to soulful sexual health education and may even have been exposed to fear- and shame-based understandings about sex. Since many Muslim women also carry shame in relation to their body and sexual health, this can leave them not only disconnected from their body, but also from having sexual health. This can result in many sexual health challenges, of which pelvic floor dysfunction is one. Let's begin by first defining what is meant by pelvic floor dysfunction and the common types that women experience.

What Is Pelvic Floor Dysfunction?

Pelvic floor dysfunction refers to a range of disorders that occur when the muscles, ligaments, and connective tissues in the pelvic floor—responsible for supporting the bladder, uterus, rectum, and other organs—are weakened, overly tight, or function improperly. For many Muslim women, the lack of knowledge about their own anatomy can make these issues even more distressing, as they may not be aware of how the pelvic floor impacts their overall sexual and reproductive health. This dysfunction can lead to painful intercourse (dyspareunia), difficulty with urination or bowel movements, and, in some cases, conditions like pelvic organ prolapse, where the organs begin to shift or descend due to the weakened pelvic support.

Given the prevalence of painful intercourse—known generally as vaginismus—the following section will go into more details.

Vaginismus

Pelvic floor dysfunction, particularly vaginismus, is a common challenge impacting women's sexual health. Vaginismus occurs when pelvic floor muscles involuntarily tighten during penetration, leading to pain or making intercourse impossible. This condition often has deeper psychological roots, particularly in Muslim communities where limited or negative sexual education may frame intercourse as shameful or fearful. Early messages emphasizing sinfulness or danger without the balance of soulful marital contexts can instill anxiety, causing the body to unconsciously guard against perceived harm. This cycle of fear and pain often perpetuates itself, with the anticipation of pain increasing muscle tension and reinforcing initial fears.

Vaginismus manifests in two types: **primary**, where discomfort has always been present during penetration, often linked to deep-seated fears or inadequate education; and **secondary**, which develops later due to trauma,

The Soulful Navigation of Female Sexual Health Challenges 233

childbirth, surgery, or medical conditions. The emotional toll can be significant, leading to feelings of inadequacy or shame and strained spousal communication. Many women avoid seeking help due to stigma or are misdiagnosed when they do. Poor advice, such as being told to "relax" or "try harder," often leaves them feeling misunderstood. Misconceptions that painful intercourse is normal, especially in environments that neglect women's pleasure, further exacerbate the issue. Table 10.2 provides insights into common symptoms, offering an opportunity for reflection and awareness before we move into soulful healing approaches.

Table 10.2. A summary of the common symptomatic descriptions of vaginismus

Symptom/Sign	Description
Pain During Attempted Penetration	Pain or discomfort with any form of vaginal penetration, including during intercourse, tampon use, or gynecological exams.
Involuntary Muscle Tightening	The pelvic floor muscles tighten involuntarily at the entrance of the vagina, making penetration difficult or impossible.
Anticipatory Fear Or Anxiety	Anxiety or fear of pain before attempting vaginal penetration, leading to avoidance behaviors.
Burning or Stinging Sensation	A feeling of burning, stinging, or soreness during or after attempted penetration.
Emotional Distress	Feelings of frustration, embarrassment, or shame due to difficulties with penetration or intimacy.
Avoidance of Intimate Activities	Avoiding situations involving penetration (sexual or medical) due to fear of pain or discomfort.
Difficulty Using Tampons	Trouble or inability to use tampons or menstrual cups; fear or anxiety arising at the thought of using vaginal menstrual products.
Involuntary Body Responses	Physical responses, such as clenching of thighs or shifting body position, to prevent penetration.

Reflections

_____
_____
_____

Soulful Healing of Vaginismus

For Muslim women, a soulful approach to healing vaginismus can be particularly empowering. By reframing sexual health as something aligned with Islamic teachings on mutual care, compassion, and pleasure within marriage, women can begin to see their bodies as valuable and worthy of respect, both in and out of intimate settings. Recognizing that sexual pleasure is part of the marital relationship in Islam, and that seeking treatment for pain is encouraged rather than shameful, can open the door for more women to seek help and heal, allowing them to reclaim their sexual health and experience intimacy without fear or pain.

The treatment of vaginismus requires a compassionate and holistic approach. Physical therapies, such as working with a pelvic floor physical or occupational therapist, can help women learn how to relax the pelvic floor muscles and retrain the body's response to penetration. This is often done through progressive exercises, such as using vaginal dilators or engaging in controlled breathing techniques to reduce muscle tension. Equally important, however, is addressing the emotional and psychological components of vaginismus. Therapy, particularly trauma-informed or sex therapy, can help women unpack the beliefs, fears, or past experiences that may be contributing to their condition. Table 10.3 provides a summary of such holistic soulful approaches for treating vaginismus.

Pelvic Organ Prolapse (POP)

Pelvic dysfunction, including pelvic organ prolapse (POP), can occur following childbirth and is often associated with aging, though younger women can also be affected. POP happens when the muscles and tissues supporting pelvic organs like the bladder, uterus, or rectum weaken or stretch, causing these organs to descend into or outside the vaginal canal. Factors like chronic constipation, heavy lifting, or genetics, in addition to childbirth, can contribute to this condition, resulting in feelings of heaviness, pressure, or discomfort, particularly during sexual intercourse.

Different types of prolapse affect various organs, such as cystocele (bladder shifting into the vaginal wall), rectocele (rectum bulging into the vaginal wall), and uterine prolapse (uterus descending into the vaginal canal). Each type can lead to pain, reduced sexual sensation, and difficulties like urinary or bowel issues, which may impact intimate relationships and overall quality of life. These physical changes often contribute to emotional strain, highlighting the need for compassionate care and awareness in addressing this condition.

The Soulful Navigation of Female Sexual Health Challenges 235

Table 10.3. A summary of holistic treatment options for vaginismus

Healing Approach	Description
Somatic/Body-Based Practices	Body-centered exercises, such as progressive muscle relaxation, deep breathing, and gentle pelvic stretches, help release tension in the pelvic floor, promote relaxation, and reduce involuntary tightening in intimate settings.
Pelvic Floor Physical/Occupational Therapy	Pelvic health therapy, led by trained specialists, uses techniques like massage, biofeedback, and guided exercises to relax and strengthen pelvic floor muscles, alleviating discomfort and improving control.
Mental Health and/or Sex Therapy	Therapy with a mental health professional or certified sex therapist addresses the emotional and psychological aspects of vaginismus, exploring past trauma, relationship dynamics, or intimacy-related anxiety. Approaches like somatic therapy and exposure therapy help reduce anxiety, process trauma, and gradually desensitize the body's response to intimacy.
Spiritual Approaches	Spiritual practices like mindfulness, prayer, and meditation foster peace, self-compassion, and acceptance, reframing intimacy as a soulful experience and aligning physical healing with spiritual well-being.
Couples Therapy	Couples therapy provides a safe space to address intimacy challenges, enhance communication, and foster empathy. By working with a therapist, partners can build trust, deepen emotional and physical closeness, and navigate healing together.
Pelvic Pain Specialists/Medical Options	A medical evaluation by a pelvic pain specialist or gynecologist experienced with vaginismus can offer tailored pain management options, such as numbing creams, muscle relaxants, or Botox to relax pelvic muscles. This assessment ensures accurate diagnosis and a targeted treatment plan.

Soulful Healing and Perspectives on Pelvic Organ Prolapse

Experiencing pelvic organ prolapse can feel overwhelming, often bringing physical discomfort and emotional challenges like embarrassment, shame, or frustration. Many women may feel isolated or question their worth and desirability, particularly in the absence of awareness and understanding about this condition, leading to silent suffering.

From a soulful perspective, prolapse is a reminder of the body as a dynamic trust (*amanah*) from Allah, meant to change over time. It invites women to practice self-care as a spiritual responsibility, seeking support through medical care, therapy, or counseling. This challenge also offers an opportunity for spiritual growth, fostering resilience, patience, and a deeper connection to Allah. By learning about prolapse and promoting open conversations, women can reclaim control over their well-being while reducing stigma and fostering a culture of compassion and support.

Sexual Intimacy Issues

Amina and Omar have been married for fifteen years and have two children aged 6 and 9. Following the birth of their children, Amina has struggled more with her sexual desire. She finds it difficult to feel any interest or desire in sexual intimacy with her husband, who often showers her with physical affection and words of affirmation. Omar has asked Amina if she's still attracted to him, and she affirms that she is—and isn't sure why she's never in the mood for sex. Amina is concerned that their marriage has lost that spark and isn't sure what to do to get it back.

For many Muslim women, challenges around sexual intimacy in marriage often revolve around issues of sexual desire and pleasure. These difficulties can arise regardless of how long a couple has been married, affecting newlyweds as well as those who have been together for years. Factors such as limited premarital education about sexual health, cultural or familial messaging about sexuality, and physical or emotional barriers can impact arousal and satisfaction, leading to struggles with desire and fulfillment. Beyond the physical, such challenges often affect women emotionally and spiritually, leading to feelings of inadequacy, shame, or frustration, and creating distance in the marital connection.

Embracing a holistic, compassionate approach to sexual health can empower Muslim women to view intimacy as a natural, soulful part of marriage, fostering emotional healing and spiritual growth along the way. In the following sections, we will explore sexual desire and pleasure issues in more detail, examining the factors that contribute to these challenges and practical approaches for navigating them within a marriage.

Challenges with Sexual Desire

As we explored in chapter 6, challenges with sexual desire are a common experience in marriage, often influenced by stress, hormonal changes, physical fatigue, and emotional dynamics within the relationship. Desire naturally ebbs and flows, but prolonged periods of low or inconsistent interest in

The Soulful Navigation of Female Sexual Health Challenges 237

intimacy can feel difficult to navigate. Cultural or religious messaging about sexuality may also contribute to feelings of guilt, uncertainty, or disconnection from personal needs. Daily responsibilities, such as work or caretaking roles, often leave little room for rest or self-care, further reducing energy and desire over time.

Emotional and relational factors, such as feelings of disconnect, unresolved conflict, or poor communication, can significantly impact desire, as emotional intimacy is closely tied to physical intimacy for many women. Hormonal fluctuations during life stages like postpartum recovery or perimenopause, along with health conditions or medications, may also decrease libido or arousal. These challenges, though complex, are deeply intertwined with physical, emotional, and spiritual aspects of well-being and can be addressed with honesty, care, and alignment with faith and values.

Challenges with Sexual Pleasure

Challenges with sexual pleasure and achieving orgasm are common in marriage, often stemming from physical, emotional, and relational factors. Stress, fatigue, and distractions can hinder relaxation and engagement in intimacy, reducing pleasure and creating a sense of disconnect. Emotional intimacy and trust within the relationship play a critical role in sexual enjoyment, as unresolved conflicts or poor communication can make it difficult for women to feel comfortable and relaxed. Cultural or personal messages about sexuality may further contribute to discomfort or self-consciousness, impacting the ability to explore and communicate needs.

Hormonal changes during life stages like postpartum recovery, breastfeeding, or perimenopause, as well as certain medications and health conditions, can also affect libido, arousal, and physical sensations. These factors underscore the complexity of women's experiences of sexual pleasure, highlighting the importance of understanding how physiological and emotional dynamics intertwine. Addressing these challenges with sensitivity and self-awareness can help couples foster deeper connection and satisfaction within intimacy.

Soulfully Navigating Sexual Intimacy Issues

Navigating challenges around sexual intimacy within marriage is deeply personal, involving physical, emotional, and spiritual dimensions. For Muslim women, these issues are often shaped by cultural, religious, and societal influences, making them complex yet surmountable with a soulful perspective. Couples can view these challenges as opportunities for growth and connection rather than barriers, reframing intimacy as a reflection of their emotional and spiritual bond. Rooted in values like *rahmah* (mercy) and *muwaddah* (love), this approach fosters healing and alignment with Allah.

Prioritize Emotional Intimacy: Emotional connection is foundational to physical intimacy. Unresolved conflicts, poor communication, or life stressors can strain relationships, making physical closeness difficult. Couples should engage in open conversations to nurture trust, safety, and vulnerability, creating a more fulfilling and pressure-free environment for intimacy.

Compassionately Collaborate: Sexual intimacy is a mutual journey of discovery. Couples can approach challenges like low desire or difficulty with arousal as opportunities to better understand one another's needs. Setting aside time for gentle, non-pressured exploration can foster relaxation and connection.

Understand the Role of Stress and Fatigue: Daily stress and fatigue often hinder sexual intimacy. Acknowledging these factors and integrating relaxation techniques, mindfulness, or shared quiet moments can help couples reconnect and approach intimacy with renewed energy.

Seek Medical or Professional Support: Life stages, hormonal changes, or health conditions may contribute to intimacy challenges. Seeking help from healthcare professionals or faith-based sexual health educators can provide clarity and align care with Islamic values.

Embrace the Spiritual Dimension of Intimacy: Intimacy within marriage is an act of worship. Reflecting on its spiritual dimension through prayer, gratitude, or supplications can shift focus from performance to partnership, enhancing emotional and spiritual alignment.

Be Patient and Gentle with Yourself: Healing and growth in intimacy take time. Embracing patience and self-compassion allows couples to view setbacks as part of the soul's journey, nurturing deeper connections with one another and with Allah.

By grounding intimacy in faith, compassion, and love, couples can transform challenges into pathways for shared growth and understanding, enriching their marital connection as part of their broader spiritual journey.

> **Reflection Questions**
>
> How often do I feel interested in or excited about engaging in sexual intimacy with my partner? Reflect on whether your level of interest has changed over time or if it varies depending on your physical, emotional, or spiritual state.

_____
_____
_____

Do I feel emotionally connected and safe with my spouse during intimate moments, and does this affect my desire for intimacy? Consider if emotional dynamics, trust, or communication within the relationship influence your feelings of desire.

_____
_____
_____

Am I able to feel physical enjoyment during intimacy, or do I find myself feeling distracted, uncomfortable, or unfulfilled? Explore any physical or emotional barriers that might prevent you from experiencing pleasure, such as stress, fatigue, or discomfort.

_____
_____
_____

When it comes to achieving orgasm, do I feel it happens naturally, or do I experience challenges or frustration in reaching this level of pleasure? Reflect on how easily you're able to reach orgasm and if there are factors that seem to influence this experience positively or negatively.

_____
_____
_____

Do I feel comfortable communicating my needs or desires during intimacy, or do I feel self-conscious or uncertain about expressing them? Think about any reservations you might have about sharing your preferences or exploring pleasure with your spouse.

_____
_____

Reproductive Challenges

Aaliyah and Saif have been trying to conceive for four out of eight years of their marriage. Both spouses have been through fertility testing, with Aaliyah being told that she has diminished ovarian reserve (i.e. the number of possible eggs) for her age. The couple decide to pursue in vitro fertilization (IVF), which results in a pregnancy. At nine weeks of pregnancy, Aaliyah experiences a miscarriage and loses her baby. The couple is devastated and wonder if this is a sign that they're not meant to be parents.

Before marriage, many Muslims discuss their hopes for starting a family, covering their ideal timeline and the number of children they envision. These conversations are often a blend of excitement and a bit of nervousness, with many assuming that conception will come easily and their plans will unfold as expected. While some couples do see their ideal timeline come to life, the reality for many is that conception can take longer than anticipated, and, in some cases, fertility challenges—including infertility—may become part of the journey.

This section covers two main topics within the realm of reproductive challenges: pregnancy loss and infertility.

Pregnancy Loss

Pregnancy loss, or miscarriage, is the spontaneous loss of a pregnancy before the 20th week of gestation, affecting 10–20% of confirmed pregnancies, though the true rate may be higher due to early, unrecognized losses (Rai & Regan, 2006). Pregnancy loss later in pregnancy—such as in the second or third trimester—may involve labor induction or a C-section, and carries its own profound spiritual and physical impacts. Miscarriage is often caused by chromosomal abnormalities or other medical factors, and in most cases, it is beyond anyone's control. Types of miscarriage include chemical pregnancy, blighted ovum, missed miscarriage, and recurrent miscarriage (three or more consecutive losses). Understanding these distinctions can help women and couples navigate this challenging experience with greater clarity and support.

Management of pregnancy loss depends on the type, timing, and health needs of the woman. A natural process may occur spontaneously, while medical intervention, such as medication like misoprostol or a surgical procedure like dilation and curettage (D&C), may be necessary in some cases to prevent complications. It's crucial to distinguish these interventions from elective abortion, as they aim to address health concerns and support recovery. Follow-up care, including tests and counseling, is often recommended to ensure comprehensive physical, emotional, and spiritual healing after a miscarriage.

Soulfully Navigating Pregnancy Loss

Muslim women experiencing pregnancy loss may struggle spiritually, grappling with feelings of sadness, confusion, or questioning why this hardship has come their way. Such a profound loss can sometimes bring about a sense of spiritual disconnection, as women may feel uncertain about how to reconcile their faith with the pain they are enduring.

The soulful perspectives within Islam, however, offer a unique path toward comfort and understanding. Islam teaches that every soul, even one lost early, has a purpose, and that Allah's wisdom encompasses all trials, even those we may not fully comprehend. Many women find solace in the belief that their unborn child will await them in Paradise and that this loss is not in vain but instead a means for spiritual growth and Divine closeness. Alongside these spiritual comforts, seeking professional emotional support or therapy can also be an important part of healing. Therapy offers a space to process grief and spiritual questions, allowing Muslim women to rebuild their connection to both faith and self-compassion while being guided through their healing journey. By combining soulful perspectives with professional support (refer to chapter 12)—whether individually for the woman and/or through couples therapy—they can honor their experience and compassionately move forward with renewed strength and peace.

For Muslim women navigating the path to motherhood, understanding the distinction between fertility challenges and infertility provides clarity and empowerment. This perspective allows women to approach their journey with patience, seeking both medical and spiritual guidance to navigate this chapter with hope and resilience.

Fertility Challenges

Fertility challenges refer to obstacles that delay conception but do not make it unattainable. Common factors include irregular cycles, hormonal imbalances, polycystic ovary syndrome (PCOS), endometriosis, or age-related declines in fertility. Stress, lifestyle factors, diet, and sleep can also contribute to these challenges. While these factors can be sensitive within the marital context, addressing them with medical interventions, lifestyle changes, or time can enhance fertility outcomes.

Spousal factors often play a role in fertility challenges, with male issues such as low sperm count, poor motility, or hormonal imbalances being common but less openly discussed. Islam encourages mutual support and open communication during trials, enabling couples to address these challenges together and strengthen their bond while exploring options aligned with their values.

Infertility

Infertility is defined as the inability to conceive after 12 months of regular attempts (or six months if the woman is over 35) and may result from various medical conditions, such as hormonal imbalances, blocked fallopian tubes, or male factors like abnormal sperm quality. Early consultation with a fertility specialist is recommended for couples with irregular cycles, known health conditions, or a history of miscarriages. Treatment options range from medications to stimulate ovulation to more advanced procedures like intrauterine insemination (IUI), in vitro fertilization (IVF), or intracytoplasmic sperm injection (ICSI) for male infertility. Alongside medical interventions, many Muslim couples integrate soulful practices such as prayer, *dua* (personal supplication), and trusting in Divine timing to foster resilience and peace. Viewing fertility challenges as part of Allah's purposeful plan allows couples to navigate this journey with faith, patience, and the recognition that trials can offer opportunities for growth and deeper connection.

Soulfully Navigating Fertility Challenges and Infertility

Muslim couples navigating infertility may consider options like surrogacy or donor gametes, both of which involve unique spiritual and ethical considerations within Islamic teachings. Surrogacy, where another woman carries the child, and donor gametes, which introduce genetic material from outside the marriage, are debated among scholars. Classical Islamic jurisprudence often limits procreation to the marital relationship, emphasizing lineage and inheritance laws, though modern scholars offer nuanced views that account for compassion and changing social contexts.

Many Muslims are encouraged to explore alternatives such as adoption or fostering, which is highly regarded within Islam. While Islamic adoption preserves the child's birth lineage, it remains a compassionate way to nurture and build a family in alignment with Islamic principles. For couples considering surrogacy or donor gametes, this journey requires balancing medical needs, ethical values, and spiritual guidance. Through prayer, consultation with scholars, and community support, couples can make thoughtful decisions rooted in love, trust in Allah, and their shared commitment to nurturing life.

Holding Soulful Space for Fertility Challenges or Pregnancy Loss

Muslims often approach others' struggles with good intentions, seeking to offer comfort or guidance. However, when it comes to fertility challenges and pregnancy loss, this well-meaning support can unintentionally manifest as spiritual bypassing—using religious or spiritual explanations to sidestep the emotional weight of another's pain. Phrases like *"At least you already have a child," "Allah is testing you, just be patient,"* or *"Have you tried this specialist?"* may be intended to console but often diminish the person's experience, leaving them feeling unseen and unheard.

Spiritual bypassing not only fails to acknowledge the depth of emotional pain but can also unintentionally reinforce feelings of isolation or inadequacy. While offering solutions or reminders of faith may seem helpful, such responses can inadvertently silence the person's need to grieve, process, and find their own soulful meaning in their journey.

Instead, Muslims are called to hold soulful space for difficult emotions without rushing into advice or explanations. This means practicing deep listening, acknowledging the pain without minimizing it, and offering empathy without imposing interpretations of the struggle. True support allows the individual to navigate their emotions and relationship with Allah in their own time and way.

Good intentions must be paired with awareness that the only person who can make soulful meaning of their struggles is the one living through them. By creating a compassionate and nonjudgmental space, we embody the Islamic values of mercy and care, fostering healing and connection rather than inadvertently adding to the weight of the struggle.

Reflection Questions

Which topics from this section would you like to learn more about?
_____
_____

If you and your spouse are navigating fertility challenges or infertility, what further information or support do you both need?
_____
_____

> How can you bring more soulful compassion to what you're experiencing?
>
> _____
>
> _____

Menopause Challenges

As discussed in chapter 8, middle adulthood brings natural shifts in the body, with menopause marking a significant physiological and spiritual transition for women around age 40. This phase is characterized by fluctuating hormone levels, the end of menstrual cycles, and symptoms that vary widely in intensity and frequency based on genetics, lifestyle, and health history. While menopause is a normal stage of life, some symptoms may disrupt daily life and require professional support.

Common Menopause-Related Challenges

Mood Swings and Depression: Hormonal changes can lead to intense mood swings, irritability, or persistent sadness. If these emotional changes interfere with relationships or daily activities, mental health support may be necessary. Therapy, lifestyle adjustments, or medication can help manage these symptoms.

Sleep Disturbances: Insomnia or disrupted sleep, often caused by night sweats or anxiety, can exacerbate fatigue, irritability, and concentration issues. Persistent sleep problems may benefit from medical treatments or therapeutic strategies guided by a physician.

Cognitive Issues: "Brain fog," involving memory lapses, difficulty concentrating, or decision-making challenges can disrupt personal and professional responsibilities. Persistent cognitive symptoms should be assessed by a healthcare provider to explore interventions that support cognitive health.

Joint and Muscle Pain: Estrogen decline during menopause can contribute to joint and muscle discomfort, limiting physical activity and affecting cardiovascular and bone health. Healthcare professionals can guide pain management, encourage an active lifestyle, and recommend supplements or medications if necessary.

Pelvic and Urogenital Health Issues: Hormonal changes can cause dryness, itching, or discomfort in the vaginal area and may lead to urinary issues like increased frequency or incontinence. These symptoms are common but treatable, with options ranging from lifestyle changes to medical interventions.

Soulfully Navigating Menopause Challenges

Menopause is a profound transition, impacting both the body and soul. As explored in chapter 8, this stage aligns with spiritual maturity, calling Muslim women to deepen their connection to Allah and embrace the wisdom life's transitions bring. While menopause often presents physical challenges, it is also an opportunity to soulfully realign with one's body, emotions, and spiritual purpose.

Embracing Active Patience and Gratitude: Menopause is part of the body's natural design and an opportunity to reflect on its remarkable journey. By practicing gratitude, women can shift their perspective from frustration to appreciation, engaging in acts of worship like prayer or reflection to anchor themselves in Allah's wisdom. Thanking Allah for the body and its changes transforms this phase into a spiritually enriching experience.

Additionally, crafting a heartfelt prayer for your body during menopause can be a powerful way to invite spiritual alignment and healing. This prayer can center your intentions, bring peace to your heart, and remind you of Allah's care and wisdom in creating and guiding you through every stage of life.

"Ya Allah, Creator of all perfection, I thank You for this body that has carried me through life. Grant me patience for its changes, strength in my body, peace in my heart, and clarity in my soul. Help me honor and nurture this trust with care and gratitude. Let this stage draw me closer to You and deepen my awareness of Your mercy and wisdom. Ameen."

Seeking Support: Menopause's challenges do not need to be faced alone. Seeking help from healthcare providers, counselors, or holistic practitioners reflects *tawakkul* (trust in Allah) and proactive stewardship of the body. Balancing physical and emotional dimensions through medical care, functional nutrition, or spiritual counseling ensures comprehensive support.

Integrating Restorative Practices: Practices such as mindfulness, yoga, or gentle exercise foster a connection between mind, body, and soul, easing symptoms while enhancing self-awareness (*muraqabah*). These practices not only promote physical health but also encourage calm and presence during this transitional phase.

Building Emotional Resilience: Menopause may bring challenging emotions, but self-accountability paired with compassion allows women to navigate them soulfully. Acknowledging feelings without judgment and processing them through journaling, therapy, or trusted conversations can maintain spiritual alignment while fostering emotional resilience.

Strengthening Relationships: Open communication with loved ones is vital, reducing isolation and fostering understanding. Sharing the menopause journey with a spouse can deepen intimacy and transform challenges into opportunities for growth. Relationships with family and friends also provide essential support during this stage.

Reflecting on Life's Bigger Picture: Menopause serves as a reminder of life's impermanence and the soul's journey toward Allah. Reflecting on the temporary nature of this world can provide perspective, turning this transition into a stepping stone for greater spiritual refinement. By adopting a soulful perspective, women can transform menopause into a stage of growth, connection, and empowerment. Honoring the body and soul as sacred trusts, they can navigate this phase with the understanding that Allah's wisdom and mercy guide every step of the journey.

Additional Sexual Health Challenges: Cancer

Understanding cancers like breast, ovarian, and cervical cancers is vital for Muslim women, as early detection and proactive care significantly improve outcomes. Many women avoid preventative exams due to fear or shame surrounding sexual health, yet addressing these concerns aligns with the Islamic value of stewardship over the body.

Breast Cancer: As one of the most common cancers in women, breast cancer may present with few symptoms initially. Early signs include a lump in the breast, changes in shape, or unusual discharge. Monthly self-examinations and regular screenings help detect the disease early, allowing for more effective treatment options.

Ovarian Cancer: Known as a "silent" cancer, ovarian cancer's symptoms—such as bloating, pelvic discomfort, or changes in bowel habits—are subtle and often overlooked. Persistent symptoms warrant consultation with a healthcare provider. Regular screenings, particularly for those with a family history, align with proactive health stewardship.

Cervical Cancer: Cervical cancer often results from persistent HPV (human papilloma virus) infections, causing abnormal cervical cells. Early stages typically lack noticeable symptoms, while advanced stages may involve irregular bleeding or pelvic pain. Regular Pap smears are crucial for catching pre-cancerous changes before symptoms arise.

Soulful Reflections on Cancer and Prevention

Navigating the potential for a cancer diagnosis can evoke fear and uncertainty, especially when it involves areas of the body often surrounded by cultural discomfort. Islam teaches that caring for the body is an act of gratitude to Allah, reflecting trust in Him and embodying self-accountability and compassion. The body is an *amanah* (trust) from Allah, and maintaining its well-being is a spiritual duty. Regular screenings for breast, ovarian, and cervical cancers honor this Divine trust, demonstrating care for the gift of life and health.

Fear of results or cultural discomfort should not deter women from fulfilling their responsibility to care for their bodies. Reframing **screenings** as acts of trust in Allah's wisdom can ease these emotions, while the power of early detection enables women to remain present for their families, communities, and spiritual growth. **Practices** like breast self-exams, Pap smears, and consulting about family history exemplify this sacred duty. Grounding healthcare routines in faith—such as reciting prayers like *"Ya Allah, guide me in fulfilling my responsibility to care for the trust You have given me. Grant me strength, patience, and clarity in all that I do"* can further align preventative care with spiritual values. By reframing screenings as acts of gratitude and responsibility, Muslim women can approach cancer prevention with confidence and purpose.

Myth Busting: The HPV Vaccine

The HPV (human papilloma virus) vaccine protects against viruses that cause cancers (e.g. cervical, throat, and genital) and genital warts. It is most effective when given before exposure, typically starting at ages 11–12, but it can be administered as early as 9. Those under 15 require two doses, while three doses are recommended for individuals 15 and older. Adults up to 26 are encouraged to get vaccinated, and some aged 27–45 may benefit based on medical advice.

Misunderstandings about the vaccine in some Muslim communities often stem from its association with sexual activity. However, Islam's emphasis on health preservation supports vaccination as a preventative measure aligned with caring for the body as a trust from God. This perspective fosters openness in discussing sexual health responsibly, enabling informed, spiritually grounded decisions for parents and young adults.

Summary

Throughout this chapter, we have reinforced the idea that Muslims have a soulful connection to their sexual health throughout their lives, even though many may not have had access to comprehensive education until faced with challenges that demanded their attention. This has often led to internalizing struggles as punishment or sin and reinforced shame-based beliefs, leaving many to feel inherently broken or flawed.

This chapter has emphasized the importance of recognizing that we are not at fault for the sexual health challenges our bodies have faced, such as pain during intimacy or hormonal imbalances. These difficulties have been understood as tests from Allah, placed on our path as part of our spiritual journey. What we are responsible for is how we have responded to these trials, ensuring that our soul continues its journey toward healing and a deeper connection with Allah.

Compassionate self-accountability has been highlighted as essential, stressing that we honor our struggles without blame or shame, while understanding that healing—whether physical, emotional, or spiritual—requires care and patience. For those who would like to learn more about soulful support-seeking for sexual health challenges, chapter 12 will be a helpful resource.

Reflections and Action Items

_____
_____
_____
_____
_____
_____

Reference List

Agarwal, A., Mulgund, A., Hamada, A., & Chyatte, M. R. (2015). A unique view on male infertility around the globe. *Reproductive Biology and Endocrinology*, 13(1), 37. https://doi.org/10.1186/s12958-015-0032-1

Mayo Clinic. (n.d.-a). *Polycystic ovary syndrome (PCOS)—Symptoms and causes*. Retrieved January 4, 2025, from https://www.mayoclinic.org/diseases-conditions/pcos/symptoms-causes/syc-20353439

Mayo Clinic. (n.d.-b). *Endometriosis—Symptoms and causes*. Retrieved January 4, 2025, from https://www.mayoclinic.org/diseases-conditions/endometriosis/symptoms-causes/syc-20354656

Mayo Clinic. (n.d.-c). *Menstrual cycle: What's normal, what's not*. Retrieved January 4, 2025, from https://www.mayoclinic.org/healthy-lifestyle/womens-health/in-depth/menstrual-cycle/art-20047186

Rai, R., & Regan, L. (2006). Recurrent miscarriage. *The Lancet*, 368(9535), 601-611. https://doi.org/10.1016/S0140-6736(06)69204-0

Walker, P. (2013). *Complex PTSD: From surviving to thriving: A guide and map for recovering from childhood trauma*. Azure Coyote Publishing.

11 The Soulful Navigation of Male Sexual Health Challenges

It's not uncommon for people to assume that my work in the field of Islam and sexual health focuses solely on women. This assumption reflects a broader societal misconception—that sexual health is somehow a "feminine" concern. However, as this book has demonstrated, sexual health is a soulful journey shared by all of us, men and women alike, from birth to death. It is a vital dimension of our holistic well-being, interconnected with our physical, emotional, and spiritual selves. Throughout my years of work in Islamic schools, Muslim communities, non-profit spaces, and now in private practice, I have witnessed a deeply moving hunger among Muslim men for soulful understanding and support of their sexual health. Despite societal narratives that often discourage vulnerability or emotional expression in men, I have encountered their openness, compassion, and genuine desire to align their sexual health with their faith and spiritual journey. This commitment reflects the beautiful balance of strength and humility that the Islamic tradition encourages. This chapter seeks to honor the courage of men who engage with this often overlooked aspect of their well-being. By addressing common challenges and offering soulful reflections, the goal is to provide Muslim men with a compassionate framework to navigate their sexual health with dignity, self-awareness, and a deepened connection to Allah.

The Journey of the Soul

| Birth | Spiritual Accountability | Spiritual Maturity | Spiritual Legacy | The Hereafter |

DOI: 10.4324/9781032675862-12

Introduction

When Muslims hear "sexual health," it is often perceived as more relevant to women. Yet, as emphasized throughout this book, sexual health is essential for all Muslims, encompassing the emotional, spiritual, and relational dimensions of life. Despite this, male sexual health education is often reduced to topics like masturbation, pornography use, and marital intimacy, neglecting men's holistic needs as whole beings on a soulful journey toward Allah. This limited, behavior-focused approach fails to provide the compassionate, faith-aligned support men need to navigate their sexual health with self-awareness and purpose.

Broader societal narratives further compound these challenges. Stereotypes portraying Muslim men as dominant or violent restrict their ability to explore nuanced aspects of masculinity, such as humility and emotional depth. Similarly, "alpha male" ideals, popularized by some public figures, resonate with young men but overlook the spiritually aligned qualities of the Prophet Muhammad (Peace and Blessings be Upon Him), such as patience, compassion, and respect. Rigid interpretations of Islamic teachings and transactional views of marriage can also create barriers for men seeking soulful guidance on sexual health.

Muslim men need compassionate spaces to unlearn harmful expectations and foster emotional and spiritual growth. Addressing sexual health as part of their broader spiritual journey enables men to develop a balanced, values-aligned connection to their sexuality. This chapter explores common challenges faced by Muslim men, including sexual trauma, pornography use, intimacy difficulties, infertility, and cancer, through a soul-centered lens that integrates emotional, spiritual, and psychological dimensions. Before continuing, take a moment to reflect on your feelings about sexual health and its place in your journey as a Muslim man.

Reflection Questions

What is your understanding of soulful sexual health education as a man? Which topics do you wish you had more access to learn about when you were younger?

_____

_____

_____

What societal messages about masculinity and sexual health for men are you aware of? How do these impact your understanding of soulful sexual health as a Muslim?

_____

_____

_____

As you reflect on your current life stage, which sexual health topics are you interested to learn more about?

_____

_____

_____

Soulful Contexts of Male Sexual Health Challenges

Before addressing common sexual health challenges, it is crucial to reframe these issues through Islamic perspectives on masculinity. Contrary to societal stereotypes that emphasize dominance or detachment, Islam centers masculinity on Divine attributes such as self-compassion, patience, and humility. The Prophet Muhammad (Peace and Blessings be Upon Him) exemplified this soulful masculinity as "a mercy to all the worlds" (Quran 21:107), demonstrating strength through kindness and nurturing rather than control.

In his interactions, the Prophet embodied respect and emotional presence, teaching that "The best of you are those who are best to their families" (Sunnah.com, n.d., Tirmidhi 3895). This highlights masculinity rooted in compassion and integrity. Through self-purification (*tazkiyah*), men are called to cleanse their souls: "He has succeeded who purifies it, and he has failed who instills it with corruption" (Quran 91:9–10). This journey of inner growth aligns external behaviors with Divine guidance, fostering soulful masculinity.

Islam also emphasizes metaphysical traits such as *rahmah* (compassion), *hikmah* (wisdom), *sabr* (patience), and *tawakkul* (trust in God). These attributes guide men to be protectors in both physical and spiritual realms, balancing emotional intelligence with strength. This holistic vision encourages men to honor their soul's needs through self-awareness, accountability, and empathy—qualities integral to sexual health as part of *amanah* (a trust) from Allah.

The concept of *futuwwah* (spiritual chivalry) enriches this understanding by providing a framework for soulful sexual health. Rooted in Sufi traditions, *futuwwah* emphasizes noble behavior, selflessness, and integrity. It reflects the virtues of the Prophet Muhammad (Peace and Blessings be Upon Him) and his companions, including generosity, courage, humility, and service to others. Beyond external acts, *futuwwah* nurtures an inner state of selflessness and steadfastness in righteousness, embodying balance between serving humanity and maintaining a connection with the Divine (Walid, 2020).

Grounded in self-accountability and self-compassion, *futuwwah* redefines masculine strength as the courage to pursue holistic well-being and faith-centered relationships. It encourages men to seek support without shame and engage with their emotional depth, shifting focus from behaviors to soul-centered growth. Through *futuwwah*, men can reclaim a chivalrous masculinity that values respect for oneself and others, fostering self-awareness and soulful connections (Walid, 2020).

Muslim men facing sexual health challenges can benefit from viewing these issues as part of their spiritual journey. Islam encourages believers to see life's challenges, including sexual health struggles, as opportunities for growth rather than as reflections of worth or punishments. This aligns with *ihsaan* (spiritual excellence), which calls for closeness to God through compassion and self-awareness.

By reframing sexual health challenges as part of the soul's journey, men can nurture both body and soul. Recognizing the body as temporary and the soul as enduring, men can approach sexual health with gentleness and see struggles as opportunities to deepen their relationship with Allah and themselves.

Masculine and Feminine Metaphysical Principles in Islamic Spirituality

Islamic cosmology emphasizes the presence of both masculine and feminine metaphysical principles within creation, reflecting a complete and balanced soul. These principles transcend physical gender, representing spiritual and metaphysical qualities essential for holistic development.

Every individual embodies both *jalal* (majesty) and *jamal* (beauty) attributes. *Jalal* is associated with qualities like strength, rigor, and power, while *jamal* reflects gentleness, mercy, and beauty. A well-rounded spiritual journey involves cultivating both attributes, enabling individuals to express the fullness of their humanity and Divine potential (Nasr, 1980).

Islamic spirituality encourages men and women to harmonize these dual principles within themselves, fostering a balance that mirrors Divine harmony. This understanding deepens one's connection with Allah and enriches the spiritual journey by integrating both *jalal* and *jamal*.

In the context of soulful sexual health for Muslim men, this framework transcends behavior-focused approaches, inviting men to see sexuality as part of a holistic spiritual journey. True masculinity is not solely defined by strength or control but also by the integration of compassion, beauty, and gentleness—qualities aligned with Divine harmony. By embracing these attributes, Muslim men can approach sexual health with self-awareness and respect, viewing it as a balanced expression of both their spiritual and physical selves.

Similar to the previous chapter, sexual health issues are often linked with unresolved trauma, including sexual trauma. Be gentle with yourself as you read the next section as the content may be triggering or upsetting.

Sexual Trauma

Hashem, a 29-year-old single Muslim professional, has struggled in his journey to seek a spouse. While he doesn't have any difficulty during the initial phase of speaking with a woman, the moment the conversations transition to commitment and marriage, Hashem finds himself feeling frozen and overwhelmed. He experiences anxiety at the mention of marriage and commitment, even though he wants this for himself. Hashem remembers an older female family member sexually touching him when he was younger, which he has never shared with anyone as he felt he wouldn't be believed. Hashem is concerned about how he'll engage with sexual intimacy in marriage and isn't sure where to start on his healing journey.

Sexual trauma encompasses psychological, spiritual, and physiological responses to sexual violence, including abuse, assault, or harassment. Trauma arises not only from the event itself but also from its impact on emotional, physical, and spiritual well-being (Herman, 2015). Research shows men often struggle to identify or accept sexual trauma due to societal expectations of masculinity, which discourage vulnerability and emphasize control (Lisak, 1994). While 1 in 6 men experiences sexual abuse by age 18 (Dube et al., 2005), many delay seeking help for decades, as acknowledging trauma can conflict with ideals of male strength and self-reliance. This disconnect often leads to denial, minimization, or misinterpretation of symptoms, with long-term mental health implications (Easton, 2013).

In Muslim communities, limited research highlights additional barriers. Cultural stigmas around male victimhood, combined with fears of racial or religious stereotyping, hinder recognition and reporting. For example, a UNHCR study on Syrian refugees found young men uniquely vulnerable to sexual violence in conflict settings but hesitant to disclose due to stigma and disbelief (UNHCR, 2017). In collectivistic Muslim cultures, with strong family ties and connections to countries in turmoil, these dynamics further complicate how trauma is processed and acknowledged.

Forms of Sexual Violence Impacting Muslim Men

- **Sexual Harassment:** Unwanted sexual advances or requests may occur in workspaces, social settings, or online, challenging men's personal boundaries.
- **Sexual Abuse:** Non-consensual acts within trusted relationships can leave deep emotional wounds, especially in contexts involving family or authority figures.
- **Sexual Assault:** Non-consensual acts, including forced or unwanted sexual contact, can lead to lasting trauma. For many men, experiences of such a nature are compounded by social stigma, creating barriers to healing.

Trauma Responses Among Men: Fight, Flight, Freeze, and Fawn

Muslim men, like others, may experience *fight*, *flight*, *freeze*, or *fawn* responses when triggered by past traumas. These natural survival mechanisms, rooted in the nervous system, aim to protect against perceived threats, whether emotional, psychological, or physical. Understanding these responses as protective rather than personal failings is key to healing.

Fight: Displays as anger, irritability, or a need for control, often intensified by societal expectations of masculinity. This may manifest as defensiveness, dominating conversations, or disproportionate reactions to criticism, masking deeper vulnerabilities.

Flight: Involves avoidance through overworking or distractions to escape emotional discomfort. Men may immerse themselves in tasks or religious obligations, avoiding emotional discussions, which can create relational distance.

Freeze: Leads to dissociation or emotional numbing, leaving men feeling "stuck" or unresponsive in relationships. This can strain connections and deepen feelings of isolation.

Fawn: Characterized by people-pleasing to avoid conflict or gain approval, often at the cost of personal needs and boundaries. This response can erode self-esteem and prevent emotional growth.

Recognizing these responses allows men to approach themselves with compassion and accountability. Seeking support through therapy, spiritual guidance, or trusted mentors can help them navigate their healing journey with balance and grace.

Societal and cultural norms often discourage emotional vulnerability in men, leading to internalized trauma that frequently goes unaddressed (Addis & Mahalik, 2003; Easton, 2013). Men may misinterpret or dismiss trauma symptoms, particularly when they differ from the externalized behaviors typically associated with trauma, such as anger or aggression. Instead, distress is more likely to manifest internally, as emotional numbness, detachment, or a lack of emotional awareness—a condition known as alexithymia (Levant et al., 2009). Societal messages to suppress emotions and "man up" further hinder men's ability to process feelings related to past trauma.

Male trauma responses, often subtle and internalized, are frequently overlooked by both men themselves and society. Symptoms like dissociation, withdrawal, and self-blame—common in internalized trauma—are less visible and, therefore, less likely to elicit help or recognition (Easton, 2013; Lisak, 1994). This cultural bias complicates men's awareness of their trauma and delays help-seeking, even when symptoms stem from significant but unrecognized events. Without acknowledgement and support, these responses can result in long-term emotional and relational difficulties.

Barriers to Healing

Research identifies three main barriers that prevent men from acknowledging and healing from sexual trauma: societal expectations of masculinity, lack of supportive spaces, and spiritual bypassing.

Societal Expectations of Masculinity: Acknowledging trauma challenges deeply ingrained beliefs about masculinity, strength, and vulnerability. Social norms discourage men from seeing themselves as victims, creating shame around disclosing abuse. This expectation of "invulnerability" leads many men to deny, minimize, or misunderstand their trauma as a form of self-preservation. Studies show men wait an average of 20–25 years to disclose abuse, if they ever do (Easton, 2013; Lisak, 1994).

Lack of Supportive Spaces: The misconception that male sexual trauma is rare or less impactful contributes to fewer resources and support systems for men (Fisher & Pina, 2013). Stigma around male victimhood often deters men from identifying as victims, reinforcing shame, self-doubt, and isolation. Discussions about men's trauma frequently focus on harm caused rather than harm endured, reducing compassion and furthering self-blame. Effective support for Muslim men involves creating spaces grounded in Islamic principles and soulful mental health frameworks, offering a compassionate and judgment-free environment for healing.

Spiritual Bypassing: Masculinity norms in Muslim communities discourage emotional expression, linking vulnerability to weakness. This fosters a "just get over it" mentality, compounding silence and shame (Addis & Mahalik, 2003). Limited emotional support for male survivors is associated with worsened mental health outcomes (Easton, 2013). Misinterpretations of Islamic teachings may also contribute to spiritual bypassing, where trauma is dismissed as a lack of faith. Reframing these teachings with compassion and soul-centered principles can foster understanding and healing that integrates spiritual and emotional dimensions.

Figure 11.1 shares a visual representation of these barriers to healing. Take a moment to reflect on your own journey with healing, noting down barriers you've encountered.

Soulful Reflections on Healing

For Muslim men, healing requires compassionate support spaces and trauma-informed education that normalize trauma responses and encourage recovery. Holistic frameworks incorporating spiritual, psychological,

The Soulful Navigation of Male Sexual Health Challenges 257

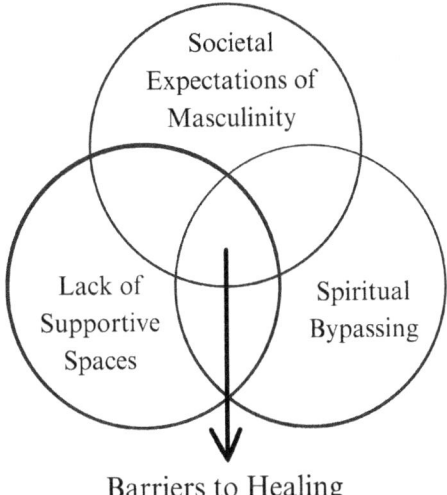

Figure 11.1 A Venn diagram representing three categories of barriers to healing that men often face

and physiological aspects promote vulnerability as a strength, restoring self-compassion and relationships.

The concept of *futuwwah* (spiritual chivalry) offers a profound lens for healing. It emphasizes virtues like integrity, humility, and selflessness, inspired by the noble character of the Prophet Muhammad (Peace and Blessings be Upon Him). *Futuwwah* nurtures inner strength, encouraging men to prioritize emotional and spiritual well-being over external displays of stoicism.

Healing through *futuwwah* involves cultivating self-compassion and self-accountability, allowing men to honor their struggles without shame or guilt. It reframes masculinity as resilience and soulful growth, fostering meaningful relationships built on empathy and spiritual awareness. By integrating *futuwwah*, Muslim men can redefine strength as the courage to embrace vulnerability and pursue a faith-centered path grounded in compassion, integrity, and a deep connection with the Divine.

Reflection Questions

As you reflect on the content, how is sexual trauma impacting your individual emotional, physical, spiritual, and/or sexual health? How about the ways in which you view masculinity?

With regards to your relationships (i.e. partner, spouse, familial, etc.), how is sexual trauma impacting them? What seems to be challenging and/or triggering?

Referring back to the four types of trauma responses, which ones are you aware of being present in your day-to-day life? Note down a few examples of when and how they showed up.

Based on the previous two questions, which aspects of your emotional, physical, spiritual, and sexual health would you like to compassionately work on?

What would you benefit from learning more about with regards to sexual trauma? Are there types of professional support you might need?

Pornography Use: A Soulful Sexual Health Challenge

Farooq, a 36-year-old single Muslim professional, has struggled with pornography use since his early teens. He has been trying for many years to stop this behavior and has accessed various support groups and programs online. While a couple of the programs did help in the short-term, Farooq finds himself slipping back into this behavior. Farooq recalls that during his childhood and teenage years, his home environment was marked by

The Soulful Navigation of Male Sexual Health Challenges 259

frequent parental arguments, a controlling father, and instances of physical abuse from his father. Farooq feels intense shame about his pornography use and isn't sure that he'll ever be able to stop.

Concerns about pornography use have grown significantly among Muslims, raising important questions for professionals and religious leaders alike. While this issue is more commonly associated with single Muslim men, its presence within marriage is also increasingly recognized. Although this section focuses on men, it is vital to acknowledge that Muslim women also face challenges with pornography use. Framing this solely as a "man's issue" limits supportive, soulful guidance for women who navigate similar struggles. Both men and women can benefit from the insights shared here as they embark on their journeys toward healing and spiritual growth.

Pornography use is a soulful sexual health challenge because it misaligns with Islamic ethical values and undermines the sacredness of marital intimacy. As discussed in chapter 4 on empowered abstinence, pornography erodes the spiritual and relational dimensions of sexuality that Islam upholds as sacred. Islam's emphasis on avoiding pornography stems from its harmful impacts, both spiritually and relationally, which far outweigh any perceived benefits.

Rather than labeling this behavior as "pornography addiction," which originates from secular psychological contexts, this chapter frames it within the Islamic understanding of the soul (*nafs*). The soul is constantly striving for refinement, accountability, and spiritual growth. Labeling challenges as "addiction" can draw attention primarily to addressing the behavior, while overlooking the underlying emotional, relational, or spiritual causes. Instead, pornography struggles are understood as opportunities for soulful growth, personal responsibility, and deeper connection with Allah.

Addressing the root causes of pornography use is essential for fostering healing and transformation. A focus solely on abstinence or fear-based strategies often creates a spiritual and emotional void, leaving individuals without the tools they need to heal comprehensively. A soulful approach integrates self-awareness, emotional resilience, and a balance of psychological and spiritual tools. This includes identifying deeper drivers such as stress, trauma, or unresolved emotional wounds that fuel the behavior. Empowered abstinence, grounded in informed decision-making and soulful understanding, reframes pornography struggles as part of the spiritual journey rather than a source of shame.

By removing stigma and approaching these challenges with compassion and accountability, individuals can cultivate resilience and seek a faith-centered path to overcoming struggles. This perspective fosters not only personal healing but also a renewed connection to Allah, reframing pornography use as an opportunity for soulful growth and alignment with Islamic values.

The Impacts of Pornography on Sexual Intimacy

Pornography use can significantly impact sexual intimacy, contributing to challenges such as erectile dysfunction (ED), premature ejaculation (PE), and performance anxiety. Understanding these effects is crucial for Muslim men seeking soulful growth and alignment with Islamic values.

1. **Erectile Dysfunction (ED)**
   Frequent pornography use can desensitize the brain to natural sexual stimuli, making real-life intimacy less engaging or satisfying. This overstimulation conditions the brain to expect heightened and unrealistic scenarios, leading to difficulties in authentic, in-real-life sexual response. For Muslim men, this disconnect can create spiritual and psychological conflicts, as intimacy—meant to express trust and connection—becomes hindered. The resulting feelings of inadequacy, guilt, and disconnection can compromise both marital and spiritual fulfillment.

2. **Premature Ejaculation (PE)**
   Pornography's portrayal of rapid, high-intensity scenes can condition men to associate arousal with swift gratification. This may lead to premature ejaculation during real-life intimacy, as the body struggles to adapt to a slower, more mindful pace. For Muslim men, this disparity between conditioned responses and Islamic teachings on intimacy can deepen frustration and anxiety. The focus shifts from mutual fulfillment to fear of inadequacy, creating tension between spiritual beliefs and behavior and leaving the soul feeling unfulfilled.

3. **Performance Anxiety**
   Unrealistic standards depicted in pornography—such as exaggerated stamina and idealized physiques—can create intense pressure for men to replicate these portrayals. This internalized anxiety about meeting such expectations can disrupt sexual function, leading to fear or avoidance of intimacy. For Muslim men,

> this anxiety undermines the soulful connection that intimacy in marriage is meant to foster, weakening both emotional bonds and spiritual well-being.
>
> Recognizing the connection between pornography use and sexual intimacy challenges allows Muslim men to soulfully reflect on how these behaviors impact their spiritual and emotional lives. Addressing these issues through self-compassion and soulful growth can pave the way for deeper healing, fostering genuine connection and alignment with faith.

Where's the Soul? Why Current Approaches to Pornography Use Are Falling Short

As concerns about pornography use among Muslims rise, many interventions focus solely on behaviors and thoughts, leaving out the deeper soulful contexts that truly address the root causes of the struggle. Community and religious leaders often emphasize behavioral strategies such as fasting, installing website blockers, or avoiding impermissible environments (Amir, 2020). While these actions may provide temporary relief, they frequently lead to cycles of relapse and shame, as they fail to explore the emotional and spiritual wounds that drive such behaviors. The heart (*qalb*) remains unaddressed, leaving individuals disconnected from the holistic healing they need. Figure 11.2 offers a visual representation of this cycle because of surface-level interventions.

Parents, often considered the primary sexual health educators, face significant challenges in navigating this topic. Studies reveal that 90% of families avoid discussing pornography altogether, while fewer than 30% of parents engage in conversations about sexual health from Islamic perspectives (Ali-Faisal, 2014; Mirza, 2019). Many mistakenly believe that Islam inherently protects youth from these struggles or fear that discussing such topics will spark unhealthy curiosity (Osman, 2020; Sanjakdar, 2011). These gaps leave young Muslims without the tools or guidance to navigate the challenges they face. As explored in chapter 7, soulful parenting approaches can provide the developmental guidance needed for such critical conversations, fostering trust and openness between parents and children.

For many Muslim men, pornography use is not merely a behavioral issue but often a coping mechanism for unresolved trauma, emotional pain, or feelings of disconnection. Research shows that compulsive

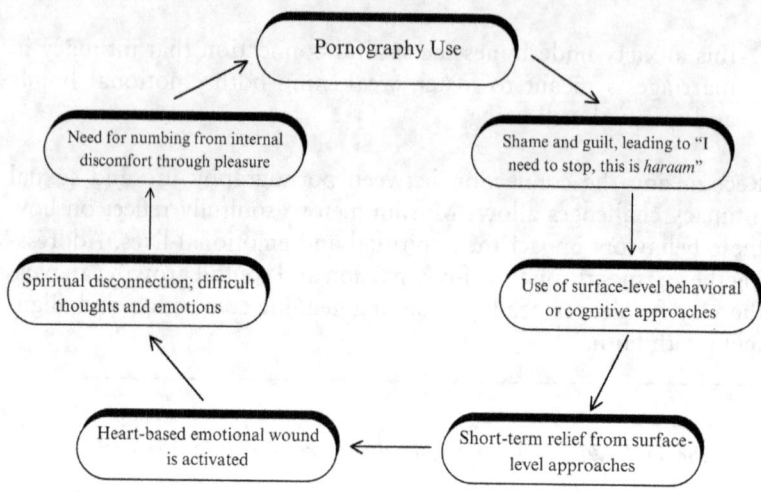

Figure 11.2 The cyclical pattern of pornography use in response to surface-level interventions that neglect the soul

pornography use frequently numbs deeper wounds, offering fleeting relief but exacerbating guilt, shame, and spiritual disconnection (Wright et al., 2017). Childhood adversity, neglect, or stress can subconsciously drive these unhealthy behaviors, further entrenching individuals in cycles of self-blame. Empowered abstinence, as discussed in chapter 4, emphasizes the need to address these underlying motivations with self-compassion, recognizing that healing begins with understanding and addressing the root causes.

The limitations of current approaches lie in their focus on controlling external actions without attending to the inner state fueling them. Islam's teachings on the *qalb* (heart) call for purification and self-reflection, offering a pathway to transform struggles into opportunities for personal and spiritual growth. True healing involves moving beyond shame and guilt toward *tawbah* (repentance), self-accountability, and spiritual resilience. Integrating trauma-informed therapeutic practices with Islamic principles allows Muslim men to address the emotional and spiritual dimensions of their behavior, fostering a renewed connection to Allah and a deeper sense of self.

A holistic approach—one that acknowledges emotional wounds, spiritual health, and the journey of the soul—empowers Muslim men to break free from surface-level interventions. By addressing the heart and embracing a compassionate, soul-centered framework, they can embark on a journey of lasting healing and transformation, grounded in faith and aligned with their purpose as believers.

Pornography Use and Shame

Addressing pornography use among Muslim men requires a compassionate understanding of the shame often associated with this behavior. The intersection of religious beliefs, personal values, and emotional responses can create significant spiritual and psychological distress.

The Cycle of Shame and Repetition: Shame often drives a cyclical pattern where self-condemnation leads to further pornography use as a coping mechanism. This feedback loop reinforces feelings of despair and isolation (Perry, 2017). Fear of judgment within the Muslim community exacerbates this secrecy, leaving men disconnected from their faith and community support.

Guilt Versus Shame: Understanding the difference between guilt and shame is crucial. Guilt focuses on behavior ("I did something wrong"), while shame targets the self ("I am inherently bad"). For Muslim men, pornography use often triggers shame over guilt, as it conflicts with their spiritual identity and values (Grubbs et al., 2015). This pervasive shame can evolve into spiritual distress, fostering feelings of unworthiness (Wilt et al., 2016).

Impact on Mental Health: Religious shame related to pornography use significantly impacts mental health, increasing the risk of anxiety, depression, and diminished self-worth (Wilt et al., 2016). Chronic shame erodes self-image and deepens spiritual despair, emphasizing the need for effective pathways to healing.

Pathways to Support: Compassionate, non-judgmental approaches are essential in addressing shame. Interventions that promote self-compassion, self-accountability, and the possibility of redemption help mitigate shame and foster healing. Religious leaders and communities can play a vital role by creating safe, empathetic spaces where men feel supported in seeking help. By addressing these challenges with understanding, men can reconnect with their faith and values, paving the way for healing and growth.

Soulful Healing from Pornography

This section explores how Muslim men can approach healing from pornography use in a way that aligns with Islamic teachings and the holistic care of the soul. It emphasizes that pornography use is often rooted in deeper emotional wounds, trauma, or unmet needs that must be addressed for meaningful and lasting change. While behavioral and cognitive approaches might help manage the external aspects of behavior, true healing comes from engaging with the soul's journey, integrating self-compassion, accountability, and a deeper understanding of one's emotional landscape.

From a soulful viewpoint, the consumption of pornography not only affects the physical and psychological aspects of a man's sexual health but also impacts the soul. The act of engaging with such content can lead to spiritual discomfort. This discomfort is often experienced as a sense of guilt or shame that, rather than promoting change, compounds feelings of inadequacy and disconnect. The soulful approach to understanding these connections is not just about acknowledging the physical and psychological impacts but recognizing how such behaviors influence one's spiritual state. This awareness helps frame these challenges as more than isolated issues—they become part of a larger dialogue about aligning one's actions with values, nurturing emotional and spiritual health, and fostering true intimacy that connects them with the Divine.

The following reflection questions invite men to see their struggles not as a failure but as an opportunity for growth and connection with Allah, encouraging a compassionate, trauma-informed approach that leads to real transformation and empowerment. As a reminder, chapter 4 on empowered abstinence shares further practical approaches aimed at balancing sexual desire, which might supplement the following reflection questions. Seeking qualified, professional support is encouraged.

Reflection Questions

What emotions or experiences in your past might be contributing to your current struggles with pornography? How have they impacted your relationship with yourself and others?

_____
_____

In what ways do you experience feelings of disconnection—from your faith, your community, or your sense of purpose? How might these disconnections be influencing your behavior?

_____
_____
_____

When you reflect on your soul's journey, what areas feel most wounded or in need of healing? How can you invite self-compassion and support into those areas?

_____
_____
_____

What role does shame play in your current experience, and how might reframing your struggles with self-compassion help you move toward healing?

_____
_____
_____

What steps can you take to address the root causes of your behavior, such as stress, trauma, or unmet emotional needs, in a way that aligns with your faith and supports your soulful growth?

_____
_____
_____

Sexual Intimacy Challenges

Nadir is a 42-year-old who has been married for seven years. During the initial stages of his marriage, Nadir and his wife enjoyed the full range of sexual intimacy, including intercourse. Over the last few months, he has been noticing challenges with maintaining his erection—he also feels anxiety rising in his body during intercourse, his mind swirling with thoughts about if he'll be able to "go all the way" this time. Nadir's wife is a supportive presence and has asked how she can help. Yet Nadir dismisses talking about and engaging in intimacy, saying that he's tired and stressed from work.

Sexual intimacy challenges are common and expected within marriage. As we explored in chapter 8, the soulful development of our sexual health continues throughout our life and may even amplify as a result of hormonal changes, life stressors, and more. And just as we explored challenges with sexual desire and pleasure that may arise for Muslim women, Muslim men may also face similar challenges. And the more we learn about what these challenges could be, the better we'll be equipped to work through them, soulfully.

While there are many other challenges that men may face related to sexual intimacy, we're going to focus on the three that are the most common: erectile dysfunction, premature ejaculation, and performance anxiety. Let's begin by defining each of these terms and what they entail.

1. Erectile Dysfunction (ED)

Definition: Erectile dysfunction (ED) is defined as the consistent or recurrent inability to achieve or maintain an erection sufficient for satisfactory sexual performance. While it is often associated with older age, ED can occur in men at any stage of life.

Signs and Symptoms: The primary sign of ED is difficulty in obtaining or sustaining an erection during sexual activity. Men experiencing ED may also notice a reduction in sexual desire and feelings of frustration or embarrassment during intimate moments. The condition can vary in severity; for some, erections may occur inconsistently, while others may find it difficult to achieve one at all.

Why It Occurs: Erectile dysfunction can be attributed to a variety of physical and psychological factors. Physically, it may result from underlying health issues such as cardiovascular disease, diabetes, high blood pressure, hormonal imbalances, or the side effects of certain medications. Psychological factors can include stress, anxiety, depression, and relationship issues, all of which can interfere with the neurological processes that trigger an erection. Lifestyle factors, such as smoking, excessive alcohol use, and a lack of physical activity, may also contribute to the occurrence of ED.

Prevalence: ED is one of the most common sexual health challenges faced by men. Studies estimate that approximately 1 in 10 men will experience ED at some point in their life. Prevalence rates increase with age, with nearly 40% of men aged 40 experiencing some form of ED, and up to 70% of men aged 70 and older being affected (Selvin et al., 2007).

2. Premature Ejaculation (PE)

Definition: Premature ejaculation (PE) is characterized by ejaculation that occurs sooner than desired, either before or shortly after sexual penetration, resulting in distress for one or both spouses. It is defined as persistent or recurrent and usually happens within one minute of penetration.

Signs and Symptoms: The primary symptom of PE is the inability to control ejaculation, leading to ejaculation that happens too quickly during sexual intercourse. This often leads to frustration, anxiety, or a feeling of inadequacy, and can cause tension within the marriage.

Why It Occurs: PE can stem from a complex mix of psychological and biological factors. Psychologically, men may experience PE due to anxiety, performance pressure, or past traumatic sexual experiences. Feelings of guilt or stress related to sex can exacerbate the condition. Biologically, PE has been linked to abnormal serotonin levels in the brain, heightened penile sensitivity, and hereditary factors. Additionally, PE may occur alongside erectile dysfunction, creating a compounded cycle of anxiety and premature release.

Prevalence: Premature ejaculation is considered the most common male sexual dysfunction, affecting approximately 30% of men at some stage in their lives. It is observed across all age groups and often results in significant emotional and relational impact, making it an important issue to recognize and address (Serefoglu et al., 2011).

3. Performance Anxiety

Definition: Performance anxiety refers to the fear of not being able to perform adequately during sexual intimacy. This form of anxiety can disrupt the ability to enjoy sexual intimacy and may interfere with erectile function, sexual desire, and overall satisfaction.

Signs and Symptoms: Men experiencing performance anxiety may notice symptoms such as difficulty achieving or maintaining an erection, rapid or premature ejaculation, and a general decrease in sexual satisfaction. This anxiety can manifest as a mental preoccupation with potential failure, leading to a cycle of worry that perpetuates sexual difficulties.

Why It Occurs: Performance anxiety is often rooted in psychological concerns such as low self-esteem, fear of rejection, previous negative sexual experiences, or a high-pressure perception of sexual performance. Societal and cultural expectations around masculinity and sexual prowess can exacerbate this anxiety, making it a recurring issue. The brain's response to stress hormones can inhibit sexual function, creating a physiological response tied to an emotional trigger.

Prevalence: Performance anxiety is common and affects men of all ages. While exact prevalence rates can vary, research suggests that many men will experience it at some point, especially during times of heightened stress or life changes. It is often a contributing factor to other sexual challenges, such as erectile dysfunction and premature ejaculation.

Understanding these common challenges—erectile dysfunction, premature ejaculation, and performance anxiety—can help men recognize and acknowledge them without stigma, creating a pathway for further exploration and soulful healing.

Soulful Approaches for Sexual Intimacy Challenges

Sexual intimacy challenges such as erectile dysfunction (ED), premature ejaculation (PE), and performance anxiety are not personal failings but opportunities for growth, healing, and deeper spiritual connection. A soulful approach reframes these issues as part of the journey toward self-awareness and alignment with faith, emphasizing compassion, understanding root causes, and integrating spiritual and professional support when needed.

Erectile Dysfunction (ED): Instead of self-blame, reflect on potential stressors or emotional triggers contributing to ED, such as life pressures, past trauma, or guilt from behaviors like pornography use. Address these without judgment, incorporating stress management practices like mindfulness, prayer, and spiritual reflection to promote inner peace.

Premature Ejaculation (PE): Recognize the role of anxiety or conditioned responses in PE. Shift focus from quick gratification to being present in intimate moments. Grounding techniques and mindfulness exercises can help foster a deeper soulful connection during intimacy.

Performance Anxiety: Acknowledge unrealistic expectations stemming from self-imposed pressures or influences like pornography use. Reflect on these and remind yourself that intimacy is about nurturing connection, not achieving perfection. Foster open communication with your spouse to create trust and mutual understanding.

When to Seek Professional Support

While reflection, spiritual practices, and self-awareness are foundational, professional help may be necessary if:

- Challenges persist and impact mental health, relationships, or spiritual well-being.
- Self-help efforts do not alleviate symptoms or address underlying causes.
- Emotional distress such as intense shame, anxiety, or feelings of inadequacy interfere with daily life.
- Deeper trauma or psychological issues require specialized interventions.

Therapists trained in sexual health, couples therapy, or Islamic psychology, as well as healthcare providers experienced in religiously responsive care, can provide targeted strategies aligned with Islamic values and beliefs.

Moving Forward

Begin addressing these challenges through introspection and soulful reflection, supported by spiritual practices and professional care when needed. By viewing intimacy struggles as part of a growth-oriented journey, men can nurture a balanced, faith-centered approach to sexual health. Use the reflection questions below to guide your process of self-discovery and healing.

Reflection Questions

When experiencing challenges like erectile dysfunction or premature ejaculation, what emotions or thoughts come up for you during or after intimacy? Reflect on whether these thoughts are tied to stress, self-doubt, past trauma, or pressure to meet certain expectations.

_____
_____
_____

How has your use of pornography influenced your arousal and response during real-life intimacy? Consider if it has set unrealistic standards or impacted the way you perceive and engage in intimate moments with your spouse.

_____

_____

What aspects of your life, such as stress from work, personal relationships, or unresolved emotional wounds, do you think might be contributing to your performance anxiety or other intimacy challenges? Reflect on whether these areas need more attention and care.

_____

_____

In what ways do you feel your connection to Islam and its practices supports or challenges your experience with these intimacy issues? Reflect on whether any feelings of guilt or shame related to your faith may be affecting your ability to engage fully and confidently in intimate relationships.

_____

_____

Male Factor Infertility

Yusuf is a 35-year-old who has been married for five years. He and his wife have been actively trying to conceive for the past three years without success. Initially, Yusuf assumed that conception would happen naturally over time, but after months of disappointment, he encouraged his wife to undergo testing, which revealed no clear issues. At his wife's suggestion, Yusuf reluctantly agreed to see a specialist. Testing revealed that Yusuf has a low sperm count and reduced motility, contributing to their difficulty conceiving. Yusuf struggles with feelings of inadequacy and shame, questioning his role as a husband and the impact this has on their shared dream of having children. He finds it difficult to share his emotions, as he believes that admitting vulnerability goes against societal expectations of masculinity. Instead, Yusuf becomes withdrawn, avoiding discussions about the future and distancing himself emotionally from his wife.

The Soulful Navigation of Male Sexual Health Challenges 271

As discussed in chapter 10, fertility challenges and infertility are common struggles for Muslim married couples, as well as for couples worldwide. Infertility, defined as the inability to conceive after 12 months of regular, unprotected intercourse, affects approximately 10–15% of couples globally (Mascarenhas et al., 2012). Male factor infertility accounts for 40–50% of all infertility cases, making it as prevalent as female factor infertility (Agarwal et al., 2015). Some research indicates that as many as 1 in 6 couples experiences infertility, with male factors contributing significantly to these difficulties (Inhorn & Patrizio, 2015).

Male factor infertility is often linked to abnormalities in sperm production, function, or delivery. Low sperm count, known as oligospermia, refers to a reduced concentration of sperm in semen, which diminishes the likelihood of successful fertilization. Poor sperm motility, even when the sperm count is normal, can hinder the sperm's ability to reach and fertilize an egg. Similarly, abnormal sperm morphology, where sperm have irregular shapes or structures, can impair their capacity to penetrate an egg. Varicocele, a condition involving the enlargement of veins within the scrotum, frequently affects sperm quality and production.

Hormonal imbalances, including disruptions in testosterone, luteinizing hormone (LH), and follicle-stimulating hormone (FSH), can also negatively impact sperm production. Genetic disorders, such as Klinefelter syndrome, may impair testicular development and sperm production. Additionally, past infections, such as sexually transmitted infections (STIs) or inflammation of reproductive organs, can reduce fertility. Lifestyle and environmental factors—such as smoking, excessive alcohol consumption, obesity, toxin exposure, and stress—are also known to affect sperm quality and overall reproductive health.

Understanding the prevalence and causes of male factor infertility fosters empathy and awareness around this sensitive topic. It highlights that infertility is not uncommon or isolated but a widespread challenge that transcends cultural, religious, and geographical boundaries. Recognizing this shared experience can help Muslim couples navigate these difficulties as part of their marital journey with greater compassion and resilience.

Soulful Approaches for Male Factor Infertility

A soulful perspective on male factor infertility encourages men to reframe the experience from one of inadequacy to a meaningful part of their spiritual journey. Infertility challenges traditional notions of masculinity, especially in cultural contexts where men are expected to fulfill specific roles. From an Islamic standpoint, masculinity is redefined by embracing vulnerability, seeking inner strength, and nurturing an understanding of self that aligns with compassion, patience, and connection to the Divine.

True strength in this context is not about the absence of struggle but the courage to face challenges with faith and integrity. For men, this means moving beyond societal pressures to appear unaffected and instead acknowledging emotions such as grief, frustration, or hope. Accepting and processing these feelings with a compassionate heart demonstrates spiritual growth and reflects a broader, more soulful understanding of masculinity.

Infertility often leads to feelings of self-blame or inadequacy, particularly when linked to male factors. In these moments, self-compassion becomes essential. In Islam, the journey of the soul involves continuous growth and striving. Recognizing the body as a temporary vessel and infertility as a trial placed by Allah encourages men to view their experience within a spiritual framework. This perspective fosters self-kindness, reminding men that their worth lies in their faith, character, and actions, rather than their reproductive ability.

The isolating nature of infertility can compel men to keep their struggles private. A soulful approach emphasizes the importance of connection—with their spouse, trusted friends, mentors, and Allah. Leaning into these relationships normalizes shared experiences and provides support, reinforcing a sense of belonging. The concept of *tawakkul* (trust in Allah) serves as a reminder that while effort is necessary, outcomes rest in Divine wisdom, offering comfort during times of uncertainty or helplessness.

Male factor infertility also challenges traditional perceptions of the male role as a provider. A soulful approach redefines provision beyond physical contributions to include emotional, spiritual, and relational support. Being a provider means offering love, patience, and unwavering partnership, nurturing a supportive and compassionate environment for both partners. This expanded understanding of provision highlights that true strength is found in character depth and the meaningful connections men cultivate with their loved ones and Allah.

Navigating Impacts on Marital Sexual Intimacy

Male factor infertility profoundly affects marital sexual intimacy, influencing physical, emotional, and spiritual dimensions of the relationship. When approached with compassion and understanding, these challenges can become opportunities to strengthen the marital bond, enhance communication, and deepen the partnership.

Infertility can evoke complex emotions like guilt, shame, and inadequacy, particularly for men grappling with the realization that their condition may contribute to conception difficulties. These feelings often impact self-esteem and confidence, leading to emotional or physical withdrawal, which can affect the quality of intimacy. For Muslim couples, societal and cultural expectations surrounding masculinity, fatherhood, and family life may intensify these struggles. Recognizing and addressing these emotions with compassion is crucial to preserving the marital bond.

Open and empathetic communication is vital for navigating the effects of infertility on intimacy. Couples should create safe spaces to share feelings without fear of judgment, fostering trust and mutual support. Islam views marriage as a partnership rooted in compassion and understanding, and reinforcing these values through vulnerable conversations helps couples maintain emotional closeness. Discussing the emotional weight of infertility and reframing intimacy as an expression of love and connection, rather than solely a means to conceive, shifts the focus from outcome-driven intimacy to shared affection.

Redefining intimacy beyond conception is essential for couples facing infertility. Viewing intimacy as an opportunity to nurture the bond and express love allows couples to reconnect in meaningful ways, relieving the pressure associated with trying to conceive. This approach aligns with Islamic values, emphasizing intimacy as a holistic connection that integrates emotional, spiritual, and physical dimensions.

Feelings of guilt or blame often arise with male factor infertility, potentially straining the relationship. Couples should approach the experience as a shared journey rather than an individual shortcoming, supporting each other with patience, compassion, and kindness. Infertility can be reframed as a test from Allah, offering opportunities for mutual growth and strengthening the relationship. Acts of worship, such as making *dua* (personal supplication) together and seeking comfort in prayer, can deepen the spiritual connection and help couples rely on *tawakkul* (trust in Allah) during uncertain times.

Strengthening the marital bond beyond intimacy fosters resilience. Shared activities, quality time, and expressions of affection help reaffirm the partnership and build a foundation of love and companionship. Shifting focus from conception to the shared journey of growth allows couples to cultivate a fulfilling relationship rooted in emotional and spiritual connection.

Male factor infertility can challenge traditional perceptions of masculinity, particularly the roles of provider and father. Redefining these roles to include emotional, spiritual, and relational support empowers men to see their value beyond biological fatherhood. Demonstrating compassion, nurturing relationships, and contributing positively to family and community life reflects true strength and provision, emphasizing the broader qualities of leadership and care within the family unit.

To deepen this soulful journey, consider the following reflection questions.

Reflection Questions

How do I understand my worth as a man considering my current struggles, and how might my faith help reframe that understanding?

_____
_____
_____

In what ways can I invite more self-compassion and release self-blame related to my experience with infertility?

_____
_____
_____

How has this journey impacted my relationship with my spouse, and how can we strengthen our partnership and shared faith during this time?

_____
_____
_____

What lessons or growth opportunities might Allah be guiding me toward through this experience?

_____
_____
_____

Male Cancers

Zaid, a 52-year-old Muslim man, was recently diagnosed with early-stage prostate cancer during a routine health screening. While treatable, the diagnosis leaves him grappling with physical, emotional, and spiritual challenges. His doctor has presented treatment options, including surgery and radiation, but the potential side effects, such as changes in sexual function and urinary incontinence, feel overwhelming. Zaid worries about how this will impact his quality of life and his intimate relationship with his wife. He avoids sharing the diagnosis with extended family, fearing stigma and pity, and feels embarrassed discussing the intimate implications, even with his wife. Zaid struggles with feelings of shame and inadequacy and wrestles with spiritual questions, wondering if the diagnosis is a test from Allah or something he could have prevented. His wife encourages him to join a support group for men with prostate cancer, but Zaid hesitates and is uneasy about speaking to strangers. Instead, he turns inward, finding some solace in prayer and reflection, though he continues to struggle with addressing the emotional and relational dimensions of his journey.

Health is an invaluable trust (*amanah*) from Allah, and caring for it is a spiritual responsibility. Prostate, testicular, and colon cancers significantly impact men worldwide. Understanding these conditions empowers Muslim men to recognize early signs, prioritize prevention, and align healthcare with their faith.

Prostate Cancer: Prostate cancer is the second most common cancer in men globally, primarily affecting those over 50. Risk factors include age, family history, and ethnicity, with African and Caribbean men at higher risk. Symptoms like difficulty urinating, blood in the urine, or pelvic discomfort often signal the need for medical attention. Early detection through regular screenings, such as PSA (prostate specific antigen) tests, is crucial for effective management.

Testicular Cancer: Affecting younger men, aged 15–35, testicular cancer is one of the most treatable cancers if detected early. Risk factors include a family history, undescended testicles, or a history of cancer in one testicle. Symptoms may include lumps, swelling, or discomfort in the testicles. Regular self-examinations are vital for early detection and prompt care.

Colon Cancer: Colon cancer, the third most common cancer in men, increases in risk after age 50. Contributing factors include genetic predisposition, low-fiber diets, sedentary lifestyles, and chronic conditions like IBD (inflammatory bowel disease). Symptoms such as bowel habit changes, rectal bleeding, or unexplained weight loss underscore the importance of routine colonoscopies starting at age 45 (or earlier with risk factors).

Impacts on Marital Intimacy

Male cancers can affect marital intimacy physically and emotionally, with challenges like reduced desire, erectile dysfunction, or altered body image impacting confidence and connection. Open communication and empathetic support are vital to maintaining intimacy during such trials. Couples can deepen their bond by emphasizing non-physical forms of affection, sharing spiritual practices, and seeking guidance from trusted medical and faith leaders. Resilience and mutual care can help couples navigate these challenges together, reinforcing their connection.

Soulful Reflections on Cancer and Prevention

Islam teaches that caring for the body honors its role as a trust from Allah. Regular health screenings for prostate, testicular, and colon cancers reflect gratitude for life and align with the soul's journey. Early detection not only saves lives but allows men to fulfill their roles in worship, relationships, and service.

Fears about potential diagnoses or societal stigmas should not deter healthcare. Reframing screenings as acts of self-compassion and trust in Allah's wisdom can shift the narrative. Seeking medical care reflects strength and faith, acknowledging Allah's plan and solutions for every trial. Proactive measures like PSA tests, self-examinations, and colonoscopies are acts of resilience and gratitude, enabling men to care for their sacred trust. Incorporating faith, such as offering prayers before screenings, transforms preventative care into worship. Reflecting on health as a spiritual responsibility empowers men to approach their well-being with purpose and confidence.

By aligning healthcare with faith, Muslim men can embrace preventative care as a pathway to honoring their bodies, nurturing their souls, and fulfilling their Divine trust.

Soulful Perspectives on Men Seeking Therapy

For many men, the idea of seeking therapy can feel unfamiliar or even daunting, shaped by societal expectations that equate vulnerability with weakness. Yet, therapy is a profound act of self-accountability and self-compassion, providing a non-judgmental space to explore thoughts, emotions, and experiences. Within a soulful framework, therapy can be seen as a step toward aligning one's inner world with one's spiritual journey—an opportunity to reflect, heal, and grow closer to Allah.

The Purpose of Therapy: A Compassionate Space

Therapy is not about fixing what is "broken" but about creating a compassionate and supportive environment to process life's complexities. It allows men to explore the layers of their experiences—whether related to stress, trauma, relationships, or personal struggles—with someone trained to listen without judgment. For Muslim men, therapy can serve as a space to reconcile personal challenges with spiritual values, helping them navigate emotional and psychological hurdles with clarity and grace.

Therapy is also a space where men can unlearn societal constructs of masculinity that discourage emotional openness. It invites them to redefine strength as the courage to face their inner struggles and to seek tools that foster resilience, self-awareness, and soulful growth.

The Role of Individual Therapy in Couples Counseling

While couples therapy can be transformative for relationships, it is essential for men to also have their own therapeutic space. Individual therapy provides men the opportunity to process their unique emotions, perspectives, and experiences without the filter of their partner's presence. This ensures that their voice is heard, and their individual needs are explored. By engaging in personal therapy alongside couples' work, men can deepen their self-awareness, fostering healthier communication and emotional intimacy within the relationship.

Therapy as a Soulful Act

From an Islamic perspective, therapy aligns with the values of self-accountability, compassion, and the journey of the soul. Seeking help is not a sign of weakness but an act of humility and trust in Allah's guidance, recognizing that human struggles are part of the Divine plan. Therapy can be a means of embodying ihsaan (excellence) by striving to be the best version of oneself—mind, body, and soul.

By embracing therapy as a tool for emotional and spiritual alignment, Muslim men can create space for healing, growth, and the cultivation of meaningful relationships. It becomes not just a path to personal well-being but also a way of fulfilling one's responsibility to oneself, one's family, and ultimately, to Allah.

Summary

The journey of navigating sexual health challenges as a Muslim man is deeply personal and intertwined with spiritual, emotional, and relational dimensions. This chapter has highlighted struggles such as sexual trauma, pornography use, intimacy challenges, infertility, and cancer, framing them within a soulful, compassionate context. Viewing these challenges as opportunities for growth and alignment with Allah's purpose transforms them from burdens into pathways for spiritual refinement.

Islam calls men to embody humility, patience, and self-accountability—values exemplified by the Prophet Muhammad (Peace and Blessings be Upon Him). True masculinity lies in compassion, emotional depth, and dedication to self-improvement. By embracing these values, men can move beyond societal stereotypes and misconceptions, nurturing a soulful connection to their sexuality that aligns with their faith and spiritual identity.

Safe, judgment-free spaces are essential for men to unlearn harmful narratives, reconcile struggles with their faith, and approach sexual health holistically. Empowered by therapy, mentorship, and education, men can explore their experiences with openness and courage, supported by a compassionate community. Soulful sexual health is a journey of resilience, self-awareness, and spiritual alignment, offering men a path to deepen their connection with Allah, foster healthier relationships, and honor the Divine trust of caring for their well-being.

Reflections and Action Items

_____

_____

_____

Reference List

Addis, M. E., & Mahalik, J. R. (2003). Men, masculinity, and the contexts of help-seeking. *American Psychologist*, 58(1), 5–14. https://doi.org/10.1037/0003-066X.58.1.5

Agarwal, A., Mulgund, A., Hamada, A., & Chyatte, M. R. (2015). A unique view on male infertility around the globe. *Reproductive Biology and Endocrinology*, 13(1), 37. https://doi.org/10.1186/s12958-015-0032-1

Ahmed, S., Abu-Ras, W., & Arfken, C. (2014). Prevalence of risk behaviors among U.S. Muslim college students. *Journal of Muslim Mental Health*, 8(1).

Ali-Faisal, S. (2014). Crossing sexual barriers: The influence of background factors and personal attitudes on sexual guilt and sexual anxiety among Canadian and American Muslim women and men (Master's thesis, University of Windsor). Electronic Theses and Dissertations. https://scholar.uwindsor.ca/etd/5051

Amir, H. S. (2020). The effectiveness of contemporary Islamic scholars in tackling pornography addiction: A case of Muslim students in Britain. *Asian Journal of Humanities, Art, and Literature, 7*(2). https://doi.org/10.18034/ajhal.v7i2.531

Dube, S. R., Anda, R. F., Whitfield, C. L., Brown, D. W., Felitti, V. J., Dong, M., & Giles, W. H. (2005). Long-term consequences of childhood sexual abuse by gender of victim. *American Journal of Preventive Medicine, 28*(5), 430–438. https://doi.org/10.1016/j.amepre.2005.01.015

Easton, S. D. (2013). Disclosure of child sexual abuse among adult male survivors. *Clinical Social Work Journal, 41*(4), 344–355. https://doi.org/10.1007/s10615-012-0420-3

Fisher, B. S., & Pina, A. (2013). Violent victimization and men's mental health: Research on male survivors of sexual violence. *Psychology of Men & Masculinity, 14*(3), 362–372. https://doi.org/10.1037/a0031836

Grubbs, J. B., Exline, J. J., Pargament, K. I., Hook, J. N., & Carlisle, R. D. (2015). Transgression as addiction: Religiosity and moral disapproval as predictors of perceived addiction to pornography. *Archives of Sexual Behavior, 44*(1), 125–136. https://doi.org/10.1007/s10508-013-0257-z

Herman, J. L. (2015). *Trauma and recovery: The aftermath of violence—from domestic abuse to political terror*. Basic Books.

Inhorn, M. C., & Patrizio, P. (2015). Infertility around the globe: New thinking on gender, reproductive technologies, and global movements in the 21st century. *Human Reproduction Update, 21*(4), 411–426. https://doi.org/10.1093/humupd/dmv016

Levant, R. F., Hall, R. J., Williams, C. M., & Hasan, N. T. (2009). Gender differences in alexithymia. *Psychology of Men & Masculinity, 10*(3), 190–203. https://doi.org/10.1037/a0015652

Lisak, D. (1994). The psychological impact of sexual abuse: Content analysis of interviews with male survivors. *Journal of Traumatic Stress, 7*(4), 525–548. https://doi.org/10.1002/jts.2490070403

Mascarenhas, M. N., Flaxman, S. R., Boerma, T., Vanderpoel, S., & Stevens, G. A. (2012). National, regional, and global trends in infertility prevalence since 1990: A systematic analysis of 277 health surveys. *PLoS Medicine, 9*(12), e1001356. https://doi.org/10.1371/journal.pmed.1001356

Mirza, S. (2019). Behind closed doors: Porn and young Muslims. *Muslim Mental Health*. Retrieved November 2024, from https://muslimmentalhealth.com/behind-closed-doors-porn-and-young-muslims/

Nasr, S. H. (1980). The male and female in the Islamic perspective. *Studies in Comparative Religion, 14*(1-2). Retrieved from www.studiesincomparativereligion.com/Public/articles/The_Male_and_Female_in_the_Islamic_Perspective-by_Seyyed_Hossein_Nasr.aspx

Osman, F. (2020). *How to talk to your Muslim child about sex*. Self-published.

Perry, S. L. (2017). Pornography use and depressive symptoms: Examining the role of moral incongruence. *Society and Mental Health, 8*(3), 195–213. https://doi.org/10.1177/2156869317728373

Sanjakdar, F. (2011). *Living West, Facing East*. Peter Lang Publishing.

Selvin, E., Burnett, A. L., & Platz, E. A. (2007). Prevalence and risk factors for erectile dysfunction in the US. *American Journal of Medicine, 120*(2), 151–157. https://doi.org/10.1016/j.amjmed.2006.06.010

Serefoglu, E. C., McMahon, C. G., Waldinger, M. D., Althof, S. E., Shindel, A. W., Adaikan, P. G., Becher, E. F., Dean, J., Giuliano, F., Hellstrom, W. J., &

Torres, L. O. (2011). An evidence-based unified definition of lifelong and acquired premature ejaculation: Report of the Second International Society for Sexual Medicine Ad Hoc Committee for the Definition of Premature Ejaculation. *Journal of Sexual Medicine*, 11(6), 1423–1431. https://doi.org/10.1111/j.1743-6109.2010.01975.x

Sunnah.com. (n.d.). Jami' at-Tirmidhi 3895. Retrieved January 5, 2025, from https://sunnah.com/tirmidhi:3895

United Nations High Commissioner for Refugees (UNHCR). (2017). *We keep it in our heart: Sexual violence against men and boys in the Syria crisis*. Retrieved from https://www.unhcr.org

Walid, D. (2020). *Futuwwah, and raising males into sacred manhood*. MI Publishing.

Wilt, J. A., Cooper, E. B., Grubbs, J. B., Exline, J. J., & Pargament, K. I. (2016). Associations of perceived addiction to internet pornography with religious/spiritual and psychological functioning. *Sexual Addiction & Compulsivity*, 23(2–3), 260–278. https://doi.org/10.1080/10720162.2016.1140604

Wright, P. J., Tokunaga, R. S., & Kraus, A. (2017). A meta-analysis of pornography consumption and actual acts of sexual aggression in general population studies. *Journal of Communication*, 66(1), 183–205. https://doi.org/10.1111/jcom.12201

12 Soulfully Seeking Sexual Health Support

We all will face sexual health challenges at some point in our lives—myself included. I have not been immune to these struggles and bring my personal learnings into this chapter. Navigating health systems, engaging with professionals, and experiencing the soulful impacts of these challenges have deepened my understanding of the complexities Muslims face in seeking support. In my work, I often encounter Muslims who are reaching out to someone for the first time about their sexual health challenges. I am deeply humbled to be that first point of connection, a role that carries both honor and spiritual responsibility. While I provide services to address their immediate needs, I also guide them in navigating broader support systems, helping them connect with other professionals when necessary. This process of seeking support often begins with building a foundation of sexual health literacy—knowing how to articulate the challenges you're experiencing and understanding the resources available to you. Yet, for many Muslims, this can feel like an uphill battle. Sexual health literacy is key to soulfully seeking support, but Muslims often struggle to describe their experiences or identify what kind of help they need. This chapter is not about perfect solutions but about creating a pathway—one that allows you to approach your sexual health with compassion, clarity, and a connection to your faith. Whether you are seeking support for the first time or learning to advocate for yourself

The Journey of the Soul

Birth — Spiritual Accountability — Spiritual Maturity — Spiritual Legacy — The Hereafter

DOI: 10.4324/9781032675862-13

more effectively, my hope is that this chapter serves as a companion in your journey, fostering a sense of empowerment and trust as you take steps toward healing and growth.

Introduction

Throughout this book, we have explored soulful sexual health as a Divine trust, empowering Muslims to navigate their journey with purpose and alignment. Previous chapters have laid the foundation for understanding sexual health as an integral part of our holistic well-being, offering tools to reframe it as a soulful responsibility deeply rooted in Islamic values. This chapter takes the next step by addressing the essential process of seeking professional support for sexual health challenges—a journey that is as much about spiritual alignment as it is about practical care.

As Muslims, our journey through soulful sexual health will inevitably bring moments of uncertainty, discomfort, or challenge—times when questions arise that we cannot answer alone. These moments remind us of the interconnectedness of our existence and the importance of seeking expertise beyond ourselves. Just as we turn to medical professionals for physical health and counselors for mental well-being, seeking sexual health support is a spiritual obligation that honors the *amanah* (trust) of our bodies. However, this process is often hindered by taboo, shame-based narratives, and myths that prevent many Muslims from taking this critical step toward care and healing.

This chapter focuses on equipping Muslims with soulful perspectives to overcome these barriers and align their efforts to seek support with their faith. It addresses common myths—such as misunderstandings about modesty, privacy, and the permissibility of seeking professional guidance—and offers practical tools to identify and connect with sexual health professionals who respect both your Islamic values and personal needs. By reframing this process as part of a soulful journey, this chapter encourages Muslims to view seeking support not as a source of discomfort or shame but as an act of spiritual integrity and empowerment.

In what follows, we will explore the challenges Muslims face in seeking sexual health support, share reflections to dismantle these barriers, and provide actionable guidance to help you build trusting relationships with professionals. Whether you are navigating questions about intimacy, health concerns, or healing from past experiences, this chapter aims to empower you to approach your sexual health with confidence, care, and alignment with your beliefs. Let us begin with some questions to guide your reflections as you prepare to take this step in your soulful journey.

Reflection Questions

How do I feel overall about my knowledge about and comfort with seeking sexual health professional support? Do I have any concerns?

_____
_____
_____

Which type of professionals do I think fits into the "sexual health support" category?

_____
_____
_____

What information am I missing about seeking professional support for my sexual health?

_____
_____
_____

Barriers and Misconceptions to Seeking Soulful Sexual Health Support

As Muslims, we face numerous barriers when attempting to seek sexual health support. Throughout the years of working in this field, I've heard from and held space for many Muslims who describe the many challenges they've faced on their sexual health journey.

Much of what Muslims need first is a reminder to be compassionate toward themselves. We need to remind ourselves that we do the best we can with what we know at the time. And while hindsight is often 20/20 and may shed light on what we could have done differently, we must remember that we were in a different place in the past. From this perspective, it's best not to "should" ourselves—when we didn't know at the time what we "should" do—and instead show ourselves compassion, as our soul is on a continuous journey of learning and unlearning.

In addition to self-compassion, it's important for us to also remember that while these barriers feel like they're within us, many of them originated from sources outside of us. As covered within the first two chapters of the book, our soul is not born with barriers and misunderstandings about sexual health, or any topic at that—these are learned. Our soulful journey with sexual health is impacted by many factors as we grow and develop, including the families, communities, and societies we were raised in. And since the soul is a witness to all that we experience in the world, we often have a lot of "baggage" within us that can prevent us from accessing sexual health support. It's important, therefore, that we separate these barriers from who we inherently are as a sacred creation of God.

To compassionately explore barriers that may be arising within our own lives, let's take a look at this from a broad perspective. Take a moment to learn more about the barriers by reading through the summary in Table 12.1, before we go into more details about them.

Barriers from Ourselves

For many Muslims, seeking support for sexual health can feel challenging due to several key barriers. First, a lack of sexual health knowledge leaves many of us unsure of where to start or what guidance is available, often preventing us from taking the first step. For example, since many Muslims aren't aware of the information presented in chapter 3 ("Foundations of Soulful Sexual Health for Muslims"), they don't have baseline information about their sexual health and therefore struggle to recognize when they may need

Table 12.1 A summary of barriers Muslims may face when seeking professional support

Type of Barrier	List of Common Barriers
Ourselves	• Lack of sexual health knowledge • Shame, fear, or anxiety • Misunderstanding Islamic perspectives of support-seeking • Challenging past experiences with professionals • Lack of sexual health literacy • Others? _____
Our Family and/or Community	• Shame or taboo toward sexual health • Mixed messaging about modesty and privacy toward sexual health • Fear of community members finding out about sexual health challenges • Spiritual bypassing (i.e. misunderstanding patience and trust in Allah as not also taking action ourselves) • Others? _____
Our Society	• Islamophobia • Lack of Muslim representation or recognition within the broader sexual health field • Others? _____

professional support. Additionally, feelings of shame, fear, or anxiety surrounding the topic of sexual health can create a sense of isolation, as many grapple with internal conflicts about whether it's appropriate to seek help at all. Fear about one's body and sexual health can result in anxiety toward having our body spoken about or examined by a professional. Misunderstanding Islamic perspectives on support-seeking is another significant barrier. Some believe that discussing sexual health might be seen as immodest or contrary to Islamic values, when in fact our faith encourages open, respectful conversations about all aspects of well-being, including sexual health. The Islamic value of privacy around marital sexual intimacy may also be misapplied to seeking well-intentioned professional support. Furthermore, past negative experiences with healthcare professionals who lacked cultural or religious humility can deter individuals from seeking further guidance. Finally, a lack of clarity about whom to turn to for help persists, as sexual health literacy within our communities is often limited, leaving people unsure of whether to approach religious scholars, medical experts, or others.

Barriers from Our Family and/or Community

Muslims often face significant family and community barriers when it comes to addressing sexual health concerns. The shame or taboo surrounding sexual health conversations can silence individuals, making it difficult to openly seek support. Many Muslims are distanced and detached from their sexual health, which is further complicated by mixed messaging about modesty and privacy. Healthy discussions about sexual health are sometimes viewed as immodest, creating confusion about what can be appropriately shared. Additionally, many fear that seeking help could lead to community judgment or gossip, which they believe reflects on their identity as Muslims. Spiritual bypassing can also act as a barrier, where trust in Allah and the concept of patience are misunderstood. Some may believe that relying on Allah means passively waiting for change without taking proactive steps, even though Islam encourages action alongside faith.

Barriers from Society

Muslims navigating sexual health often encounter significant societal barriers that make seeking support even more challenging. Islamophobia plays a central role, manifesting in healthcare settings through discrimination or biased assumptions about Muslim beliefs and practices. This leaves individuals feeling misunderstood or judged, leading to reluctance in accessing sexual health services. Additionally, the lack of Muslim representation or recognition within the broader sexual health field creates a gap in culturally and spiritually sensitive care. When the unique needs of Muslim communities are overlooked, it can reinforce feelings of exclusion and isolation, leaving many unsure of where to turn for guidance.

> **Reflection on Barriers**
>
> Addressing these barriers requires us to identify which ones we're facing, exploring all three areas of individual, family/community, and societal layers. With this context in mind, take a few moments to answer the following questions to deepen your awareness of which barriers may exist for you. We will then transition to explore Islamic soulful perspectives of support-seeking.
>
> Which barriers, whether personal, family-based, or societal, have I encountered when seeking or attempting to seek sexual health support, and how have these barriers affected me?
>
> _____
> _____
> _____
>
> How can I start to compassionately reframe these barriers, using the soulful perspectives I've learned from earlier chapters?
>
> _____
> _____
> _____
>
> What knowledge is missing for me to address these barriers? What questions do I have about sexual health support-seeking?
>
> _____
> _____
> _____

Seeking Sexual Health Support: The Soulful Islamic Context

Now that we've gained insights into barriers we may be facing with seeking sexual health support, it's important that we explore and reflect on Islamic soulful perspectives, which will be quite helpful in our unlearning journey. Because by exploring why our holistic tradition encourages taking care of our sexual health, we can learn to give ourselves permission to take steps toward seeking support.

Islam is a faith tradition centered on compassionate self-accountability and intentions. Our soul, as framed in chapter 1, is a Divine responsibility that has been entrusted to us from Allah, and our soul contains our body—and all aspects of our emotional, physical, spiritual, and sexual health. Alongside the Divine responsibility we each have toward our soul, Allah has also entrusted us with free will, through the gift of our intellect. And

Allah has also created and gifted many professionals with expert information and skills that can support our spiritual and sexual health.

While the nature of how Muslims conceptualize sexual health continues to be reactive and limited to certain milestones in life—namely marriage and reproduction—this book has outlined the soulful and developmental nature of sexual health across our lifespan. As such, our emotional and physical health foundations as younger Muslims prepare us for deeper spiritual and sexual health as we enter puberty onwards. And since puberty marks the transition into individual accountability toward Allah, this encompasses all aspects of our soul, including our sexual health.

In addition to soulful perspectives of our sexual health, many Muslims are also aware of a set of guidelines, or *shariah*, that we try to abide by in daily life. *Shariah* is often understood as Islamic law, but, in a practical sense, it encompasses much more than legal rulings. *Shariah* is a holistic guide that Muslims follow to live a life that is pleasing to God, covering every aspect of daily living, from worship and ethics to personal and social interactions. *Shariah* is derived from the Quran and the sunnah (the teachings and practices of Prophet Muhammad, Peace and Blessings be Upon Him) and aims to help Muslims cultivate a just, moral, and spiritually fulfilling life. In practice, *shariah* provides principles on how to pray, fast, give charity, conduct business, resolve disputes, care for family, and maintain ethical behavior in all situations. At its core, *shariah* is about aligning one's actions and intentions with Divine guidance, promoting justice, compassion, and the well-being of individuals and the community (Kamali, 2008).

The five core principles of Islamic law, known as the *Maqasid al-Shariah*, include the protection of faith, life, intellect, lineage, and wealth. Protection of faith (*Hifz al-Deen*) ensures the right to practice religion and promotes spiritual growth. Protection of life (*Hifz al-Nafs*) safeguards the sanctity of human life through laws that protect individuals from harm. Protection of intellect (*Hifz al-Aql*) promotes education and critical thinking while protecting the mind from harmful influences. Protection of lineage (*Hifz al-Nasl*) preserves family structures and moral relationships, while protection of wealth (*Hifz al-Mal*) ensures economic justice and fairness in financial matters (Kamali, 2008).

Since *shariah* relates to all aspects of our lives, it encompasses all dimensions of our soul—including our sexual health. As we reflect on the five objectives of *shariah*, you may be making connections between information that you've been learning throughout this book and our obligation toward our soul. For example, you may reflect on how sexual health struggles—such as sexual health decision-making before marriage—can have impacts on our spiritual and mental health. Or how protecting our life includes our physical body, and interplays with our sexual and reproductive health, and taking preventative steps for wellness exams as we age. And you may also relate the objective of preserving lineage toward chapter 7, which explored how parents can center soulful approaches to educate children about sexual health.

As this book has explored and demonstrated, our sexual health is not separate from our soul, but intertwined with it—which means that challenges, questions, or issues with our sexual health can impact our emotional, physical, and spiritual health. It is therefore even more important to center a collaborative model for all aspects of our health, and to take steps to address anything that arises that brings us concern.

Ultimately, as Muslims, we are continually encouraged to "tie our camel" by actively seeking resources and professionals, and to simultaneously place our trust in Allah with regards to the outcome. This concept is rooted in a hadith in which the Prophet Muhammad (Peace and Blessings be Upon Him) advised a man to "tie your camel and trust in Allah," emphasizing the balance between taking action and relying on Divine wisdom (Sunnah.com, n.d., Tirmidhi 2517). By doing what we can in the moment and actively addressing our Divine responsibilities toward our soulful sexual health, we tie our camel and allow the future to unfold with trust in Allah's plan.

With these soulful perspectives in mind, let's explore common myths that often prevent Muslims from seeking support with their sexual health, and how we can compassionately unlearn these myths.

Myth Busting: Seeking Sexual Health Support

Myth: We are taught as Muslims to have patience during challenges, which is a means to test our faith in God. My sexual health challenges require patience over taking action to seek professional support.

Fact: As we've explored throughout this book, we have responsibilities toward our soulful sexual health which requires us to take action. This means holding ourselves compassionately self-accountable to learn about our bodies; gain skills to take care of our bodies; and to take steps to seek support from trusted professionals. Patience/*sabr* from soulful perspectives is with regards to the outcome, not in terms of stopping ourselves from taking steps and action. We tie our camel and do what we can, while we pray to God for guidance, outcomes, and have patience with regards to the outcome.

Myth: Seeing an OB/GYN for my sexual health means that I'll need a Pap smear and pelvic exam, and I don't want to lose my virginity.

Fact: Not all women who visit an OB/GYN will need a Pap smear and pelvic exam—it really depends on the intention of your visit; what the issue or question you have may be; and whether you are comfortable with these procedures if the OB/GYN thinks that it would be an important diagnostic tool to gain insights about your reproductive health. In addition, as we explored in chapter 3, virginity is not related to medical exams that involve the vaginal canal, just as virginity is not related to menstrual hygiene products that are inserted into the vagina. The hymen is a piece of membrane that naturally changes and stretches during everyday activities, and its presence or absence is not an indicator of virginity.

Myth: It is not permissible to seek professional support related to marital sexual intimacy or other sexual health topics because it's a breach of the Islamic values of privacy and modesty.

Fact: While Islam has values of privacy and modesty, these are related to casual conversations and sharing of intimate information and details that are not for the sake of seeking professional support. For example, a group of married men must hold with great responsibility any information about their intimate lives with their wives and not partake in sharing any details. On the flip side, trusted professionals are there to support our soulful sexual health journey, and since Islam values the sanctity of our body and life, we are responsible to seek support. Furthermore, since marital sexual intimacy holds such a sacred value within the Islamic tradition, seeking professional support can amplify its blessings.

Myth: Our sexual health is not important until we have an issue or concern, so there's no need to seek preventative measures.

Fact: As Muslims, we tend to be reactive with many aspects of our health, since we may not have had soulful contexts to empower ourselves with what we need to know to be proactive. Since we are gifted with a Divine responsibility to take care of our soul, this means being proactive to prevent issues from arising that may further impact our spiritual development. Therefore, we must try as much as possible to "get ahead" of our sexual health by seeking knowledge throughout our lifespan, and seeking support when we notice something is a challenge.

> **Myth:** Non-Muslim providers often push Muslims to do what they don't agree with and may hold judgments toward my religious beliefs and values. I don't think I can be helped.
>
> **Fact:** Having held therapeutic space with Muslims, I have heard that some Muslims have had unhelpful and harmful interactions and experiences with non-Muslim providers. At the same time, it is best not to generalize this to all professionals, which may lead us to feel isolated and hopeless. And left to struggle alone. If you have had a negative experience or interaction, it's best to process how you felt and feel as a result, and to reflect on what is important to you moving forward. The rest of this chapter will share compassionate reflections and information to confidently empower your support-seeking journey.

Empowering Your Soulful Support-Seeking Journey

Having supported Muslims to access a range of sexual health professionals and services, I have seen firsthand the many obstacles we face with receiving soul-centered care. At the same time, this work has demonstrated a few key components that can help Muslims feel more empowered and confident with navigating various forms of support for their sexual health journey.

There are three key steps for your soulful sexual health journey—the first is knowing when to reach out for professional support; the second is knowing whom to reach out to; and the third is how to prepare for receiving support for your sexual health. Let's take it one step at a time, with moments to reflect on how each part relates to your sexual health journey.

Step 1: Knowing When to Reach Out for Professional Support

As we've been exploring throughout this book, our sexual health is a combination of our spiritual, mental, and physical health. From a broad perspective, Muslims engaging in soulful, sexual health work can recognize the need to seek professional support when they encounter challenges that disrupt their emotional, physical, or spiritual well-being.

Depending on the life stage you are actively in, there are signs and indicators that may gently nudge you to seek professional support. For example:

For *young children* who have not reached puberty, any complaints or difficulties with bowel and bladder movements; changed behaviors around certain family members; accidental exposure to pornography; or repeated sexual behaviors after initial intervention may warrant seeking support from a pediatrician.

For *teenagers*, young women experiencing painful and unpredictable menstrual cycles; boys who experience pain during erections or difficulty with bladder or bowel; or noticeable mental health challenges, such as anxiety or depression, may benefit from accessing physical and emotional health services.

As Muslims mature into *adulthood* and begin the search for a spouse, you may benefit from soulful mental health support when experiencing persistent feelings of guilt, shame, or confusion about sexual decisions you're making that conflict with Islamic values; to work through unresolved trauma; when you notice difficulties in maintaining healthy relationships; or struggle with self-worth and confidence as you think about preparing for marital sexual intimacy.

For Muslims who are *married* and are entering into family planning stages, questions about fertility and infertility; understanding birth control and contraception; and challenges related to erectile dysfunction or premature ejaculation may warrant a healthcare visit.

As you have read through these stages and examples, have you noticed anything? They have been presented in a developmental manner similar to the way in which the chapters are organized in this book and the journey of our soul. This book has been organized in this intentional way to build your foundation of sexual health knowledge as you grow and develop. Therefore, as you continue to access this book throughout your soulful sexual health developmental journey, it can hopefully help bring awareness to questions or concerns that may be arising. Let's check in now.

Reflection

Based on where I currently am in my soulful sexual health journey, what questions or concerns do I have? If I think ahead 3–5 years to my future soulful development, what may I want to learn more about or seek guidance on?

_____
_____
_____

Step 2: Exploring Sexual Health Professionals and Areas of Expertise

A second common barrier I find Muslims facing when trying to navigate sexual health concerns is feeling unsure about which professional(s) to access. Understandably, our sexual health feels quite vulnerable, and we often hold the value of privacy, so knowing who to turn to can greatly ease the process of receiving support.

Let's begin your empowerment journey by exploring a list of common sexual health professionals and their typical areas of expertise. Table 12.2 offers an overview of these roles; however, since licensure and professional titles can vary across countries, you may need to cross-check the information based on your local context. After reviewing the table, use the space below to reflect on what stands out to you and make any personal notes.

Table 12.2 A summary of sexual health related professionals and their role description

Professional	Common Reasons to Access
Sexual Health Educator	Guidance on sexual health, education on healthy relationships.
Sex Therapist	Addressing sexual dysfunction, intimacy issues, or improving sexual communication.
Psychologist/Counselor	Support for emotional concerns, trauma, anxiety, or guilt related to sexuality.
Medical Doctor (GP)	Physical health concerns related to sexual well-being, contraception, and sexual infections.
Gynecologist/Urologist	Specific reproductive or genital health concerns, hormonal issues, fertility support.
Social Worker	Support for navigating relationship dynamics, domestic issues, or abuse.
Occupational Therapist	Holistic and practical support for addressing spiritual, physical, emotional, and functional challenges impacting sexual health, including those related to disability, injury, or overall well-being.
Pelvic Floor Physical Therapist	Treatment for pelvic pain, incontinence, or physical discomfort/pain during intercourse.
Pediatrician	Guidance on children's sexual development, bowel, or bladder issues, etc.
Reproductive Endocrinologist or Medical Fertility Specialist	Fertility issues, hormonal imbalances, reproductive challenges, or family planning.

Reflections

_____
_____
_____

Can't I Just Speak to My Medical Doctor?

For many Muslims seeking professional support for their sexual health, a medical doctor is often the first point of contact. This is a practical and necessary step, as doctors can rule out physical or medical conditions that may be contributing to your sexual health concerns. For example, hormonal imbalances causing low sexual desire or erectile dysfunction in men (discussed in chapter 11) or conditions like endometriosis and pelvic floor dysfunction in women (covered in chapter 10) can be identified and addressed by a qualified medical professional. Having a clear understanding of your physical health can often be the first step toward healing and managing sexual health challenges.

However, it is essential to recognize that not all medical doctors have specialized knowledge in sexual health. Physicians vary greatly in their understanding, approach, and ability to address nuanced concerns in this area. This variability can sometimes lead to frustration or discouragement, particularly if a doctor dismisses your concerns or tells you that "everything is fine" while you're still grappling with unresolved issues. For example, a woman experiencing painful intercourse may be told her physical exams are normal, leaving her with unanswered questions about vaginismus or emotional factors impacting intimacy. Similarly, a man struggling with premature ejaculation might be offered a generic solution without addressing underlying emotional, relational, or psychological contributors.

To navigate these challenges, it's important to take a proactive and informed approach to your sexual health journey. If a doctor is unable to provide adequate guidance or if you feel your concerns are not being taken seriously, consider seeking a referral to a specialist. For women, this might include consulting an OB/GYN with expertise in pelvic floor therapy or hormonal health. For men, a urologist or andrologist may provide targeted insights into concerns like infertility or erectile dysfunction.

Additionally, while medical doctors are an invaluable resource for diagnosing and managing physical aspects of sexual health, many issues also require emotional, relational, or spiritual exploration. Challenges such as sexual trauma (chapter 10), performance anxiety, or pornography use (chapter 11) often benefit from a more comprehensive approach that includes mental health professionals or faith-aligned counselors. Viewing sexual health from a holistic, soulful perspective allows you to address not just the symptoms but the underlying causes, leading to deeper healing and alignment with your values.

Preparing yourself to access professional services is an empowering step in your journey. Whether you are consulting with a medical doctor, mental health professional, or specialist, being informed and ready to advocate for your needs ensures that you can take full advantage of the resources available to you. Let's explore how to prepare for these conversations and build a supportive network for your soulful sexual health.

Step 3: Empowering Yourself for the First Visit, and Beyond

Preparing to visit a sexual health professional is an act of courage and self-compassion. Mentally preparing for the visit is one step, but taking the next step to attend and navigate the first appointment, and subsequent ones, requires thoughtful preparation. Let's explore how to approach this process with clarity and soulful alignment.

Research

Empowering yourself begins with choosing the right professional, someone who aligns with your needs and values as a Muslim. Here are some actionable steps to help you find a suitable provider.

Seek Recommendations: Start by reaching out to trusted sources—family members, friends, or community leaders—who may have experience with culturally sensitive and faith-aligned professionals. This can provide reassurance and a strong starting point.

Research Professional Backgrounds: Investigate the credentials, certifications, and areas of expertise of potential providers. Many professionals list their specializations—such as sexual health, reproductive health, sex therapy, fertility, or pelvic health—on their websites or profiles. Verifying their qualifications and memberships in reputable organizations can offer additional confidence in their ability to provide expert care.

Gauge Cultural Sensitivity: Explore reviews and testimonials from other patients or clients to gain insight into the provider's approach. Positive feedback, especially regarding cultural and religious sensitivity, is a good indicator of their ability to meet your unique needs.

Evaluate Alignment with Islamic Values: Whenever possible, review the professional's communication style and treatment approach to ensure they are respectful of your values. A provider who acknowledges and accommodates Islamic perspectives on modesty, privacy, and spiritual well-being can create a more comfortable and empowering experience.

By investing time in research and preparation, you set the foundation for a successful first visit and a professional relationship that respects your needs, values, and journey toward soulful sexual health.

Developing Confidence: Communicating Your Sexual Health Concerns

After finding a professional to seek services from, the next step is to gain increased confidence in your ability to communicate about your sexual health and ask questions. While you may also be concerned about how the professional will respond, and what their insights will be (more to come on this), let's focus more on what we can do to feel more confident about our first visit.

Review the preparation steps in Table 12.3 and make a few notes on a separate piece of paper noting how you feel as you work through each step.

Table 12.3 A summary of preparation steps for Muslims for those seeking soulful sexual health support

Preparation Step
Clarify Intentions and Concerns: Reflect on the specific reasons for seeking help and list any specific questions or issues related to your sexual health.
Ensure Islamic Compatibility: Research faith-sensitive professionals or prepare to explain Islamic perspectives during your visit. Ask yourself how much energy you're willing to place into educating a non-Muslim provider about Islam.
Review Medical and Personal History: Summarize your past medical or sexual health concerns to discuss with the professional.
Consider Privacy and Modesty: Think about how to maintain modesty and privacy during the appointment and inquire about practitioner gender preferences if necessary.
Prepare Emotionally: Reflect on any feelings of anxiety or concern and consider how to manage them during the visit.
Understand Confidentiality: Ensure you are comfortable with the confidentiality policies of the professional.
Involve a Trusted Support Person: Consider speaking with a friend or family member before your visit, for support.
Set Spiritual Intentions: Align the visit with the intention of seeking wellness for the sake of Allah and your soulful journey.

> **Reflection Question**
>
> How are you feeling at the end of working through Table 12.3? Which steps do you need more time and support with?
>
> _____
> _____
> _____

When the Visit Doesn't Go as Planned . . .

Hannah is a newly married Muslim woman who has been engaging in sexual intimacy with her husband for a few months. However, she experiences sharp pain in her vulva when intercourse is attempted, prompting her to seek professional help. Hannah finds an OB/GYN through her insurance provider and schedules an appointment to address her concerns. At the appointment, the OB/GYN, without performing an examination, suggests that Hannah needs to "relax more" during sex and recommends using a vibrator to masturbate alone to become more comfortable. The doctor also suggests adding alcohol into her intimacy routine to help her relax. Hannah explains that she doesn't drink alcohol for religious reasons and feels relaxed and comfortable with her husband. Despite this, the OB/GYN dismissively advises her to "try harder" through the pain, leaving Hannah feeling unheard, invalidated, and unsupported in her effort to address her sexual health challenges.

Steve is a recent convert to Islam who is working to align his lifestyle with his newly embraced soulful sexual health journey. Concerned that years of casual pornography use and sexual relationships may have impacted him negatively, Steve wants to explore abstinence until marriage and prepare himself for a soulful and meaningful marital relationship. Steve researches therapists and schedules an online consultation with a Muslim licensed counselor. During the session, Steve shares his concerns, but the counselor appears visibly uncomfortable with mentions of pornography and premarital sexual experiences. The counselor emphasizes the sinfulness of premarital sex and pornography, stating that such behaviors are haraam *and carry severe Afterlife consequences. He advises Steve to limit his screen time, avoid interactions with women, recite more Quran, and fast to "control" his sexual desires. Steve leaves the session feeling overwhelmed and filled with dread, reflecting on what he'll have to do to "stop sinning as a Muslim." Instead of feeling encouraged and supported, Steve feels judged and unprepared to navigate his challenges.*

Both within and beyond the Muslim community, it is not uncommon to encounter professionals who may not be the right fit in terms of personality, approach, or the insights they provide. These experiences, while disheartening and frustrating, do not reflect on your worth or effort. It is crucial to acknowledge any feelings that arise without assuming that all interactions with professionals will follow the same pattern. Most importantly, do not blame yourself for the outcome—you took the steps available to you at the time and acted with the knowledge and preparation you had.

As the case studies above illustrate, challenges may arise with both Muslim and non-Muslim providers. Professionals, like all individuals, are on their own inner journeys and may unintentionally project their personal triggers or biases onto clients. This can be especially hurtful, frustrating, or confusing for Muslim clients who place significant trust and respect in professionals. When such interactions evoke further guilt or shame, it is important to remember that these feelings do not define you or your efforts. You are navigating a vulnerable space with courage, and challenges with providers are not a reflection of your value as a person or as a Muslim.

Approaching Challenges with Care and Reflection

When difficulties arise with a sexual health professional, it's helpful to reflect on whether the issue stems from personal discomfort or a professional concern.

Addressing Personal Discomfort

If the challenge feels personal, such as discomfort with how a topic was approached or discussed, take time to evaluate whether this discomfort is linked to your cultural or religious values. For example:

- If a professional recommends practices that conflict with your faith, such as alcohol use to relax during intimacy, reflect on how this contradicts with your values.
- If discussions feel too clinical or dismissive, consider whether the tone of the conversation resonated with your emotional needs.

In these cases, seeking guidance from trusted religious or health professionals can provide clarity and direction. This could include consulting a scholar or a culturally sensitive health professional who understands Islamic values.

Navigating Professional Concerns

For more significant concerns, such as a professional failing to provide adequate support or crossing ethical boundaries, consider these steps:

Consult Trusted Sources

- Reach out to an Islamic scholar, a knowledgeable family member, or a trusted Muslim health professional for advice on how to proceed.
- Explore community resources, such as Muslim health networks or local organizations, that can offer recommendations or support.

Reflect on Communication

- Consider whether expressing your concerns to the professional could lead to mutual understanding. For instance, if a provider seemed dismissive, a follow-up conversation might clarify expectations and improve the dynamic.
- If you decide not to communicate your concerns or if the issue remains unresolved, remember that seeking support from a different professional is a valid and proactive choice.

Align Efforts with Your Values

- Remind yourself that self-advocacy is an act of self-accountability and aligns with Islamic principles of caring for the *amanah* (trust) of your body.
- Turn to prayer to seek guidance and strength as you continue your journey toward finding support that aligns with your soulful needs.

A Soulful Perspective on Challenges

While such experiences can feel like setbacks, they are also opportunities to deepen your self-awareness and resilience. Every step you take—whether addressing discomfort, seeking a second opinion, or finding a better fit—demonstrates your commitment to honoring your well-being as part of your spiritual journey. Trust in Allah's wisdom and mercy as you navigate these challenges, knowing that the effort you make in caring for your sexual health is an act of worship and a reflection of your trust in the Divine. Now, let's review this in the box on the next page to gain a sense of steps you can take when issues with your provider/professional arise.

Soulfully Navigating Challenges with Professionals

When facing challenges with a sexual health professional, the first step is to identify the nature of the issue—whether it stems from personal discomfort or a professional concern.

If the discomfort is personal, take time to evaluate your personal beliefs to see if the issue relates to your cultural or religious values. In such cases, it may be helpful to consult religious guidance from a trusted Islamic scholar or authority to gain clarity.

If the challenge is a professional issue, such as inadequate support or a lack of alignment with Islamic values, it's important to address the professional concern by reflecting on whether it involves a violation of ethics or principles. Next, reflect on whether to communicate concerns with the professional to see if mutual understanding can resolve the issue. If you choose to communicate concerns, engage respectfully and seek resolution. If not, or if the issue persists, seek alternative support by finding a professional who better aligns with your needs.

Throughout this process, it can be helpful to explore community resources, such as Muslim health networks or local support groups, for additional guidance. Finally, practicing self-advocacy and prayer can help you stay grounded, empowered, and spiritually aligned as you navigate these challenges.

Reflections

Frequently Asked Questions: The First OB/GYN Visit

Is it okay to request a female OB/GYN?
Yes, it's completely within your rights to request a female OB/GYN. Many Muslim women feel more comfortable with a female provider,

and this preference is respected. You can ask for one when booking your appointment.

Can I wear my hijab during the visit?
Absolutely. You can wear your hijab throughout most of your visit. During exams, you may need to remove some clothing, but your comfort and modesty will be prioritized. Let your provider know your preferences.

How should I handle physical examinations that require undressing?
The provider will ensure privacy and modesty by using drapes or gowns during exams. Feel free to communicate your concerns about modesty so your needs are respected during the examination process.

Can I bring a family member or friend into the room with me?
Yes, you can request to bring a family member, spouse, or friend for support. Having someone with you can make the experience more comfortable, and clinics might be able to accommodate this.

How can I discuss intimate health issues without feeling embarrassed?
It's natural to feel hesitant discussing personal health but remember that your OB/GYN is here to help without judgment. You can start by sharing what feels most comfortable and know that your provider will guide the conversation with care and sensitivity.

Can I decline certain procedures that make me uncomfortable?
Yes, you have the right to decline any procedure or examination that makes you uncomfortable. Share your concerns with your OB/GYN so they can work with you to find alternatives that honor both your health and your values.

How do I maintain my modesty during pregnancy checkups or childbirth?
Communicate your desire for modesty with your healthcare team. Most professionals are sensitive to cultural and religious needs and will help you maintain as much modesty as possible, especially during intimate exams or childbirth.

Do I need to remove all pubic hair or shave/wax my legs before the visit?
There's no requirement to remove all pubic hair or shave/wax your legs before an OB/GYN visit. Doctors are focused on your health, not your grooming choices. You can decide what makes you feel comfortable, and your OB/GYN will respect that.

Can I visit the OB/GYN during my menstrual cycle?
Yes, you can still have an OB/GYN visit during your menstrual cycle. For certain exams, such as a Pap smear, it may be better to reschedule, but routine checkups or addressing concerns can still take place. Let your doctor know if you're menstruating so they can adjust the exam if needed.

Summary

We've explored the delicate balance between the personal, spiritual, and professional dimensions of sexual health within an Islamic framework. Acknowledging the barriers Muslims face in seeking sexual health support is essential for breaking down the myths and stigmas that often hinder individuals from prioritizing this critical aspect of their well-being. By framing professional help-seeking as not just a practical necessity but also a spiritual responsibility, we've emphasized that caring for our sexual health is an integral part of our soulful journey as Muslims.

For those seeking support, this chapter has provided soulful guidance to overcome barriers, encouraging reflection and intentionality in choosing sexual health professionals who honor both faith and personal needs. It has also highlighted the importance of building relationships with healthcare providers that respect Islamic values, ensuring Muslims can receive the care they deserve without compromising their spiritual beliefs.

For professionals, this chapter serves as a reminder of the unique cultural and religious sensitivities involved in supporting Muslim clients. By fostering compassion and understanding, professionals can provide care that aligns with the soulful needs of their clients. Ultimately, this chapter is a call for Muslims and professionals to collaborate with openness, respect, and trust, bridging the gap between Islamic teachings and professional expertise. In doing so, sexual health can be approached with empowerment, care, and spiritual integrity.

302 Soulful Sexual Health for Muslims

The next chapter shifts focus to soulful considerations specifically for professionals supporting Muslim clients.

Reflections and Action Items

_____
_____
_____
_____
_____

Reference List

Kamali, M. H. (2008). *Shari'ah law: An introduction*. Oneworld Publications.

Sunnah.com. (n.d.). Jami' at-Tirmidhi 2517. Retrieved January 5, 2025, from https://sunnah.com/tirmidhi:2517

13 Soulfully Providing Sexual Health Support

It's interesting to reflect on how my work in the realm of sexual health has led me to navigate two worlds—one being Muslim and the other the "mainstream." I've thoroughly enjoyed presenting at conferences and leading workshops for a variety of professionals in medicine, sexual health, mental health, and counseling. The humility and openness with which these professionals have compassionately reflected on what I've shared has been heartwarming. In many cases, professionals have shared that my workshop or session was the first time they gained nuanced, accurate knowledge about Islam—and that, more than anything else, was eye-opening for them. Muslims seeking sexual health support may turn to either Muslim or non-Muslim professionals, depending on their comfort level and the accessibility of services. However, many are deeply concerned about privacy and confidentiality, especially when discussing sensitive topics like sexual health. The fear of being morally judged for their struggles often compounds the difficulty of reaching out for help. This underscores the critical need for professionals to create safe, nonjudgmental spaces where Muslims feel seen, respected, and understood. To those I've met in the past at such learning opportunities who are now reading this, thank you! And to those who may be learning about sexual health for Muslims for the first time, I'm equally grateful you're here. I hope this section deepens your understanding, confidence, and skill set in supporting Muslim clients and patients.

The Journey of the Soul

Birth | Spiritual Accountability | Spiritual Maturity | Spiritual Legacy | The Hereafter

DOI: 10.4324/9781032675862-14

Introduction

So far, this book has explored soulful, nuanced contexts of sexual health for Muslims. And in the same light, this same nuanced and soulful approach is helpful for professionals who support Muslims with their sexual health.

It is not uncommon in my work with Muslim clients to refer them to a variety of sexual health professionals—most of which tend to be outside of the Muslim faith. At the same time, I have heard experiences from Muslim clients who have sought support from Muslim professionals who have had mixed experiences. There are unique complexities and considerations for both Muslim and non-Muslim professionals to compassionately work through, and for the sake of this chapter both of these groups will be referred to as "professionals."

For professionals, this chapter explores soulful, unique cultural and religious sensitivities that come into play when supporting Muslim clients. By fostering understanding and compassion, professionals can better serve the Muslim community in ways that resonate with their clients' soulful needs. Ultimately, this chapter is a call for both Muslims and professionals to work together with openness, respect, and trust, creating a bridge between Islamic teachings and professional expertise. By doing so, we can ensure that sexual health is approached not with shame or discomfort, but with a sense of empowerment, care, and spiritual integrity.

Reflection for Professionals: Deepening Your Approach with Muslim Clients

Working with Muslim clients on sexual health requires more than just technical expertise—it demands a thoughtful, compassionate understanding of their cultural, spiritual, and personal contexts. Many Muslim clients may feel hesitant or vulnerable discussing such sensitive topics, especially in spaces where they fear being misunderstood or judged. By reflecting on your own practices and adapting your approach, you can foster a therapeutic environment that not only supports but also empowers Muslim clients.

Below are a few reflective questions to help you consider how you can enhance your practice to better serve Muslim clients in their soulful sexual health journey.

As you engage with Muslim clients, take a moment to reflect on these questions:

How does your understanding of Islam and its values impact the way you approach sexual health issues with Muslim clients?

___

___

What steps can you take to create a culturally and spiritually affirming space for Muslim clients to discuss their sexual health without fear of judgment?

___

___

How might incorporating questions about faith, spirituality, and personal values into your intake forms make Muslim clients feel seen and understood before they even walk through your door?

___

___

These reflections invite you to align your practice with a values-based, culturally humble approach, centering compassion and understanding in the therapeutic relationship. Consider how integrating these questions into your practice could foster trust, provide clarity, and ensure that your Muslim clients feel heard, respected, and empowered to share their journey with you. By creating an intentional space that acknowledges their spiritual and cultural context, you honor your clients' unique needs and set the foundation for meaningful, transformative support.

Why May Muslims Be Hesitant to Seek Professional Support?

Muslims may hesitate to seek mental and sexual health support due to concerns about cultural and religious sensitivity. Research highlights fears that non-Muslim professionals may not respect Islamic values around modesty, gender segregation, and sexual conduct, creating discomfort when discussing sensitive topics (Ali & Ushijima, 2005). A preference for seeking guidance from religious figures or Muslim professionals often arises from the association of sexual health with religious morality (Ali & Ushijima, 2005). Additionally, a lack of culturally tailored services and fear of judgment around practices like abstinence, arranged marriage, or contraception can act as barriers (Inhorn, 2006).

When seeking support from Muslim professionals, clients may fear breaches of confidentiality, especially in close-knit communities where personal disclosures risk becoming known in social or religious circles (Goforth, 2014). Concerns about judgment, particularly regarding taboo topics like premarital sex or sexual orientation, and a perception that advice might be overly religious rather than therapeutic, also contribute to hesitation (Dialmy, 2010; Obermeyer, 2000).

To address these challenges, providers must prioritize cultural competence and humility, explore misappropriation bias, and implement values-based approaches that align with clients' needs for soulful and respectful sexual health support.

Reflection Questions

What comes to mind, in terms of words or images, when I hear the words "Muslim" and "sexual health"?

_____
_____
_____

Where has my knowledge about Muslims and Islam predominantly come from, and what is my assessment of the sources' accuracy?

_____
_____
_____

What stands out to me from reading through this book? What am I curious to learn more about that would serve my professional skill building?

_____
_____

Exploring Beliefs and Values-Based Approaches: Who Are Muslims?

As discussed in chapter 1, Muslims are a globally diverse population, reflecting significant demographic and cultural variations. Asia hosts the largest Muslim population, with countries like Indonesia, Pakistan, India, and Bangladesh accounting for a substantial portion of the global Muslim community (Pew Research Center, 2015). Indonesia, the most populous Muslim-majority country, represents about 12% of the global Muslim population. South Asia, Central Asia, and the Middle East—regions such as Turkey, Iran, and Saudi Arabia—have historically been centers of Islamic civilization and remain influential in Islamic thought and practice.

In Africa, Islam has a strong presence, particularly in North and Sub-Saharan regions, with countries like Egypt, Nigeria, and Sudan hosting significant Muslim populations (Pew Research Center, 2017). In Europe and the Americas, Muslim communities are smaller but growing due to migration and higher birth rates, with countries like France, Germany, the United States, and Canada seeing increasing visibility of Muslims (Bagby, 2012; Cesari, 2014).

This diversity underscores Islam as one of the most culturally and ethnically varied Abrahamic faiths. While core principles like the Five Pillars of Islam and the Oneness of God remain consistent, lived practices differ widely. Some Muslims identify as more cultural than religious, others adhere to literal Quranic interpretations, and many are still exploring their faith, especially regarding sexual and spiritual health. Understanding this diversity and distinguishing between beliefs and values allows practitioners to adopt a values-based approach tailored to the unique needs of Muslim clients.

What Are Beliefs and Values?

Beliefs and values are interconnected yet distinct concepts influencing how individuals navigate life. Beliefs are convictions about reality, existence, and the Divine, forming the foundation of faith. In Islam, the six core beliefs—Allah, angels, holy books, prophets, the Day of Judgment, and Divine predestination—shape a Muslim's worldview and relationship with God (Esposito, 2011). For example, belief in the Day of Judgment emphasizes accountability and the Afterlife. Values, on the other hand, are principles guiding behavior, rooted in beliefs but focused on practical actions. Values like justice, compassion, and humility stem from Islamic teachings and dictate how faith is lived daily. For instance, belief in Allah's mercy may inspire compassion in interactions.

For professionals supporting Muslim clients in sexual health, exploring the alignment—or misalignment—between beliefs and values is crucial.

A client struggling to uphold abstinence before marriage may feel distress when actions conflict with beliefs, warranting a compassionate exploration of their decision-making process. Similarly, a couple navigating religious guidance on using donor gametes in IVF may balance beliefs with their desire to conceive, reflecting differing priorities between their values and religious rulings.

Centering both beliefs and values empowers Muslim clients to reflect on their struggles without judgment. Consider this exchange:

Client: *"I feel ashamed about having sex with my partner, even though we plan to marry. I feel like a hypocrite because I can't follow a belief I've always held."*

Professional: *"It sounds like you're struggling because your actions don't align with your belief in abstinence. Would it help to explore this further?"*

Client: *"Yes, I'd like to understand why it's so hard."*

Professional: *"Your belief in abstinence is clear, but the challenge lies in living it out. Actions aren't who we are, and it's okay to feel guilty without letting shame define you. Exploring emotions and reasons behind your actions may help realign them with your beliefs."*

Client: *"That's helpful. I'd like to understand what's driving my behavior and how to stay abstinent before marriage."*

This approach reframes shame, fosters self-compassion, and aligns actions with beliefs. The PLISSIT model later in this chapter will provide tools for supporting Muslim clients with a values-based framework.

Having just read through this conversation between a client and therapist, take a few moments to reflect on the following questions.

> **Reflection Questions**
>
> How did it make you feel reading through the dialogue? What does this interaction bring up for you with regards to your own beliefs and values about abstinence and sex before marriage? How did the therapist gently guide the client to reflect on their beliefs and values?
>
> _____
> _____
> _____

Culture Versus Religion

Before diving into how professionals can provide care to their Muslims clients through cultural humility, let's take a moment to distinguish between culture and religion.

The distinction between religion and culture is often blurred, especially when discussing Muslim communities. This has led to the common and (sometimes) dangerous misuse of these terms. Religion refers to the system of faith and worship, with Islam being a comprehensive belief system based on the teachings of the Quran and the hadith, guiding Muslims in their relationship with God, moral conduct, and religious practices (Esposito, 2011). On the other hand, culture encompasses the social customs, traditions, and behaviors that evolve within particular communities, which can vary significantly across Muslim populations. While Islam provides universal religious principles, cultural practices differ based on geography, ethnicity, and history. For example, the practice of wearing a headscarf (*hijab*) is a religious mandate in Islam, but the way it is styled varies widely across cultures, such as between Muslims in Indonesia, the Middle East, and West Africa. The common misuse of these terms arises when cultural practices are mistaken for religious requirements, or when certain cultural norms are incorrectly assumed to be Islamic. This conflation can lead to stereotyping and misunderstandings, particularly when cultural traditions are mistakenly viewed as universally Islamic practices (al-Sharify, 2020).

Understanding the distinction between religion and culture is crucial when addressing the diverse experiences of Muslims around the world, and especially as it pertains to soulful sexual health for Muslims. Let's debunk some misconceptions and stereotypes surrounding the Islamic faith.

Dismantling Stereotypes: Muslims and Gender

Muslim men and women often face harmful stereotypes that distort their identities and experiences. Muslim women are frequently objectified through narratives portraying them as submissive, sexually repressed, or entirely controlled by men—whether through choices like wearing the *hijab* or assumptions about sexual dynamics in marriage. Conversely, Muslim men are villainized as controlling, aggressive, and hypersexual, reducing their character to simplistic and harmful tropes.

For professionals supporting Muslims, it is essential to recognize the impact of these stereotypes. They not only misrepresent Islamic teachings but also affect how Muslims navigate their identities, relationships, and well-being. Professionals can help clients challenge these narratives by fostering environments of trust and compassion, offering nuanced support that aligns with faith-centered values, and validating the unique experiences of Muslim individuals. By approaching these topics with cultural humility and sensitivity, professionals can empower Muslims to reclaim their authentic identities and build resilience against stereotypes.

Misappropriation Bias

Fatima is a 35-year-old Muslim woman engaged to be married in a few months. She has decided to seek sexual health education from a professional who came recommended by a friend. Fatima discloses to the educator that she has never been sexually active or explored her body, and while she has some anxiety about marital sexual intimacy, she's motivated to learn about her body and sex before marriage. The professional reacts in a shocked manner when Fatima discloses her abstinence, and says, "You mean, you've never even masturbated?" Fatima feels her face flush and her stomach drop, as she responds, "No." The educator then shares that masturbation is the best way to get to know her body before marriage, and it's common for young women to do this. "By getting to know your body this way, you can catch up and be ready for sex." Fatima isn't sure what to say—she's feeling ashamed and confused.

This scenario highlights misappropriation bias, where cultural or religious beliefs are misunderstood, generalized, or dismissed, leading to inappropriate or harmful professional responses. Stereotypes about Muslim men and women—such as viewing men as oppressive and hypersexual or women as repressed and submissive—fuel these biases. These misconceptions overlook the diversity within Muslim communities and Islamic teachings, which emphasize mutual respect, consent, and sexual satisfaction in marriage. Misappropriation bias prevents meaningful engagement with individual experiences, reducing sexual health discussions to preconceived notions rather than nuanced, client-centered care.

Bias can also manifest as viewing Muslims as "behind" Western norms, equating conservative values like modesty or abstinence with repression. This perspective overlooks Islamic sexual ethics, which prioritize consent, mutual satisfaction, and spirituality in marriage. Implicit biases—unconscious stereotypes shaped by societal narratives—further reinforce misappropriation bias, leading professionals to dismiss culturally informed approaches or view clients like Fatima as "lacking."

Addressing these biases requires active self-reflection, ongoing education, and a commitment to understanding clients as individuals. Practitioners should focus on personalized, empathetic care that respects the client's values and beliefs. By doing so, professionals can move beyond harmful assumptions, fostering trust and providing effective support for Muslim clients' soulful sexual health needs.

To place this context into practical action, let's take Fatima's case study and break it down into steps, pausing to reflect as we go. After which we'll explore a series of conversation starters and questions professionals can use to deepen their understanding of a Muslim's soulful sexual health contexts.

Fatima is a 35-year-old Muslim woman engaged to be married in a few months. She has decided to seek sexual health education from a professional who came recommended by a friend. Fatima discloses to the educator that she has never been sexually active or explored her body, and while she has some anxiety about marital sexual intimacy, she's motivated to learn about her body and sex before marriage.

Check-in: How do you feel after reading this context about Fatima? What feelings and thoughts do you notice arising? Do you feel anything arise in your body? Make a note of what you notice.

___
___
___
___
___

Next, ask yourself how you can acknowledge that Fatima's context might be different from yours, and how you can suspend judgment and actively place yourself in Fatima's shoes, so to speak.

___
___
___
___

Rather than—*The professional reacts in a shocked manner when Fatima discloses her abstinence, and says, "You mean, you've never even masturbated?"*—What would you say to Fatima sharing her background and goals for support?

___
___
___

312 *Soulful Sexual Health for Muslims*

How can you gain more context about Fatima's beliefs and values with regards to *how* she wants to learn about her body and sex before marriage? What compassionate, soulful questions can you ask to gain more understanding about Fatima, while ensuring that she feels comfortable sharing this with you?

If you do happen to make a mistake and say something and you're unsure how Fatima feels as a result, what could you say and do in the moment to check in about this? How would you repair the therapeutic relationship?

Cultural Competence Versus Cultural Humility

While professionals are trained in culturally responsive care, applying this knowledge without projecting personal feelings requires intentional effort. Two frameworks—cultural competence and cultural humility—help address clients' cultural and spiritual needs effectively.

Cultural competence involves understanding and respecting a client's cultural context by acquiring knowledge about their background, beliefs, and practices (Campinha-Bacote, 2002). However, it risks oversimplifying culture and reinforcing stereotypes if viewed as static knowledge (Tervalon & Murray-García, 1998).

Cultural humility, on the other hand, emphasizes self-reflection, openness, and collaboration. It acknowledges the limits of a practitioner's knowledge and prioritizes learning directly from clients, viewing them as experts in their cultural experiences (Mosher et al., 2017). This approach is particularly effective with Muslim clients in sexual health contexts, given the diversity within the global Muslim community and individual variations in how faith influences sexuality.

By practicing cultural humility, professionals can engage respectfully with clients, fostering trust and meaningful dialogue. This adaptability is essential for addressing sensitive topics like sexual health in ways that honor each client's unique spiritual and cultural identity. Let's consider the case study below to see how a therapist engages in meaningful, respectful dialogue with a client going through challenges with marital sexual intimacy.

Case Study: Navigating Cultural Humility in Practice

Hafsa is a 30-year-old Muslim woman seeking therapy to address challenges with intimacy in her marriage. During the initial session, she shares that she feels disconnected from her husband and experiences guilt due to cultural messaging around being a "good wife." Hafsa explains that she grew up in a family where discussions about sex were taboo, and her understanding of marital intimacy was limited to what she learned from her Islamic studies classes and cultural norms. She expresses hesitation in opening up fully, as she fears judgment from the therapist regarding her faith and personal struggles.

The therapist, aware of the importance of cultural humility, refrains from making assumptions about Hafsa's experiences or beliefs. Instead, they ask open-ended questions, such as, "How has your faith shaped your understanding of intimacy?" and "What feels most challenging for you in navigating this aspect of your relationship?"

This approach allows Hafsa to share her unique perspective and feel validated. Rather than relying solely on generalized knowledge about Islamic teachings, the therapist acknowledges that Hafsa is the expert on her own experiences. They collaborate to explore how her faith can serve as a source of strength and guidance in addressing her concerns. By practicing cultural humility, the therapist fosters a safe, respectful space for Hafsa to navigate her challenges without feeling reduced to stereotypes or oversimplified interpretations of her faith.

As this book has explored, sexual health for Muslims is deeply intertwined with spiritual, emotional, and physical contexts. As one example, marital sexual intimacy is often seen not only through a biological lens but also as a spiritual and moral practice. Through the lens of cultural humility, practitioners can better support clients' soulful sexual health by respecting the importance of modesty, privacy, and religious adherence in their lives. This approach also opens up the space for mutual learning and understanding, where clients feel empowered to share their experiences and needs without fear of judgment. For example, clients may appreciate discussions around sexual health that align with Islamic values, such as conversations about premarital abstinence or marital sexual rights and responsibilities (Ali & Ushijima, 2005). Cultural humility, therefore, allows providers to tailor their care in a way that aligns with the client's religious and spiritual needs, fostering a therapeutic environment that is both respectful and effective.

Table 13.1 compares cultural competence with cultural humility. After summarizing the table's content, use the space below to make any notes that relate cultural humility to your practice as a professional. We'll then transition to explore values-based approaches and cultural humility in practice.

Table 13.1 A summary of the key features and differences between cultural competence and cultural humility

Aspect	*Cultural Competence*	*Cultural Humility*
Approach to Culture	Assumes that the provider can gain a complete understanding of the client's culture through education and experience.	Views culture as dynamic, complex, and individualized; recognizes that the provider cannot fully know the client's culture.
Knowledge Acquisition	Focuses on acquiring specific knowledge about the client's cultural background, beliefs, and practices.	Emphasizes ongoing learning and openness to being taught by the client about their unique cultural context.
Client–Provider Relationship	The provider is seen as the expert who applies cultural knowledge to the client's case.	Sees the client as the expert of their own experience, encouraging a partnership between client and provider.
Power Dynamics	May reinforce a top-down approach where the professional holds more power based on their knowledge.	Encourages a balanced power dynamic, with both the provider and client contributing to the understanding and treatment process.
Flexibility	May be more rigid in applying learned cultural norms or practices.	Encourages flexibility, adapting to the client's expressed needs and values rather than applying generalized cultural knowledge.
Self-Reflection	Limited emphasis on the provider's ongoing reflection or awareness of their biases.	Promotes continuous self-reflection and awareness of the provider's biases, assumptions, and limitations.

Reflections

_____
_____
_____

Incorporating Values-Based Approaches and Cultural Humility into Practice: Questions and Conversation Starters for Professionals

While each professional has their own approach to build rapport, comfort, and trust with their clients, it may be helpful to incorporate conversation starters and questions to build awareness about a Muslim client's soulful sexual health landscape.

One useful framework for navigating these discussions is the PLISSIT model. This model provides a structured approach to sexual healthcare by breaking it into four levels: Permission, Limited Information, Specific Suggestions, and Intensive Therapy. The PLISSIT model was developed by psychologist Jack S. Annon in 1976 as a way to guide professionals in addressing sexual concerns within therapeutic settings. It has since become a widely used framework in sexual healthcare, providing a structured approach to help professionals assess and address the varying levels of sexual health needs of their clients. This model offers a flexible yet comprehensive approach to addressing the sexual health needs of Muslim clients, facilitating discussions that honor both their beliefs and values (Annon, 1976; Badran, 2017).

In the context of values-based care for Muslims, the PLISSIT model can be adapted to respect Islamic teachings while addressing sexual health concerns with sensitivity to soulful contexts:

1. At the **Permission** stage, the provider creates a safe space where clients feel comfortable discussing sexual health within the boundaries of their faith. This might involve explicitly inviting the client to share how their religious beliefs and values intersect with their sexual well-being.
2. Moving to **Limited Information,** the provider offers general education that aligns with Islamic values, such as the importance of sexual health within marriage and the integration of physical desires with spiritual growth.
3. **Specific suggestions** might involve tailored advice on sexual practices within the parameters of what has been learned about the client's beliefs and values, ensuring that recommendations honor the client's soulful sexual health journey.
4. Finally, the **Intensive Therapy** level involves more in-depth interventions, perhaps in collaboration with Muslim professionals or

counselors who are versed in both Islamic soulful contexts and sexual health, ensuring that the client's care is holistic and congruent with their belief and values system.

Professionals are encouraged to use the PLISSIT model to frame how and when they open and approach soulful discussions about sexual health with their Muslim clients. And as many professionals know, the initial stages with a new client are greatly impactful not only with regards to supporting the client with making sense of their sexual health struggles and needs, but also for building a soulful connection and establishing rapport.

Therapeutic Use of Soul

The concept of "therapeutic use of self" is common within the literature, involving the mindful and intentional application of the therapist's own personality, insights, and emotional responses. Central to this practice is the ability to build rapport, where the therapist fosters a connection that allows the client to feel safe and understood, facilitating open and honest communication. Empathy, self-awareness, authenticity, and maintaining appropriate professional boundaries are often key elements of therapeutic use of self, and these elements are very applicable to the work you will do with Muslim clients.

At the same time, given the soulful worldview of Muslims and their sexual health, a slight enhancement to the therapeutic use of self might be helpful. We'll call this model the "therapeutic use of the soul," since its aim is to deepen how we as professionals show up for our clients.

The therapeutic use of the soul for professionals who work with Muslim clients centers two key components: heartfelt compassion and self-accountability. You may be familiar with these terms, since they've made appearances throughout numerous chapters in this book. So let's explore what each of these components entail.

Heartfelt compassion moves beyond empathy that is intellectual or thought-based, toward that which is attempted to be felt internally. Heartfelt compassion by professionals requires a suspension of thoughts, biases, or perceptions, to be truly in the moment with your Muslim client. It is important to note that this form of compassion is not at all the same as feeling pity or sorry for your clients but rather seeing your role as helping them to uncover their sexual health issues and how they may be hindering them actualizing their desired goals. Compassion that comes from the heart is about "being with" the client, rather than "doing to" the client.

Self-accountability as professionals is crucially important to ensure that we are not projecting what is inside us onto clients. It is not uncommon for us as humans to project implicit biases, stereotypes, and our discomfort onto clients, often unconsciously. Self-accountability as professionals who work with Muslim clients means that we are compassionately calling ourselves into question when our thoughts and emotions about and toward Muslim clients need investigating. Self-accountability as professionals ensures that we "walk the talk" as we show up in helping roles with our clients.

Let's explore a few conversation starters that may help demonstrate heartfelt compassion and self-accountability with Muslim clients:

"I'd like you to know that I've worked with a few Muslim clients, and from what I've learned, there can be a range of beliefs and values. Would it be alright if I asked you some questions about this, as we complete our consultation?"

"I'm deeply sorry for the struggles you've had over the years, and that feeling of being stuck is what stood out to me from what you shared."

"I'd like us to have an open dialogue and for you to be comfortable with raising any questions or concerns about this process together. If I ask too many questions about Islam, or say something that doesn't feel good to you, please let me know. I also send post-session surveys, if you prefer to write this down. I'm open to improving how I show up to support you."

With these suggestions in mind, perhaps think back to Muslim clients you've worked with, or imagine yourself with a future Muslim client—what questions or conversation starters do you think would be beneficial to demonstrate heartfelt compassion and self-accountability?

_____
_____
_____
_____

How do you plan to hold yourself accountable to ongoing inner work and learning related to supporting Muslim clients with their soulful sexual health?

_____
_____
_____
_____

What Happens When I Can't Help My Client?

Having explored these contexts to build the therapeutic relationship, professionals often wonder what to do when they have reached the limit of their knowledge about Islam, and how to approach the conversation with their Muslim client. For example, both Muslim and non-Muslim fertility specialists may feel unsure what to do when a couple is stuck deciding whether to pursue surrogacy or donor egg or sperm. As much as the fertility specialists have their own beliefs and values about what to do, their role is to work with their clients' beliefs and values.

In the case of reaching an impasse with a Muslim client with regards to religious decision-making, or when you feel as though your expertise has reached its limit, the same approaches of heartfelt compassion and self-accountability can be used. While it's understandable to worry that the Muslim client may think that you can no longer help them, it is important to clarify that you are suggesting additional support to supplement what you are offering.

The following conversation openers may help professionals broach these conversations in a way that continues to be supportive of their Muslim clients:

"As we spoke about last time, we're at a point where a decision does need to be made, and I know how challenging this is given the religious concerns you've brought up. Do you have access to religious resources or scholars that could help you learn about reproductive assistance when navigating infertility?"

"I've been reading more about Islam and sexual health, and I have to admit, there's still so much I don't know. Shall we create a plan to support you with getting information you need?"

"It can be frustrating when you speak with a few different scholars and community leaders, and they give you different perspectives. I'm sure it can make things confusing. I remember you telling me about the 'tying your camel' concept within Islam. Does this apply here? If you feel like you've tied your camel, how can you move forward with deciding what to do and trusting in God, as you've been doing throughout our work together."

Take a few moments to perhaps reflect on your work with Muslim clients. After reading this chapter, how would you use self-accountability and compassion to broach challenging situations and topics with them?

_____
_____
_____
_____

Soulful Metaphors in Therapy: Tie Your Camel

Muslims often use metaphors to articulate complex emotional and spiritual experiences, connecting their internal states with familiar imagery from Islamic traditions. Metaphors like "the heart as a garden" or "the soul's journey" integrate spiritual values with emotional healing, fostering self-awareness and insight (Abu-Raiya & Pargament, 2015). They also facilitate communication in therapy, particularly when discussing sensitive topics that may feel culturally challenging (al-Krenawi & Graham, 2000).

Professionals supporting Muslim clients are encouraged to explore metaphors their clients resonate with or introduce relevant Islamic ones. A well-known example is the hadith, "Tie your camel and trust in Allah," which emphasizes balancing personal responsibility with reliance on God (Sunnah.com, n.d., Tirmidhi 2517). This metaphor can help clients understand the interplay between action and faith in their healing journey. For instance, a therapist might encourage practical steps like mindfulness or learning about one's body, framed as "tying your camel" while trusting in Allah's plan. By using such metaphors, therapists can create a meaningful connection between therapeutic practices and the client's spiritual values, making the healing process both practical and soulfully aligned.

Summary

This final chapter provided professionals with tools to offer soulful and culturally sensitive sexual health support to Muslim clients. Recognizing the unique barriers Muslims face—whether working with Muslim or non-Muslim professionals—the chapter emphasized fostering trust, compassion, and understanding to create safe and empowering care environments that honor spiritual and cultural needs.

Muslims often hesitate to seek support from non-Muslim professionals due to concerns about cultural insensitivity, judgment, and a lack of understanding of Islamic practices. Muslim professionals, meanwhile, face challenges like confidentiality in close-knit communities, addressing taboo topics, and avoiding overly rigid religious frameworks that might not meet holistic client needs.

To address these gaps, the chapter encouraged cultural humility, values-based care, and adaptive approaches that align with clients' spiritual and cultural frameworks. Strategies included addressing unconscious biases, understanding faith-informed decisions, and fostering nonjudgmental, respectful therapeutic relationships. By adopting this soulful approach, professionals can empower Muslim clients to navigate sexual health challenges with dignity and spiritual alignment.

Reflections and Action Items

Reference List

Abu-Raiya, H., & Pargament, K. I. (2015). Religious coping among diverse religions: Commonalities and divergences. *Psychology of Religion and Spirituality,* 7(1), 24–33.

Ali, K. (2006). *Sexual ethics and Islam: Feminist reflections on Qur'an, Hadith, and jurisprudence.* Oneworld Publications.

Ali, M. M., & Ushijima, H. (2005). Perceptions of men on the role of religious leaders in reproductive health issues in rural Pakistan. *Journal of Biosocial Science,* 37(1), 115–122. https://doi.org/10.1017/S0021932003006473

Annon, J. S. (1976). The PLISSIT model: A proposed conceptual scheme for the behavioral treatment of sexual problems. *Journal of Sex Education and Therapy,* 2(1), 1–15. https://doi.org/10.1080/01614576.1976.11074483

Badran, H. (2017). Culturally sensitive approaches to sexual health counseling for Muslim clients. *Journal of Muslim Mental Health,* 11(2), 45–60.

Bagby, I. (2012). *The American mosque 2011: Basic characteristics of the American mosque, attitudes of mosque leaders.* Council on American–Islamic Relations. Retrieved from https://hirr.hartfordinternational.edu/wp-content/uploads/2024/11/The-American-Mosque-2011-web.pdf

Bouhdiba, A. (1985). *Sexuality in Islam.* Routledge & Kegan Paul.

Campinha-Bacote, J. (2002). The process of cultural competence in the delivery of healthcare services: A model of care. *Journal of Transcultural Nursing,* 13(3), 181–184. https://doi.org/10.1177/10459602013003003

Cesari, J. (2014). *The awakening of Muslim democracy: Religion, modernity, and the state.* Cambridge University Press.

Dialmy, A. (2010). Sexuality and Islam. The European Journal of Contraception & Reproductive Health Care, 15(3), 160–168. https://doi.org/10.3109/13625181003793339

Esposito, J. L. (2011). *What everyone needs to know about Islam.* Oxford University Press.

FitzGerald, C., & Hurst, S. (2017). Implicit bias in healthcare professionals: A systematic review. *BMC Medical Ethics, 18*(1), 19. https://doi.org/10.1186/s12910-017-0179-8

Goforth, A. N., Oka, E. R., Leong, F. T. L., & Denis, D. J. (2014). Acculturation, acculturative stress, religiosity and psychological adjustment among Muslim Arab American adolescents. Journal of Muslim Mental Health, 8(2), 3–19. https://doi.org/10.3998/jmmh.10381607.0008.202

Hasnain, M. (2005). Cultural approach to HIV/AIDS harm reduction in Muslim countries. *Harm Reduction Journal, 2*(1), 1–9. https://doi.org/10.1186/1477-7517-2-23

Inhorn, M. C. (2006). Making Muslim babies: IVF and gamete donation in Sunni versus Shi'a Islam. *Culture, Medicine, and Psychiatry, 30*(4), 427–450. https://doi.org/10.1007/s11013-006-9027-x

Krenawi, A., al-, & Graham, J. R. (2000). Culturally sensitive social work practice with Arab clients in mental health settings. *Health & Social Work, 25*(1), 9–22.

Mosher, D. K., Hook, J. N., Captari, L. E., Davis, D. E., DeBlaere, C., & Owen, J. (2017). Cultural humility: A therapeutic framework for engaging diverse clients. Practice Innovations, 2(4), 221–233. https://doi.org/10.1037/pri0000055

Obermeyer, C. M. (2000). Sexuality in Morocco: Changing context and contested rights. *Culture, Health & Sexuality, 2*(3), 239–254. https://doi.org/10.1080/136910500422232

Pew Research Center. (2015). *The future of world religions: Population growth projections, 2010–2050.* Retrieved from https://www.pewforum.org/2015/04/02/religious-projections-2010-2050/

Pew Research Center. (2017). *Europe's growing Muslim population.* Retrieved from https://www.pewforum.org/2017/11/29/europes-growing-muslim-population/

Roald, A. S. (2001). *Women in Islam: The Western experience.* Routledge.

Sharify, T., al- (2020). Cultural versus religious practices: The case of Muslim communities. *Journal of Islamic Studies, 12*(2), 145–162. https://doi.org/10.1093/jis/ett005

Sunnah.com. (n.d.). *Jami' at-Tirmidhi 2517.* Retrieved January 5, 2025, from https://sunnah.com/tirmidhi:2517

Tervalon, M., & Murray-García, J. (1998). Cultural humility versus cultural competence: A critical distinction in defining physician training outcomes in multicultural education. *Journal of Health Care for the Poor and Underserved, 9*(2), 117–125. https://doi.org/10.1353/hpu.2010.0233

Conclusion
A Soulful Vision for Sexual Health

This book has been an invitation to journey toward soulful sexual health—an integrative, lifelong process that connects the physical, emotional, and spiritual dimensions of our being. Centered on the Islamic framework of the soul, it emphasizes that sexual health is not merely a matter of physical behaviors or biological functions, but a sacred part of our journey toward Allah. Grounded in compassion, self-accountability, and the alignment of our actions with faith, this book aspires to transform the way Muslims approach sexual health in their lives, families, and communities.

To you, the reader, I offer my deepest gratitude. By engaging with this book, you have taken an essential step in contributing to a future where soulful sexual health is a natural and celebrated part of the Muslim journey. Your willingness to reflect, unlearn, and embrace these teachings demonstrates your commitment to aligning your actions with Allah's guidance. May Allah continue to guide you on your journey.

Barriers to Change

As we move forward, we must also recognize and address the barriers that stand in the way of this transformation. The taboos, shame, and misinformation surrounding sexual health are deeply entrenched in cultural narratives and often reinforced by societal and systemic stigmas. Misinterpretations of Islamic teachings, fear of judgment, and limited access to faith-aligned resources further complicate the journey.

On a personal level, unhealed wounds can cause our hearts to constrict at the mention or thought of sexual health. Past experiences of shame, trauma, or fear leave emotional scars that make it difficult to engage with this topic openly. Unless we address these wounds with self-compassion and a commitment to healing, the cycles of silence and stigma will persist, preventing meaningful growth.

This book is designed to address these barriers, offering soulful tools and frameworks that empower individuals and communities to navigate the challenges of sexual health with resilience and intentionality. By confronting our own discomfort and actively seeking healing, we can create environments where sexual health education is normalized, compassionate, and grounded in Islamic values.

A Soulful Vision for the Future

"Indeed, Allah will not change the condition of a people until they change what is in themselves" (Quran 13:11)

True transformation begins with the individual. If we wish to see a shift in our families, communities, and societies, we must first embark on the journey of our own soul. This book centers on your personal journey toward soulful sexual health, knowing that its ripple effects will extend to those around you and beyond.

My vision for the future of soulful sexual health for Muslims is one of collective empowerment and systemic change. People, families, and communities recognize that investing in soulful sexual health for Muslims is not merely a practical choice but a spiritual one. They understand that this investment supports the journey of the soul, which is an obligation for every Muslim. Caring for our sexual health is not separate from our faith; it is an essential part of aligning with Allah's guidance and fulfilling our responsibility to nurture the body and soul He has entrusted to us.

I imagine a world where professionals are trained in soul-based frameworks for sexual health, integrating soulful Islamic principles with the practical realities of contemporary life to provide therapy and educational approaches that truly resonate with Muslims. In this world, Islamic schools, weekend programs, and community centers seamlessly incorporate sexual health education into their curricula, equipping the next generation with the knowledge, compassion, and resilience they need to navigate their journey with confidence and connection. Educational institutions at all levels would offer courses on soulful sexual health for Muslims, acknowledging the profound intersections between religion and sexual health as a source of spiritual growth and connection.

Collaboration would thrive, bringing together the expertise of scholars, imams, therapists, educators, and holistic healers to create comprehensive and compassionate approaches to sexual health. Communities would invest in training imams, resident scholars, chaplains, teachers, and volunteers to approach sexual health discussions with confidence and nuance, bridging the gap between faith and lived experiences. In this imagined world, every individual would have access to a soulful, well-rounded approach to sexual health, fostering a deeper connection to themselves, their faith, and their Creator.

An Ongoing Journey

This book is a step toward realizing this vision, but it is far from the final word. The field of soulful sexual health for Muslims is in its infancy, and there is much work to be done. Together, we can nurture this field, creating spaces for research, education, and dialogue that uphold the sacredness of our bodies and souls. I hope that you will join me on this ongoing journey.

Throughout this book, you have encountered reflection questions designed to help you deepen your understanding, explore your emotions, and take steps toward personal growth. Now, as you close this book, there is one final reflection question to consider: **What are you walking away with?** Think about the insights, tools, and inspirations you've gained through this journey. How will they shape your approach to your own sexual health, your relationships, and your connection to Allah?

Whether you are embarking on personal healing, fostering openness within your family, or contributing to community change, remember that this journey is a sacred trust and an act of worship.

May Allah guide us all to embrace our sexual health with dignity, self-awareness, and faith, and may this work serve as a means of benefit for generations to come. Ameen.

Additional Readings

Chapter 1: Contextualizing Islam and the Soul

Helwa, A. (2020). *Secrets of divine love: A spiritual journey into the heart of Islam.* Naulit Publishing House.
Nasr, S. H. (2002). *The heart of Islam: Enduring values for humanity.* Harper San Francisco.
Nasr, S. H. (2007). *The garden of truth: The vision and promise of Sufism, Islam's mystical tradition.* Harper One.
Nasr, S. H., Dagli, C. K., Dakake, M. M., Lumbard, J. E. B., & Rustom, M. (Eds.). (2015). *The study Quran: A new translation and commentary.* HarperOne.
Prince Ghazi bin Muhammad. (2018). *A thinking person's guide to Islam: The essence of Islam in 12 verses from the Qur'an.* Turath Publishing.
Rahman, J. (2013). *Spiritual gems of Islam: Insights & practices from the Qur'an, Hadith, Rumi & Muslim teaching stories to enlighten the heart & mind.* Sky Light Paths Publishing.

Chapter 2: A Soulful Model of Sexual Health for Muslims

El Fadl, K. A. (2001). *Speaking in God's name: Islamic law, authority and women.* Oneworld Publications.
Sidek, O., & Mansor, E. (2021). *Sex, soul and Islam.* Claritas Books.

Chapter 3: Foundations of Soulful Sexual Health for Muslims

Boston Women's Health Book Collective. (2011). *Our bodies, ourselves: A new edition for a new era.* Touchstone.
Madaras, L., & Madaras, A. (2007). *What's happening to my body? Book for boys: A growing-up guide for parents and sons* (3rd ed.). William Morrow Paperbacks.
Madaras, L., & Madaras, A. (2007). *What's happening to my body? Book for girls: A growing-up guide for parents and daughters* (3rd ed.). William Morrow Paperbacks.
Vitti, A. (2020). *In the FLO: Unlock your hormonal advantage and revolutionize your life.* HarperOne.

Chapter 4: A Soulful Model of Empowered Abstinence

Ghazali, A. H., al- (1995). *On disciplining the soul and on breaking the two desires: Books XXII and XXIII of the Revival of the Religious Sciences (Ihya' 'ulum al-din)*. (T. J. Winter, trans.). Islamic Texts Society.

Making Sense of Islam & Sexual Health for Muslims. (n.d.). *Making Sense of Islam and Sexual Health for Muslims* video series [YouTube playlist]. YouTube. www.youtube.com/playlist?list=PL8VghbPE-c_NtexjK94f5R-UTMYJ4svj1

Chapter 5: The Soulful Search for a Spouse

Abugideiri, S. E., & Magid, M. H. (2014). *Before you tie the knot: A guide for couples*. CreateSpace Independent Publishing Platform.

Kawthari, M. I., al- (2010). *Islamic guide to sexual relations*. White Thread Press.

Nadir, P. A. (2021). *Before the nikah: Proven principles to help single Muslims choose wisely and build strong marriages*. Book Power Publishing.

Chapter 6: Soulful Sexual Intimacy in Marriage

Chapman, G. D. (2010). *The five love languages: The secret to love that lasts*. Walker Large Print.

Nagoski, E. (2024). *Come together: The science (and art!) of creating lasting sexual connections*. Harper Wave.

Nagoski, E. (2015). *Come as you are: The surprising new science that will transform your sex life*. Simon & Schuster.

Chapter 7: Soulful Parenting Approaches for Sexual Health

Osman, F. (2020). *How to talk to your Muslim child about sex*. Self-published.

Sanders, J. (2015). *No means no!* Educate2Empower Publishing.

Sanders, J. (2017). *Let's talk about body boundaries, consent and respect: Teach children about body ownership, respect, feelings, choices and recognizing bullying behaviors*. Educate2Empower Publishing.

Shoatz, S. (2019). *My voice is my superpower*. Self-published.

Starishevsky, J. (2009). *My body belongs to me*. Safety Star Media.

Chapter 8: Soulful Sexual Health and Spiritual Maturity

Hill, M. (2021). *Perimenopause power: Navigating your hormones on the journey to menopause*. Green Tree.

Northrup, C. (2021). *The wisdom of menopause: Creating physical and emotional health during the change* (4th ed.). Bantam.

Chapter 9: A Spiritual Legacy of Soulful Sexual Health

Smith, L., & Grabovac, I. (Eds.). (2023). *Sexual behavior and health in older adults*. Springer.

Chapter 10: The Soulful Navigation of Female Sexual Health Challenges and Chapter 11: The Soulful Navigation of Male Sexual Health Challenges

Cohen, S. (2017). *Pelvic pain explained: What everyone needs to know*. Rowman & Littlefield Publishers.
Hari, J. (2018). *Lost connections: Uncovering the real causes of depression—and the unexpected solutions*. Bloomsbury Publishing.
Levine, P. A. (1997). *Waking the tiger: Healing trauma*. North Atlantic Books.
Marcus, B. S. (2021). *Sex points: Reclaim your sex life with the revolutionary multi-point system*. Hachette Go.
Maté, G., & Maté, D. (2022). *The myth of normal: Trauma, illness, and healing in a toxic culture*. Avery.
van der Kolk, B. (2014). *The body keeps the score: Brain, mind, and body in the healing of trauma*. Viking.

Chapter 12: Soulfully Seeking Sexual Health Support

Minaa B. (2023). *Owning our struggles: A path to healing and finding community in a broken world*. TarcherPerigee.
Tawwab, N. G. (2021). *Set boundaries, find peace: A guide to reclaiming yourself*. TarcherPerigee.

Chapter 13: Soulfully Providing Sexual Health Support

Ahmed, S., & Amer, M. M. (Eds.). (2012). *Counseling Muslims: Handbook of mental health issues and interventions*. Routledge.
Ellis, K., & Ungco, J. (Eds.). (2023). *Sexuality and intimacy: An occupational therapy approach*. AOTA Press.
Jacobson, C. (2024). *Sex therapy with religious patients: Working with Jewish, Christian, and Muslim communities*. Routledge.

Index

abstinence: challenges and difficulty 78–81; empowered versus fear-based 81–3; Islamic perspectives 76; Islamic texts 34–5; sexual desire and the soul 76–8; shame and guilt 81; see also marital sexual intimacy

Badri, M. 20
breast cancer 246–7; see also female sexual health challenges

cervical cancer 246–247
childbirth: Islamic traditions 35–6
children see parenting
colon cancer 275
conception 36, 240–1, 270, 272–3
consent 147–8; see also sexual intimacy

dating 104–6, 108–9, 174–5; see also marriage, premarital phase

emotional health definition 39; see also abstinence, parenting, pornography
empowered abstinence: al-Ghazali's 6M framework 92–6; emotional processing 90–2; levels of the soul 84–5; self-awareness and lifestyle alignment 85–90; soulful sexual decision-making 85; theology, ethics, and spirituality 82

fertility 35–6, 56, 58, 192; see also female sexual health, female reproductive challenges, male reproductive challenges

female cancers 246–7
female reproductive challenges: fertility and infertility 240–1; navigating medical and spiritual support 290–6; pregnancy loss and miscarriage 240–1
female sexual health: genitalia 56–8; internal reproductive system 58–9; myth busting 54–5; sexual development 55–6; soulful foundations 52–4; see also menstruation
female sexual health challenges: cancer 246–7; menopause 244–6; myth busting 220–1; navigating sexual intimacy challenges 236–9; pelvic floor dysfunction 231–2; pelvic organ prolapse 234–6; sexual desire 236–7; sexual pleasure 237; soulful perspectives 219–20; vaginismus 232–4
female sexual trauma: definition 221–3; healing 226–8; impacts 224–6; trauma responses 223; see also female sexual health challenges
fitrah 24

heart: definition 21–2; purification of 25–7
hormones: female midlife changes 189–94; menstruation 60; male midlife changes 195

Islam: colonization and disruption 16–17; historical context 13–14
Islamic psychology 20–1

LGBTQ+: supporting parental conversations 179–182; *see also* parenting

male factor infertility 270–4; *see also* male sexual health challenges
male cancers 274–7; *see also* male sexual health challenges
male sexual health: ghusl 71; hormones 69; midlife changes 195–6; nocturnal emissions 69–71; preventative care 200–2; reproductive system 67–9; social support 198; soulful foundations 67; soulful navigation 197; spiritual maturity 194–6
male sexual health challenges: cancers 274–7; erectile dysfunction 266–7; infertility 270–4; performance anxiety 267–8; pornography use 258–65; premature ejaculation 267; sexual trauma 221–8; soulful approaches 268–70
male sexual trauma: barriers to healing 256–8; definition 222–3; healing 226–8; impacts 224–6; trauma responses 223
marital rape 132; 147–8; *see also* angels cursing *ḥadīth*
marital sexual intimacy: collaboration 148–9; communication (before and after marriage) 140–7; consent 147–8; definition and soulful model 126–9; diverse needs 151; foreplay 129–31; gaining confidence 150; Islamic guidelines 128; myths 124–5; pleasure mapping 150–2; post-intimacy care 153; supplications 129; unhealthy or abusive dynamics 132–3; wedding night 128; *see also* abstinence
marriage: dating and physical attraction 104–7; heart-based intentions 104–5; Islamic framing and expectations 101–3; qualities in a spouse 103; *see also* sexual intimacy
men *see* male sexual health *and* male sexual health challenges
menopause: challenges 244–6; overview 190–1; professional and spiritual support 191; soulful navigation 193–4
menstrual challenges: absent periods 229–30; endometriosis 230; heavy bleeding 229; irregular cycles 229; myths about pain 230; painful periods 229; PCOS 230; PMS and PMDD 229; *see also* menstruation
menstruation: *ghusl* (major purification) 65–6; hygiene and products 62–5; Islamic perspectives and soulful framing 60; phases and infradian rhythm 60–2; *see also* menstrual challenges
middle adulthood: changes in marital intimacy 202–5; spiritual transitions 187–9; *see also* spiritual maturity
miscarriage *see* pregnancy loss
Muslim demographics 15–6

OB/GYN visit 299–301
see also pap smear
older adulthood: communities and families 212–14; sexual health contexts 211–12; sharing wisdom 214–16; soulful perspectives 208–11
oral sex 128
ovarian cancer 246–7

parenting: adult Muslim children 182; age-based approaches 168–78; aligning as caregivers 160–2; answering children's questions 178; children with unique needs 165; Islamic perspectives and approach 157–8; LGBTQ+ conversations 179–82; myth busting 162; natural learning moments 164–6; preventing child sexual abuse 167; soulful model 163–4; unlearning shame 158–60
pelvic floor dysfunction 231–2
pelvic organ prolapse 234–6
perimenopause: overview 189–90; professional and spiritual support 191; sexual development 56; soulful navigation 193–4
physical health definition 40–1
pornography use: cycle of use 261–2; healing 264–5; shame 263; soulful perspectives 258–60; *see also* abstinence

pregnancy loss 240–1
premarital phase: assertive communication and self-accountability 113–14; empowered abstinence 115–17; marriage apps 112; relationship in limbo 118; search for a spouse 107–9; setting boundaries 111–14; sexual health and reproductive conversations 118–20; sexualized behaviors 109–10
premarital sex *see* abstinence
preventative exams: mammograms 200; men's health screenings 200–202; pap smears 200
professionals: beliefs vs. values 307–8; culture vs religion 309–10; cultural competence vs humility 312–15; gender stereotypes 309–10; hesitation to seek support 305–7; misappropriation bias 310–12; Muslim demographics 15–16, 307; PLISSIT 315–16; referring clients 317–18; self-reflection 304–5; therapeutic use of soul 316–17; using soulful metaphors 319
Prophet Muhammad 13–14
prostate cancer 275
puberty: connection to sexual desire 66–7; definition 50–1; onset and Islamic perspectives 51–2; spiritual accountability 51; Islamic texts 34

reproductive challenges *see* female reproductive challenges *and* male reproductive challenges
Rothman, A. 20

sex *see* sexual intimacy
sexual response 133–8; *see also* sexual intimacy

sexual intercourse *see* sexual intimacy
sexual health support: barriers 283–6; empowerment 290–2; medical support 293–4; myths about 288–90; preparatory steps 294–6; problem solving 296–9; sexual health professionals 292–3; soulful lens 286–8
sexual abuse prevention (children) 167; *see also* parenting
sexual desire: definition 133; desire discrepancy 138; dual control model 134–5; female sexual response 136–7; types of desire 135–6; *see also* sexual intimacy
sexual health: common myths 32–3; definition 32; Islamic traditions 33–6; soulful model 37–42; soulful values 42–5; theology, ethics, and spirituality 37–8
sexual health challenges *see* female sexual health challenges, male sexual health challenges
soul: definition 18; journey 22–4; model 20–2; purification and discipline 27–8; stages of life 18–19; *see also* Islamic Psychology
spirit 21–2
spiritual bypassing 44
spiritual health 38–39
spiritual maturity: enhancing intimacy in marriage 202–5; soulful Islamic perspectives 187–9

testicular cancer 275
therapy for men 276–7

vaginismus 232–4
vibrators 128

zina see premarital sex